FINDING BIX

finding BIX

THE LIFE AND
AFTERLIFE OF A
JAZZ LEGEND

**BRENDAN
WOLFE**

UNIVERSITY
OF IOWA PRESS,
Iowa City

University of Iowa Press, Iowa City 52242
Copyright © 2017 by the University of Iowa Press
www.uipress.uiowa.edu
Printed in the United States of America

Design by Richard Hendel

The University of Iowa Press is a member of Green Press Initiative
and is committed to preserving natural resources.

Printed on acid-free paper

Library of Congress Cataloging-in-Publication Data
Names: Wolfe, Brendan, 1971–
Title: Finding Bix : the life and afterlife of a jazz legend / Brendan Wolfe.
Description: Iowa City : University of Iowa Press, [2017]
Identifiers: LCCN 2016040306 | ISBN 978-1-60938-506-4 (pbk) |
ISBN 978-1-60938-507-1 (ebk)
Subjects: LCSH: Beiderbecke, Bix, 1903–1931. | Jazz musicians—United States—
Biography.
Classification: LCC ML419.B25 W65 2017 | DDC 788.9/6165092 [B]—dc23
LC record available at https://lccn.loc.gov/2016040306

For Mom, of course

ACKNOWLEDGMENTS

I am grateful to the following people for helping to make this book possible: Charles Abplanalp, Chris Beiderbecke, Scott Black, Brandi Bowles, Eric Brandt, Irwin Chusid; Catherine Cocks and Jim McCoy at the University of Iowa Press; Susan Parker Coleman, Ana María Correa, Emrah Erken; John and Kerry Fanning of La Muse Writers and Artists Retreat in Labastide-Esparbairenque, France; Tony Field, Sue Fischer, Patricia Foster, Joanne Gabbin, Megan Fishmann Getten; Matthew Gibson, Peter Hedlund, and Donna Lucey at *Encyclopedia Virginia*; Ted Gioia, John Grant, and Stacey Evans; Kate J. Grossman; Albert Haim and the Bixography Discussion Group; Jack Hamilton, Michael Heckman, Matt Hedstrom and Sarah Mullen, Rob Hill, Hilary Holladay, Trevor Jackson, Will Jennings and Sue Futrell, Brad Kay; Jane Kulow, Sarah Lawson, and Tori Talbot at the Virginia Festival of the Book; Preston Lauterbach, Geoff Muldaur, Susan H. Perdue, Shelley Post, William H. Roba, Lisa Ryan, Mark Saunders, Michelle Taylor, Terry Teachout, Flemming Thorbye, Nicole VanderLinden, Jay Varner; Rob Vaughan, Kevin McFadden, Maggie Guggenheimer, and the Virginia Foundation for the Humanities; Lisa Zavala Wagner, Debbie White, and Fredrick Woodard.

Thanks to Barbara Wascher, whose lively conversation and sharp insights made the book better and more fun to write; to Julia Kudravetz and Sheila McMillen, who inspired and also helped me to revise; and to Rick Zollo, who read every draft with enthusiasm and encouragement.

And loving thanks to my family: Beatrix Wolfe, Molly Minturn, Fran Wolfe, Bridget Wolfe; Sara, Albert, Sienna, and Indigo Womble; Jake Minturn, Richard Minturn and Suzanne Freeman; and the late Tom Wolfe.

Finally, special thanks go to Amiri Baraka, Rich Johnson, Jean Pierre Lion, and Richard M. Sudhalter, who in the time since I interviewed them have gone to that place where, according to Louis Armstrong, Bix Beiderbecke always blows first trumpet.

When you leap from the womb, we'll teach you how to play croquet, and how to clean bookcases, and how to write your name, and how to make mudcakes and who Bix Beiderbecke was and all about whiskey and wine and all about Eve and Adam and where to mail your letters.

— DONALD BARTHELME, in a letter to his unborn daughter, 1981

He is the ideal of the Romantic jazz musician, the first one that we have, the Romantic, self-destructive musician, and you know how influential that must have been. He did a lot of damage. Bix Beiderbecke killed a lot of people.

— TERRY TEACHOUT, in an interview with the author, 2006

We had been listening to a woman in costume pretend to be the mother of the early jazz legend Bix Beiderbecke. She read a script from note cards and once or twice mistakenly referred to herself in the third person. When the trolley finally deposited our group in front of 1934 Grand Avenue we politely applauded and I leaped to the curb.

"I want to welcome you to here," our new guide said as we stood outside the Beiderbecke family home in Davenport, Iowa. She was Italian and spoke with long Mediterranean vowels, motioning our group into an air-conditioned living room. The house was remarkably unremarkable—hardwood floors except where there was carpet or tile, original fixtures except where there was plastic, antique furniture except for the pieces from Walmart. It could have been my own home, except that, judging by a few scattered piles of documents on a folding table, it looked also to be an office. On the fireplace mantle, a few copies of the film *Bix: An Interpretation of a Legend* (1991) stood on display, for sale. Its Italian director, Giuseppe "Pupi" Avati, had purchased Bix's house and shot several scenes here. Now its star, Bryant Weeks—wearing a stained wife-beater, his head haloed in yellow—gazed out from the front of the DVD cases, looking sweaty and mercurial.

"This is where Bix grew up," our guide said. "And this is like the piano he learned to play as a boy." She motioned to an upright against the wall. "You are wondering if it is the original, no? I am sad to report it's not. For many years, the owners have tried to convince the local museum to bring it home, but they must not trust us." She winked conspiratorially. "We also don't have the phonograph machine that he played his first jazz records on. There are so many things we don't have. Sometimes," she sighed, "I would be happy just to have a plumbing man. The toilets are so much trouble!"

As historic sites go—and Bix's childhood home is listed on the

National Register of Historic Places—this was not terribly impressive. It barely hinted at Bix's importance to the music world. Where, for instance, was the sign proclaiming that he and Louis Armstrong were the most innovative jazz soloists of the 1920s, "the twin lines of descent from which most of today's jazz can be traced," to quote the critic Terry Teachout? Armstrong, of course, was one of the great geniuses of American music; he helped to invent jazz and popular music as we know it today. Bix, for his part, was the first important white soloist and the first to heavily influence black musicians. Where Satch blew hot and high, Bix, on tunes like "Singin' the Blues" from 1927, stuck it out in the middle register, exploring the melody with improvised solos that were breathtaking and nearly perfect. He invented the jazz ballad and pointed the way to "cool" jazz. He also loved classical music, and in his own handful of compositions, the most famous of which was the piano piece "In a Mist," he channeled as much Debussy as boogie-woogie. His was a hybrid musical sensibility, mixing low culture and high, black and white, Davenport and New York. It was a fully *American* sensibility, or so Amiri Baraka claimed back in the 1960s, creating "a common cultural ground where black and white America seemed only day and night in the same city." "And that's a profoundly racist argument," Teachout snaps in response, but I'm getting ahead of myself. The point is, Bix accomplished all of this in a career that consisted of a few hundred recordings and lasted a mere six years.

When the end came, he was twenty-eight and gin-soaked.

"I remember the day we heard Bix was dead," a saxophone player once told an interviewer. "It went around the musicians in whispers, as though nobody dared say it out loud. We couldn't believe it—it was like saying the Pope was dead. If it was true, if Bix was really gone, what the hell were we all going to do?"

That quotation appears on the first page of *Bix: Man & Legend*, the definitive Beiderbecke biography, published in 1974. The authors, Richard M. Sudhalter and Philip R. Evans (with William Dean-Myatt, who contributed to a discography), go on to wonder what it was about the death of "this quiet, deferential young man" that provoked "almost apocalyptic bereavement" among both his friends and people who knew only his recordings. They suggest it may have been Bix's music, with its "capacity to reach a listener and move him emotionally even at first contact," but then they decided, no, that couldn't be it; lots of jazz does that. So what was it? Sudhalter and Evans seem as dumbfounded about it as other writers, but they note that whatever it was, in the years following Bix's death it transformed their well-behaved young man into one of jazz's original and most enduring legends. It's a turn of events neither they nor anyone else seems too pleased about.

Part Keats and part Fitzgerald, Bix the legend is a nineteenth-century Romantic hero refitted for the Jazz Age. He comes in with the flappers and checks out not long after the Great Crash, a baby-faced foot-shuffler who can't read music and carries his instrument around in a brown paper bag. He is a "cardboard martyr," complains the cantankerous British critic Benny Green; "a beatific figure before whom the idolators kneel in reverence, and at whom the debunkers heave giant brickbats." He is "jazz's Number One Saint," and to boot he's got Kirk Douglas's chin. "Someday, when I'm really good, I'm gonna do things with this trumpet nobody's ever thought of doing," a wide-eyed Douglas tells Doris Day in the 1950 film *Young Man with a Horn* (based on the Bix-inspired novel of the same name). "I'm gonna hit a note that nobody ever heard before."

Never mind that Bix didn't play trumpet; he played cornet. Or that he didn't go for the high notes—the whole point of his style! The legendary Bix is the artist shooting for something he can't quite reach. "Bix was as usual gazing off into his private astronomy," Ralph Berton writes in his memoir *Remembering Bix*, also published in 1974. (On *that* book's first page, Berton one-ups the old saxophone player and compares Bix to Jesus himself; a young James Dickey, in an unpublished essay dated 1943, throws in Napoleon, Alexander the Great, and Beethoven for good measure.) "Bix did not let anything at all distract his mind from that cornet," Armstrong recalled. "His heart was with it all the time."

In the movie, this sort of behavior clearly concerns Doris Day. "You've got to have some other interest or you'll go off your rocker," she advises her young man. "I know, you need a hobby, like collecting stamps or a dog."

Poor Kirk! I always feel bad for him at this moment—*stamps?!?*—even as I am left wondering what part of all this is Bix and what part is legend. Sudhalter and Evans's answer is to focus their book—rather

3

tediously sometimes, for Bix's life was not terribly exciting—only on what they know to be true. And in a way, their instincts are just as maternal as Doris Day's. They hope to protect Bix not from himself but from his legend, which they compare to "40 years of underbrush" and at which they solemnly promise to hack away, "destroying the popularly accepted image to get at the person of fact, flesh and blood." (One suspects that Benny Green would approve.) That in the end the underbrush always wins is, of course, hardly surprising. Sudhalter, who did the writing, and Evans, who contributed the research, squabbled so much—over the use of invented dialogue, over the question of whether one of Bix's girlfriends had an abortion, even

over the order of names on the book's front cover—that after *Man & Legend*'s publication they suffered a dramatic falling out. Already a contentious bunch, Bixophiles happily chose sides and began to call each other names. In a 2003 interview, I asked Sudhalter about the controversy. "For twenty-five years, Phil Evans never stopped spewing anger, vituperation, and venom," he said. "I'm still surprised when I come across people whose opinions of me have been shaped by him."

Evans died in 1999, Sudhalter in 2008. And because of their conflict, *Bix: Man & Legend*, the first jazz biography to be nominated for a National Book Award, remains out of print. Bix, however, manages to live on—just not here on Grand Avenue. This place seems strangely empty of any Bix, real or imagined.

"Come," our tour guide said, grabbing my arm. "I will show you upstairs."

I grew up with Bix. All of us from his hometown did, and still do, although we never actually knew him. In Davenport he exists in two dimensions only, everywhere on posters for the annual Bix Beiderbecke Memorial Jazz Festival, on the side of a downtown parking garage, on sweaty T-shirts and plastic beer cups, his image cast forever in the same pose, lifted from the most famous photograph of him: face round, hair perfectly parted down the middle, his tux perfectly pressed. Perfectly recognizable, he has over the years become part town mascot, part Golden Calf. Bill Wundram, white-haired columnist for the local *Quad-City Times*, insists on calling him "Bixie," as if he were still in knickers, sneaking away from the large family home on Grand Avenue and down the steep hill to the Mississippi River, where he could listen to riverboat musicians from New Orleans. There's his name on a thousand bumper stickers—in block serif letters, white on red: "Bix Lives!"—as if he hadn't already died a slow, pathetic death in a Queens boarding house back in 1931, so young, so far away from his family, and screaming, said his landlord, "that there were two Mexicans under the bed, with long daggers, waiting to kill him." "Jazz's Number One Saint" is right: in a city where the Mexicans now have largely displaced the Germans, he rises again, every third weekend in July. Kitschy Dixieland musicians in red-and-white-striped shirts and suspenders crowd the band shell to blow their clarinets at seniors in lawn chairs, while many more folks crowd Third and Fourth streets for the arts festival, browsing craft booths and eating tenderloins. Bix bobblehead dolls can be picked up farther down River Drive at John O'Donnell Stadium, home of the minor league baseball team that until recently was known as the Swing of the Quad Cities. (The team logo depicted baseballs floating out of the bell of a pastel saxophone.) Most popular of all, however, is the Bix 7, an elite seven-mile road race independent of the music festival but until recently held each year on that same Saturday. It was a regular excuse for my aunt Sara to host an early morning cocktail party, her house conveniently situated on a bluff near the turnaround on McClellan Boulevard, where tens of thousands of runners, invariably led by a Kenyan or two, passed by, and then passed by again, before heading back down to the river. For that reason, I suppose, the word "Bix" for me has always carried with it the salty smell of sweat and the taste of mimosas. Bix is a season. Bix is a party. Bix is a great Davenport reunion. The colorful posters change every year, but Bix is always the same. His cornet, which rests on an unseen knee, is always silent.

If this were Borges, there might be talk of *el asombro*, or *la sagrada horror*—that "holy dread" in the face of meaningful words, in the face of what the Kiowa essayist N. Scott Momaday calls "that ancient and irresistible tradition of *vox humana*"; in other words, there might be the observation that the sound, the wonderful *sound* of Bix's instrument, "like a girl saying yes," as Eddie Condon famously put it, what made Bix *Bix*, for crying out loud, is largely absent. Or at least it was from the Bix I knew growing up in Davenport, and from the Bix everyone else I knew knew. Who *was* Bix? We didn't know.

Bix was a genius, and I learned this, it turns out, from the Italians.

"What are you-a doo-ing in my film?" he howled. "Oh, Christ!" he howled, such that even his modish eyeglasses, which hung suspended from a string around his thick and hairy neck, trembled. This was Pupi Avati. *Pooooo*-pee, as it was pronounced. And his pidgin squawking impressed its victim. His spittle flew the short distance from his neatly cropped beard to my bare, eighteen-year-old cheeks, speckling an otherwise adequate makeup job. "Oh, good God!" Pupi raged. "Please, makeup," while, for a brief moment, the tape continued to roll "My Pretty Girl" at full volume, oblivious. I was on the set of *Bix: An Interpretation of a Legend* (it would later screen at Cannes), which Pupi and his brother, the producer Antonio Avati, had traveled all the way from Rome to Davenport to make, and which I had come to participate in through the good offices of my high school orchestra teacher, who was serving as a consultant to the film. My job each day was to get my hair slicked back, don a period suit, and pretend to play the fiddle in a re-creation of the mid-1920s St. Louis band fronted by C-melody sax-man Frankie "Tram" Trumbauer and his protégé Bix Beiderbecke. "My Pretty Girl": what a great dance number, with extras flailing about doing the Charleston, the band bouncing up and down on the stand, shiny black shoes tapping, and Tram and Bix up front trading solos. The fiddle player, meanwhile, got a solo break, too, and on this day Pupi was filming a tight close-up, that huge camera of his wheeled up against my jaw like an X-ray machine at the dentist's office. "Now, don't-a look," he begged me, before yelling, "Playback!" and then, "Action!" I pretended to play with the music, but I couldn't help it. "Jesus goddamn Christ!" he howled. I always turned and looked, take after take. And "My Pretty Girl" rolled on.

I fell head over heels for "My Pretty Girl" that day and, on another afternoon of shooting, for "Singin' the Blues"; I fell in love with Bix's bell-like tone ("surefooted as a mountain goat," according to Mezz Mezzrow; "like a mallet hits a chime," according to Hoagy Carmichael), the cool reserve, the exquisitely controlled improvisation; I fell in love with the romance of Bix, the jazz and swing of Bix ("I just sat there," said Max Kaminsky, "vibrating like a harp to the echoes of Bix's astoundingly beautiful tone. It sounded like a choirful of angels"); I fell in love with my seemingly exclusive discovery that Bix existed outside of Davenport, that he was a musician of heroic stature. Only later did I learn that it wasn't actually Bix on the tape. It was a Dixieland band imitating Bix, a displaced Dixieland band somewhere in Italy—Tom Pletcher on cornet, joined by names like Fabrizio Cattaneo and Fabiano Pellini—blowing Bix's solos note for note, the DNA of their choruses an almost perfect match.

No matter. It might as well have been Bix. For me, it *was* Bix.

Bix was a kid from the cornfields. Bix is a guy named Tom. Bix is Italian. As I unintentionally and rather haphazardly began my quest to unmask the many faces of Bix, I learned this lesson over and over again: the closer I got to Bix, or at least to someone I thought might be Bix, the more he retreated. Even his recordings weren't to be trusted. "One cannot hear Bix Beiderbecke from the tall corn of Iowa without feeling this is singularly ours and it is about time we wake up to the fact," declared the program notes to a Carnegie Hall concert, "From Spirituals to Swing," performed several years after his death. But *can* one hear Bix? According to his contemporaries, those crackly old 78s sounded nothing like him; such primitive technology never came close to capturing his horn. How could it? This is particularly frustrating to accept in our cocksure age of compact discs and digital technology, although it's worth noting that sound geeks can just as easily use their computers to correct a faltering pitch as illuminate a perfect one. (Without such programming, one suspects that—*poof*—Top 40 would cease to exist.) Upon hearing digital sound for the first time, the German conductor Herbert von Karajan reportedly exclaimed, "all else is gaslight!" "Well, what's wrong with gaslight?" retorts the Irish poet and 78 aficionado Ciaran Carson in his book *Last Night's Fun* (1996). "For you can use your imagination, make figures out of shadow."

Bix is a specter, then, flitting in and out of the snaps and pops of a wax record. Even while listening to Bix, to the real, honest-to-god Bix, he is a shadow.

The first full-length biography of Bix Beiderbecke, titled *Bugles for Beiderbecke*, was published in 1958. The writers were two courtly and condescending Englishmen, Charles Wareing and George Garlick, who, like the Avati brothers several decades later, were exasperated by the hayseeds in Bix's hometown. "Although the majority of its citizens might falter if taxed for the reason," they write, "Davenport does, in fact, claim a modest degree of fame." Even taking into account a certain aristocratic understatement, their choice of words is poor. There is nothing modest about the legacy of Bix Beiderbecke. Shortly after the Avatis broke set, I read *Remembering Bix* by Ralph Berton, a former editor of *Down Beat* magazine and by all accounts a precocious storyteller, a man who had no interest whatsoever in English reserve. His older brother Vic had been Bix's drummer, and for a summer Ralph had followed Bix around like a puppy, doing literally what I had done only virtually, lapping up the improvisations, the legendary bits on piano; to him, Bix was something holy. "Like Jesus, van Gogh, and other gifted outcasts, Bix found the world uninhabitable," Berton writes in his book's second sentence,

> and left it, I think, without regrets, dying as he had lived—casually, without ceremony, and of course broke.
>
> Bix's work has influenced, directly or indirectly, two generations of musicians and music-lovers so far, in many countries, and left a permanent imprint on jazz; thirty years before there was a word for it, he was the first "cool" jazzman. How many of his contemporaries came under his spell it is impossible even to guess.

One of them said somewhere, in print, that once you hear Bix blow four notes on that horn, your life would never be the same. I know how irritating that sort of rhetoric can be, especially to those who weren't there; but for us who were, it was the simple truth.

I purchased my copy of *Remembering Bix*—mine is the first British edition, as it happens—in a tiny used bookstore in the Village of East Davenport, which is just a few cross streets on the bank of the Mississippi. During the Civil War, this was Camp McClellan. During the 1910s, Bix supposedly trotted down this way to ogle the ragtimers on the riverboats, traveling men like Louis Armstrong. "The first time I heard Bix," Armstrong remembered, "I said these words to myself, 'This man is as serious about his music as I am.'" I couldn't resist *Remembering Bix* after spying it in the window, its cover a psychedelic yellow, orange, and green, with that same familiar picture: round face, hair parted, perfect tux, cornet on an unseen knee. I picked it up recently and found folded inside the front cover a newspaper clipping, from the *New York Times* obituaries, July 18, 1998: "James Flora, 84, Author and Album Cover Illustrator, Dies." To the right of Mr. Flora's stately, gray-goateed photo, without comment or cutline, is an extraordinary, Picassoesque album cover showing two characters blowing colored beads from their horns. It is called *Bix and Tram*.

I listened to Bix. Overcoming my own Karajanesque skepticism, I bought cassettes and wore out their magnetic tape rewinding and re-playing his solos on "Davenport Blues," "I'm Coming Virginia," "Way Down Yonder in New Orleans," "Sorry," "At the Jazz Band Ball," "Royal Garden Blues," "Jazz Me Blues," "Goose Pimples," and perhaps the most effortlessly elegant statement in the history of jazz, "Singin' the Blues." *This* was Bix Beiderbecke, goddammit, and while I'd by no means gotten all Hoagy Carmichael about it—in one of his memoirs, the songwriter had recalled that, upon first hearing Bix play, he "rose violently from the piano bench and fell, exhausted, on to a daven-port"—Bix and I nevertheless slummed together in our own private Idaho for close to a decade, cold-shouldering everyone else. I read Berton's book, but otherwise declined to overthink the problem of "jazz's Number One Saint." All that mattered was the music. And as for the Avatis—they were dead to me after I showed up to their black-tie premiere only to discover that my much-anticipated solo had been ignominiously, even vindictively, snipped out of the final cut. (The movie, it turns out, was a finalist for the Palme d'Or.)

For all those years—through high school, college, and graduate school, through a long love affair with Shostakovich and an utterly typical, if mercifully brief, Rush phase—Bix's music remained. And his shadow meant nothing to me. Then, in the summer of 2000, something astonishing happened: I received in the mail an angry but neatly typed letter.

It was signed "Bix Beiderbecke."

I was a newspaper editor in Iowa City by then, and I had published a long, largely positive review of a new edition of Berton's *Remembering Bix*; there's a lot of great energy in that review, but also a lot of ignorance, not simply of the facts of Bix's life, but of the passion with which people regard him. (Example: I once requested an interview with a jazz musician on the subject of Bix. His e-mailed reply included the unsolicited and enthusiastic observation that Bix, when socializing, "got more ass than a toilet seat.") Without quite knowing it, I had rehashed as the truth what I since have come to call the Great Bix Myth, a story that is neither entirely false nor entirely true, but an ingenious and persistent blend of the two. Although there are countless variations, a classic version might begin something like this:

> Leon "Bix" Beiderbecke is born in the obscure river town of Davenport, Iowa, to a family of uptight Germans who worship Beethoven and despise jazz. When he grows up to neglect his studies in favor of teaching himself the cornet, Mom and Pop Beiderbecke send him to a military academy outside Chicago. A little discipline goes a long way, they figure, but fate cruelly intervenes. Chicago, they should have known, is the thumping heart of the jazz world, and after he is caught sneaking off campus one too many times to go hear the likes of King Oliver and Louis Armstrong, Bix is expelled. He soon moves to the Windy City to join his idols, and there begins his professional career.

There are certain established conventions to this story. Davenport, for instance, must be "obscure" in order to emphasize the irony of a genius such as Bix emerging from the cornfields ("snatched out of a cradle in the cornfields," as Mezz Mezzrow wrote). Also, it conveniently allows Brits like Wareing and Garlick to sigh in disbelief at the indifference of the locals and especially those tightly puckered

Beiderbeckes. This is foreshadowing of a sort: Bix will always be the consummate outsider—among his own kind in Dullsboro and soon among the black musicians in the world of hot jazz. (Judging by Berton's description of Bix "gazing off into his private astronomy," he was something of an outsider even among his fellow *white* musicians.) Armstrong, meanwhile, is often said to play for and even meet Bix on the Mississippi riverfront. His presence, first in Davenport and then in Chicago, makes for a satisfying first-act symmetry.

In Chicago and then Detroit, Bix's fatal flaw—a weakness for bathtub gin—first reveals itself; however, he also makes the fortunate acquaintance of one Frank Trumbauer. Part bandleader, part fairy godmother, "Tram," as he is known, helps our brilliant but woefully undertrained hero achieve stardom. After a long engagement in St. Louis, the two join the Jean Goldkette Orchestra. An East Coast tour ends triumphantly in the Big Apple, where the Goldkette boys famously outplay the black musicians in Fletcher Henderson's band. At the height of the Roaring Twenties, this kid from Iowa who can't please his parents, who can't even read music, is idolized by fellow artists, including Louis Armstrong. When Goldkette disbands, Bix and Tram hire on with America's most famous and prestigious popular music outfit, the Paul Whiteman Orchestra. Bix is now in the high country, where the air's thin and the booze plentiful.

The Great Bix Myth has traditionally demanded that Bix's decision to join Whiteman be characterized as a sellout of colossal proportions, as sacrificing his genius on the altar of mammon. So why does he do it? Bix is mysterious, that's why. He's forgetful; he doesn't eat much; he doesn't talk much; he doesn't look at girls (all comments about toilet seats notwithstanding); he carries his expensive horn around in a brown paper sack and accidentally puts his shoes on the wrong feet. When the other guys are finally getting some shut-eye, Bix is up working out weird, modernist piano compositions. The story about Bix is that he's the kind of guy you tell stories about.

Whiteman's music is screechingly bad, his schedule extremely demanding. When Bix looks for solace in a bottle, his health starts to fail. On a recuperative trip back to Davenport, he finds in a closet all the records he has sent home to his folks, records that would change jazz history; they're tucked away in the back, unopened and unlistened-to. Poor Bix! The drinking gets so bad that Whiteman sends Bix to rehab, but each night during his absence, our hero's chair is set up and left empty in his honor. After that, his attendance in the band is spotty. He finally ends up in Queens, strung out and broke. As a favor to some buddies, he plays a date at Princeton but catches a nasty cold. A few weeks later, with the Jazz Age over and the United States plunging into depression, Bix Beiderbecke dies. He was only twenty-eight.

Take note here that the Great Bix Myth demands that Bix's death be characterized as a tragedy, that even as he is being sanctified, those jerry-loving Beiderbeckes be vilified. They're hopelessly bourgeois, after all. They're uncaring parents. "The family ignored and deplored Bix's musical career when he was alive," Berton wrote and I quoted in my review, "but after his death had belatedly apprised them of his fame in the outside world, they all developed a tendency to make a prudent buck out of it by exploiting his memory, shedding crocodile tears over his genius, his sweetness, &c."

Back, then, to the letter. It arrived in a cream-colored envelope with a preprinted return address: lovely serif letters that spelled out "Bix Beiderbecke."

> Brendan Wolfe's article "The Davenport Blues" dated July 11, 2000 was interesting reading but contained numerous errors and, as Clinton's spin doctors would say, frequently gives a "false impression." I'd like to correct some of them.
>
> His first mistake was to use Ralph Berten's [sic] book as a reference. Most real students of Bix consider his work right along with Pupi's movie: Bix biographies liberally sprinkled with fiction, which is often demeaning to him and his family. For his next article I'd suggest he use *The Leon Bix Beiderbecke Story* by Phil and Linda Evans, as his source material.

What followed was a brief and likely incomplete list of factual errors and alleged misinterpretations that included Bix's name (it was Leon Bix Beiderbecke and *not* Leon "Bix" Beiderbecke), his education (he attended prep school and *not* a military academy), his family (the Beiderbeckes did *not* exile him for pursuing jazz), his death (he died of pneumonia and *not* alcoholism), and his afterlife (the Beiderbeckes did *not* attempt to profit from his fame). The letter, finally, was signed, "R. Bix Beiderbecke, Jacksonville, Illinois." Many of Mr. Beiderbecke's claims, I would come to learn later, were far more complicated than he was letting on. At the time, though, I was embarrassed to receive such a spirited correction, but also thrilled. Bix's nephew had introduced me to yet another Bix, this one appealingly independent of the legend, a Bix who was disputed, attacked, and defended—an object of history, in other words.

As if on a dare, I ordered the Evanses' book. At 602 pages, it's a big red doorstop with poor binding and, on its cover, a painting of a dreamy-eyed Bix. (By accident or design, this Bix also comes outfitted with a Mona Lisa smile and a shimmering orange nimbus.) The book itself is a singularly thorough, even compulsive work of scholarship. Meticulously organized into a day-by-day, year-by-year chronology of Bix's life, it reads more like the authors' research notes than a traditional biography. A day may occupy pages or, in the instance of Thursday, March 18, 1926, a mere nine words: "**Bix** and Pee Wee Russell had dinner at Ruth's." Telegraphic descriptions are accompanied by info-laden charts and tables, newspaper clippings, orchestra programs (Bix often attended the St. Louis symphony), set lists, personal letters, photographs (including a family album of far-flung, present-day Beiderbeckes), and verbatim transcripts from interviews with friends and acquaintances. "**Bix** came in and borrowed some cigarettes," the aforementioned Ruth recalled in 1973. "I was smoking Camels and I think that was his brand, too." There is an index of song titles and a section devoted to the particulars of Bix's cornets. And lest you wonder why the boldface print, Philip Evans explains in his foreword: "So as not to confuse the reader, we have bolded **Bix**'s name/names when it is referring to the **Bix**. Also his words whether in comments, his letters or newspaper articles, have also been bolded."

While explicitly declaring war on all things "anti-**Bix**"—from the Evanses' perspective, a short list would certainly include the Avatis' film and Berton's memoir—the ironically titled *The Leon Bix Beiderbecke Story* is also at war with narrative itself. It is a colossus of facts, filled with information of all kinds, both pertinent and otherwise. It is not, however, a story.

And that, I suppose, disappointed me. I had become attached to Berton's Bix, to the exile and the drunk. He suited the Romantic in me who assumes that pain fuels all great art, and he spoke powerfully to the young man in me who had battled his own father and the bottle in what seemed like equal measures. More than anything, though, Berton's Bix struck me as a complex figure. Listen to "Singin' the Blues," which opens with a solo by Trumbauer, one marked by what in 1927 was unprecedented lyricism. "Trumbauer always told a little story," the saxophonist Lester Young explained. The music was not about dancing, in other words, or virtuosity; it was about narrative. And when Bix chimes in, jazz changed forever. Here was the music's first balladeer, his solo like a finished composition—restrained, precise, governed by melody instead of chord changes and tempo. Yet it was entirely improvised.

As he did in "Singin' the Blues," the Bix of my imagination dwelled inside that narrative while somehow transcending it. His solo blew smooth as polished glass but underneath it roiled with all the ruffled alienation and unseemly longing of a Keats or a Charlie Parker; it's something the music itself only hints at, a shadow the listener reaches for but never quite obtains.

This was *my* Bix, but was it *the* Bix?

In Evans and Evans, the authors and their editor, Norman Gentieu, decline the difficult challenge of telling a story or of stitching together, from the cloth of so many sources, a full and complete character, a living human being. Instead, they rail against the many "flawed," "unfortunate," "self-serving," "imaginary," "reckless," "arbitrary," and "often politically correct" novels, biographies, memoirs, and movies about Bix. "Happily," their book tells us, "the error-ridden glut has now been rendered kaput, obsolete—fit only for a hungry paper-shredder and a bottomless compost pit."

Noting well the oddly defensive tone of this declaration, I wondered what on earth they could be so afraid of. Yet the more I read about Bix's life—research that over the next several years consumed me as much as the music ever did—the better I understood the answer.

Perhaps it was on that trip of mine to 1934 Grand Avenue—the Beider-becke family home, just a mile or two west of where I grew up—that I first conceived of trying to write my own story of Bix's life, of trying to connect music, history, and legend. I blame the house's emptiness—it moved me in some strange way.

When we finally made it upstairs, our guide introduced us to the room once shared by Bix and his older brother, Burnie. She pointed across the hall to the newly bought department-store bed in the exact spot where their parents had slept. Now our guide slept there. "I'm sometimes in the house for weeks at a time," she said, throwing up her hands. "The owners give us work and we can't finish it!"

At night, when the house is quiet, she thinks about Bix. "He drank too much," she said. "He died from it, poor boy. So young. But now he is in heaven, no?" She lightly touched the cross around her neck. "I think so."

For a moment the group silently fidgeted. It was tough to tell where Bix was right then, or where he was going.

"One of the things I like about jazz, kid," Bix once told his fellow cornetist Jimmy McPartland, "is I don't know what's going to happen next. Do you?"

We filed back downstairs, where our guide's mother, an elegant gray wisp in her nineties and armed with nary a word of English, showed us to the door, smiling.

"Okay," she said. "Beeeeex."

I might as well say it—that name!

Bix. B*eeeee*x. Leon B*eeeee*x.

Bix's brother Burnie claimed that this was the boy's given name and presented to the Evanses a birth certificate from the county registrar, which is dated January 1963 and reads "Leon Bix Beiderbecke." This, however, was not sufficient for Rich Johnson, a tall and ornery Bixophile whom I first met in 2005, when he was eighty-three. (He died three years later.)

"Well, his name wasn't Bix; it was Bismark," Johnson said, "and I have so much proof, it's unbelievable." The longtime musical director of the Bix Beiderbecke Memorial Jazz Festival, Johnson cited Bix's elementary school registration, as well as the will of a great aunt. "You know what happened? It was altered," Johnson said, referring to the birth certificate. "I have those records. It was altered in the fifties. Burnie did it. Why, I don't know."

Neither do I, of course. But I do think it's worth mentioning that Bix's name matters in a way that perhaps others' don't. "What a wonderful, impossible name!" cries out a character in Anton Myrer's novel *A Green Desire*. It's one of "The Fantastic Names of Jazz," according to the poet Hayden Carruth, who wedges it right in there between Stuff Smith and Bunny Berigan. And on February 18, 1995, Bix's name was the subject of a "Family Circus" cartoon, wherein Dolly holds up a Beiderbecke vinyl and remarks to her brother Billy, "Daddy's listening to an old trumpet player named Big Spider Beck." Not exactly sidesplitting, but it caused me to wonder (a) whether any of the cartoon's readers under sixty had any idea who this Bix fellow was; and (b) whether Bix would still be Bix were he not, in fact, named "Bix" and "Beiderbecke." Certainly these difficult and slightly ridiculous four syllables are central to the mystique. They're "mouth-pleasure," as the poet Donald Hall might put it—alliterative, abrupt, declamatory. That Saxon-y cross-like *x* sounds so pleasingly foreign; it's a Romantic legend all by itself. And if the clipped-ness of *–becke* rehearses a kind of sudden death, then the sibilance of *x*—*kssssss*— and the way it seems to echo across the peaks and valleys of "Beiderbecke," rehearses immortality. Mezz Mezzrow was really Milton; Stuff Smith was Hezekiah, Leroy, *and* Gordon; Bunny Berigan merely Rowland. Bix Beiderbecke, though, for what it's worth, and with all due respect to Rich Johnson, was *really* Bix.

So there you have it. Leon Beiderbecke was born on March 10, 1903—Leon Bix, Leon Bismark, Leon Bismark "Bix"—and already he's a bit out of focus. What remains uncontested, however, is that Bix's parents, Bismark and Agatha, whatever in fact they named the boy, actually *called* him Bix, and when they welcomed him into their two-story house at 1934 Grand Avenue, they set about worrying over more important issues, like whether his ears stuck out. (They did, according to Aggie, and she bobbed little Bickie's hair in an effort to mitigate the effect.) They also worried about his dangerous habit of "waddling"—to borrow Burnie's verb—out onto the streetcar tracks, which vibrated from use and so hummed, making a kind of music. "Even then the lad heard what the rest of us missed," Burnie sighed.

From the outside, the Beiderbecke home is sturdy and elegant. On the upper level, a small turret opens onto a false rounded balcony—opposite to it was Bix's bedroom—while the lower level is dominated by an expansive front porch. When it was built in 1893, Bismark and Agatha were newly married and likely flush with Beiderbecke money. Bismark's father had made a small fortune first in groceries, then in banking, and shortly after Bix was born, Bismark took over the East Davenport Lumber & Fuel Company. While it wasn't nearly as impressive as the elder Beiderbecke's mansion, the house on Grand must have been smartly furnished and impeccably kept. Mrs. Beiderbecke, who played the organ at First Presbyterian Church, kept a piano in the well-lit front parlor, and when he was two Bickie stood high on his tiptoes and with a single chubby finger plunked out "Mister Dooley." By the time he was three, Bix had graduated to Liszt, and on the occasion of his seventh birthday the *Davenport Democrat* dispatched a reporter, an anonymous fellow who claimed that this "is the most unusual and the most remarkably talented child in music that there is in this city."

Bix was a mother's dream, in other words, although calling him "most unusual" has always struck me as hyperbolic. Was being gifted on the piano really so unusual for a young boy, even one who "has never taken a music lesson and . . . does not know one key from another"? Further into the article, the reporter observes that "when 'Bickie' is playing the piano, he never looks at the keys; he never watches his hands."

> It might seem that the child's mind was not on what he is playing, because his eyes are centered upon objects about the room or he is looking into space with apparently no thought of the piece he is playing. But a careful observation of that gaze and of the child indicates that his mind is absorbed in the music, in the melody that he is playing.

Ralph Berton would later describe Bix as "gazing off into his private astronomy," and here we see that he was the same way even as a child. Perhaps this *was* unusual, or at least unusual enough that the reporter finds himself drawn into "a careful observation of that gaze."

In 1931, just weeks before Bix's death, the guitar player Eddie Condon visited Bix at his apartment in Queens, concerned that his old friend was ill from the drink. "His feet were swollen and dragged when he walked," Condon recalled in a memoir; "his thoughts were often muddled." But when Bix sat to play, nothing had changed, his fingers producing, as they always had, "the same effortless, unbelievable" music. "It was only when I looked at his face," Condon wrote, "and saw the absence there that things got cold and tight around me and I stiffened my drink."

The same blank expression—what Condon described as "the absence" and what Berton dubbed his "private astronomy"—that had marked Bix at seven marks him no less at twenty-eight. We can't help but wonder where he's off to and, if we could, would we want to follow him there?

For Bix, though, the true beginning of it all came post-Liszt. It was 1918, and a few days before Christmas Burnie arrived home from the army carrying a Victrola phonograph and records by the Original Dixieland Jazz Band (ODJB). He may as well have set off a bomb.

The ODJB were five white boys from New Orleans who had distinguished themselves the year before for having been the first to record so-called hot music. Their cornetist, an underclass Sicilian named Nick LaRocca, would later insist that whites, not blacks, had invented jazz—that *he* had invented jazz—but either way, the Victor Talking Machine Company scandalized God-fearing Americans with sides like "Tiger Rag" and "Skeleton Jangle." (The trombone "chokes and gargles," the *New York Sun* protested, while LaRocca bragged of whinnying like a horse during the band's live performances as women "raise[d] their dresses above their knees and carr[ied] on, men shrieking and everybody having a good time.") Not particularly scandalized himself, fifteen-year-old Bix was inspired to pick up a cornet for the first time—a dented loaner from a neighbor—so he could learn the parts by ear.

"Bickie!" Agatha must have wailed. "What about the piano? What about Liszt?"

Those records, by the way, mark an important and perhaps underappreciated moment in the history of jazz music. For the first time, aspiring performers such as Bix could learn their craft from speakers and not in smoky, booze-filled barrooms. It meant they could be influenced by styles and traditions across the country and even world, played by men they had never seen perform. From the relative quiet of 1934 Grand, Bix could now slow the music down, repeat it, and closely study it. Absent the sometimes restrictive context of the music's original time and place of recording, he likely felt more free to interpret it, expand it, and make it his own. Music was no longer

21

ephemeral; it was an artifact. The jazz historian Scott DeVeaux has noted that this very fact may have helped jazz become understood as an art form. While the records themselves were "meant to be used up"—as Bix certainly used his up—many still survived. And these remnants, which were collected, organized, and even fetishized, became the basis for jazz history and criticism. The recordings, in other words, proved to be a necessary testament to jazz as an art form.

Of course, jazz was far from being considered an art form when Bix started listening. *Shrieking? Whinnying like a horse?* One can only imagine how good, oompah-loving Presbyterians like Mr. and Mrs. Beiderbecke must have felt about such nonsense. Just the word—*jazz*—screamed impropriety. A footnote tucked away in a later edition of H. L. Mencken's *The American Language* tells us that according to a South Carolinian, "the announcement, in 1919, of the first *jazz band* to play in Columbia, where he was then serving in the state legislature, inspired feelings of terror among the local Baptists such as what might have been aroused by a personal appearance of Yahweh. Until that time *jazz* had never been heard in the Palmetto State except as a verb meaning to copulate."

1919. That was the same year Bix bought his first cornet.

It's worth remembering, meanwhile, that Davenport, Iowa, was *not* Columbia, South Carolina. Nor was it entirely the caricature that many historians and biographers have rendered, "a community steeped in—what else?—corn fields," as one has written. When I was growing up, Davenport was a small city that was nevertheless part of a much larger, river-straddling metropolitan area known as the Quad Cities. In the 1970s these were factory towns, manufacturing everything from supermarket bread to heavy farm equipment and airplane parts. They were smelly and sooty and loud with trains, although by the time I reached high school, much of that had disappeared, replaced with riverboat gambling and drug gangs expanding out from Chicago. Davenport wasn't a farming town or a cultural backwater then and it wasn't in Bix's day, either.

Granted, from a distance it could be hard to tell. On a trip up the Mississippi in 1882, Mark Twain caught a "glimpse at Davenport, which is another beautiful city, crowning a hill." The phrase, according to Twain, "applies to all these towns, for they are all comely, all

22

well-built, clean, orderly, pleasant to the eye, and cheering to the spirit; and they are all situated on hills." As it happens, though, Twain didn't stop in Davenport. If he had, he might have been greeted by hookers. And lots of beer.

In 1839 the half-French, half-Indian Antoine LeClaire founded Davenport on a westward bend in the river and named it for his friend, Colonel George Davenport, from whom he had purchased the land. By the time Bismark and Agatha married in 1893, Davenport had grown into a full-fledged, freewheeling city of 30,000, part of what was known then as the Tri-Cities. In no sense was it a small town; rather, it was, in the words of one historian, "a regional entrepôt," with a high school, two passenger-train depots, a bridge to Illinois, and under the bridge and running along and just north of what is now River Drive, a red light district. In 1884 the state legislature had prohibited the manufacture or sale of all alcoholic beverages, including wine and beer—the very lifeblood of the city's large and boisterous German population. Davenport responded by electing its first German mayor, whose father had been a leader of the Schleswig-Holstein independence movement back in the home country. Like the elder, the younger was unbowed by central authority, and he led Davenport on a five-year revolt against state-sanctioned priggishness. Not only did the city ignore Iowa's prohibition law, it flaunted it, licensing and collecting fees from 130 of its saloons. Scott County was being called *die Frei Staat Scott* after *die Frei Staat Schleswig-Holstein*. Then, in 1893, city officials decided to license the downtown prostitutes, too, a practice that lasted until Bix was in kindergarten.

Storyville was the name of New Orleans's red light district and the area near where Louis Armstrong grew up. Davenport's Storyville was called Bucktown, and the historian Sharon Wood describes a hard-drinking neighborhood so disreputable that a wife might attack her husband just for being seen on the wrong street corner. (One such wife, when she spotted her husband at the corner of Fourth and Brady streets flirting with two young women, "pounded" one of the women before grabbing a horsewhip from a nearby buggy and attempting to finish off the husband.) The year Bix was born, the *Chicago American* newspaper proclaimed Davenport to be "the wickedest city in America." One Davenporter, an actress, had fled to the

Windy City after claiming to have been forced into prostitution by a theater owner. "If it is true that God has forsaken Chicago," she wrote, "then He has never even visited Davenport, Iowa."

Far from being comely or cheering to the spirit, Davenport was the kind of place where local organizers of the Women's Christian Temperance Union griped that their national counterparts always left the city "with the same expression on their faces which we interpret, 'Can't do anything in Davenport.'" And by the time Bix began experimenting with the ODJB—Liszt be damned, he spun those records so many times the grooves wore smooth—it was the kind of place where a kid could idle down by the river and take in the real stuff off the boats. (How appropriate that "Beiderbecke," in German, actually means "by the brook.") Davenport, in other words, probably allowed Bix just enough breathing room, a chance to teach himself a few crude fingerings and noodle along in a band organized by his buddy Fritz Putzier. A chance to disappear, if need be, into his own private astronomy. To be sure, Bismark was a no-guff kind of father, insisting on hard work and a stiff collar, but the river always beckoned just down the hill; it was always within earshot. "The pulse of that wonderful music reached deeply into Bixie's heart," an old friend told Phil Evans, "and he spent his lifetime trying to solve the riddle of it."

To do that, Bix would need a better horn. Fritz, who had switched to C-melody saxophone, sold Bix his Conn Victor for thirty-five dollars and together they made music that was known less for its quality than its fearlessness. Bix, in particular, was pretty rough around the edges, his fingering unorthodox and entirely self-taught, the product of his ear and not the well-meaning instruction he had received. At least one biographer has suggested that this may have contributed to his unique sound, but a more typical reaction comes from the historian Richard Hadlock, who accused Bix of being just plain lazy. He was lazy at school—"barely scraping through at the last moment"—and he was lazy with his horn: "Bix got by on a vast natural talent for music and a quick, searching mind, adding to these as little hard work as possible." At the same time, though, the kid could be something of an intellectual. Hadlock reports an anecdote in which a much older Bix is sitting at the piano when a friend asks him who this fellow Proust is. Bix hits a chord, pauses, and then answers, "A French writer who lived in a cork-lined room. His stuff is no good in translation."

Which is pretty funny, actually, but also leaves you wondering. Bix is too lazy to read music but ambitious enough to read hundreds of pages of Proust in English *and* in French? Or maybe he was just a great wit. Hadlock published his essay in 1965; perhaps he viewed Bix as a kind of proto-hippie, a long-haired type who indulged himself in the artsy-fartsy without knowing a damn thing about discipline and an honest day's work. Or, as the music historian Ted Gioia has argued, maybe the anecdote illustrates "the cool ethos in formation," that is, Bix was cool before cool even existed, a fact that comes through in the contradiction of his being both a know-it-all and a shoulder-shrugger. He cares but wouldn't be caught dead caring.

Bix's story is full of these sorts of contradictions. He's lazy and unschooled but well read and intellectual. He's a musical prodigy, and although we know *when* he learns his art, we don't know how. The story is silent on whence this gorgeous music comes, and the empty space that results, this thing that we don't know, is central, I think, to understanding Bix.

Another historian, James Lincoln Collier, has filed the above conundrum under the rubric of Bix's "Tragic Temperament" and chalks it up not to laziness but to something else, some "internal resistance": "Obviously, even at an early age Bix was finding something in music that was his own, and he was determined, on whatever level of consciousness, to preserve it from the controlling hands that were so busy in other parts of his life." This is such a rich and elliptical image—*controlling hands?*—that you can't help but wonder what, specifically, Collier is talking about. Note that Bix was, at this point, a teenager, one who always forgot his horn down at Maher's Confectionary and Ice Cream Parlor and who undoubtedly caused all sorts of other problems. Of course there were hands controlling him! There were his parents, his teachers, even his friends forever worrying about what to do with that instrument Bix left behind. This strikes me as more typical than tragic, although biographers, with some justification, tend to read their subjects in hindsight. And the next couple of years would not be at all kind to Bix Beiderbecke.

Still, what about his parents? Ralph Berton's venomous accusations notwithstanding ("prudent buck," "crocodile tears"), what was Bix's relationship to them? He played jazz, after all, and the Beiderbeckes were nothing if not churchgoing and squarely middle class, their tastes predictably conservative. Against the notorious chokes and gargles of that newfangled rhythm, they were like a fortress of musical propriety: grandfather Carl sang in the choir, sister Mary Louise bought popular sheet music, and mother Agatha played the organ at First Presbyterian. Certainly the neighbors must have presented a challenge—"Aggie, what kinds of records is that boy *playing* over there?"—and who could have blamed the Beiderbeckes if they had been sensitive to the fact that they were a family of recent immigrants—from Germany on Bismark's side and Ireland on Agatha's? Fitting in mattered, especially, as we'll see, during the tumultuous years of World War I. There also may have been a dab of racial anxiety mixed in. In proclaiming Bix's aesthetic sensibility to be "catholic" as opposed to "Teutonic," Hoagy Carmichael rather too blithely added, at a time when the Ku Klux Klan had entered its second phase and was recruiting in Iowa, that "the tom-tom from the jungle beat in his pulse."

All things considered, the Beiderbeckes may have been unwilling or unable to escape the constraints of their class enough to fully support a son for whom "Tiger Rag" had become an ongoing obsession. Multiple biographers, their condescension as ruthless as it is unsurprising, have long suggested as much, although none goes so far as Berton. He declared that Bismark and Agatha were more anxious to receive the fickle approval of Davenport "society" (Berton's scare quotes, not my own) "than about the fate of their one black-sheep son, who might as well have been a two-headed creature from Venus, for all they knew or cared about what was going on inside him."

In some ways, Bix *was* a two-headed creature from Venus, disappearing into his music the way he did. The blank stare. The private astronomy. When I was a kid my weakness was Shostakovich, and his Fifth Symphony in particular, which he wrote in the first part of 1937 while under enormous pressure from Stalin to simplify his compositions and align them with a more heroic vision of the Soviet Union. "Enormous pressure" is a euphemism here. In fact, Shostakovich worried that on any given night he might be spirited away and shot, and I convinced myself that I could detect that fear in the black ice of the first movement, in the shimmering spaces between the notes. I also convinced myself, because I was seventeen years old, that this was a lot like high school. And more than once, with the symphony's triumphant finale still ringing in my ears—it purportedly sounded false to Shostakovich and he thought himself a fool for writing it, but to me, again because I was seventeen years old, it sounded positively orgasmic, a necessary release from all of my seventeen-year-old suffering—I burst onto the streets of Davenport, as I imagine Bix must have done, too. I took Middle Road down to McClellan Boulevard and then climbed the bluffs overlooking the wide Mississippi, still consumed by the music, surveying a vista that included slow-moving barges and paddleboats and the sprawling federal installation on Rock Island, before finally descending toward the smell of diesel and seaweed. Of course, unlike me, when Bix shuffled riverward he also shuffled musicward—down, down, down.

My room was in the basement, and Mom would stand at the top of our stairs and shout over the music, "Well, at least the boy is listening to something decent down there," but Bix enjoyed no such luxury. And worse yet, he could play. He could really *play*! I enjoyed no such luxury. Barely above average on the violin and viola, not even that on the piano and guitar, my obsessions encountered a natural roadblock, while Bix's, alas, did not. Sure, Mom and Pop Beiderbecke could dress him up and point him in the direction of school, but they couldn't force him, any more than my parents could, to avoid the lure of beer and cheap wine. They couldn't force him back up and out of his head.

And prior to that infamous moment when Bix's parents sent him off to prep school, they may have tried—which makes me curious about this whole idea of Davenport "society." What sort of constraints might it have worked on Bismark and Agatha as they tried to figure out what to do with their wayward, jazz-loving son? In search of an answer, I met William H. Roba for coffee. A historian on the faculty of a community college, Roba specializes in Davenport's German-Americans and for the last year he had been researching an article on Bix.

"It's not so much that he disappointed his family," Roba said, brushing muffin crumbs from his sweater. "It isn't so much that they didn't want him to play music. But they were worried about how it would impact business." Think about it, Roba said. Bix's grandfather was a wealthy banker, his father a businessman—both of them Germans doing their best to assimilate and move up the social ladder. Notice, too, how Bix's father married a woman of Irish stock and moved from the west, or German, side of town to Grand Avenue. "That was the mixed side of town," Roba said. "People were poorer, true. But they were American. It was the American side of town."

Bismark's best efforts, however, nearly sank with the *Lusitania*. At first, Americans had resisted intervention against the Germans, but when Woodrow Wilson finally received his declaration of war, anti-German sentiment spiked. German-Americans were no longer neighbors; they were Huns and spies. There were dire warnings about subversion and a total impatience for those reticent about war. Iowa governor W. L. Harding banned any language other than English from being spoken in public or in church, and in the town of Denison, an anti-German mob threatened to burn down the offices of the German-language newspaper and lynch its editor.

Governor Harding also ordered that "English must be the medium of instruction in all schools." This was Bix's freshman year in high school. "Seeing no need to teach German anymore at school, the authorities basically took it upon themselves to round up all the German textbooks or geography books—anything that might have a picture of the German Kaiser on it—and gather them all up in the parking lot of Davenport High," Roba said. It was May 8, 1918. "Everyone was let out of school, and you can just imagine the scene. They're out there smoking and laughing. They're singing patriotic songs. They're doing cheers for their class. And they're burning books. They burned all the books. All the German teachers, meanwhile, were summarily fired. They ended up keeping one who could also speak French."

So where's Bix in all this? He's keeping a low profile. Said Roba: "His whole life he could not run away from his name: Leon Bismark. The Iron Chancellor. It's like that line from *The Third Man*: 'She ought to go careful in Vienna.'" The Beiderbeckes, in other words, went careful in Davenport. Even three years later, Bix's antics may have been bad for business—the business of fitting in, of not making waves. The business of being American.

The biographers Richard Sudhalter and Philip Evans argue that most of Bix's "adult life may be viewed as a long unconscious struggle to eradicate a sense of guilt by striving for 'respectability' within his chosen field." That's why he wanted to join Whiteman; that's why he later showed interest in playing and composing classical music. "There was little hope of flexibility or real understanding from Bismark or Agatha; they were too intrinsic a part of Davenport and its culture for significant insight," write Sudhalter and Evans. "Nor was Bix's understanding of himself and his circumstances sufficient to cope. His ultimate destruction, viewed in this light, was all but inevitable."

At least with the information we have to work with so far in the story, this strikes me as gross overstatement. In the end, what did it really matter whether his parents truly understood him? What good did that do Bix? He wanted to play jazz and, from all accounts, he did play jazz.

On the last day of his sophomore year of high school—this would have been May 1920—Bix performed for Vaudeville Night at the Grand Opera House, singing first with the Boy's Glee Club choir and then with a vocal quintet called, at that time unremarkably, the Black Jazz Babies. The number "Ma Punkin Sue" was billed as a "jazz specialty" and featured the African American student Raymond Moore tap dancing while Bix unleashed a few riffs on his horn.

"It was the first time many of us had heard him play the cornet," Bix's sweetheart Vera Cox remembered. "It stunned everybody— nobody realized how good Bix had become since he started playing. He was quiet, you know, never made much of a show about things . . . He really thought he didn't have any real talent, and was honestly surprised when he got to be famous."

Fritz Putzier, meanwhile, had invited Bix to join Neal Buckley's Novelty Orchestra, and the following Christmas the group landed a nightclub gig worth, in Bix's words, "piles of jack." The job almost fell through, though, when a veteran conductor placed a call to Local 67 of the American Federation of Musicians, alerting the union that certain "punk kids" were working without union cards. Now, in order to obtain proper memberships and so keep their gig, Buckley, Bix, and the boys were required to audition as a band and take turns sight-reading. This was especially bad news for Bix, who played almost exclusively by ear and therefore was a terrible sight-reader. (One can almost picture Hadlock shaking a fat finger: "If only the boy weren't so lazy . . .")

When the big day arrived, everyone was full of nerves. One of Harvey Berry's violin strings broke while he was tuning up, and Dick Woolsey took forever to set up his drums. As for Bix, Sudhalter and Evans describe him as "shaky," and the implication is that this ought to be read literally. Presiding over the scene, meanwhile, was the union exec Roy Kautz—heavily starched, generally disapproving, and, in all ways that mattered, German. To Sudhalter and Evans he exemplified a later description of Davenport proffered by one of Bix's musician friends. In those days, he said, Davenport was a *"very* predominantly German town, whose music was *over* legitimate . . . a dotted eighth was a dotted eighth, and a vibrato was *verboten*, only excusable in a solo and then used sparingly . . . we punks who played jazz were frowned on and ridiculed as 'chassers,' German accent for 'jazzers.'"

Buckley's Novelty Orchestra performed its one memorized number competently enough, but then Herr Kautz distributed some sheet music and, sitting himself down at the piano, invited each musician to step forward and sight-read. All passed the test except for Bix, who rather than read his own part copied by ear Kautz's piano part. After stopping him, Kautz "put his arm around Bix because he was beginning to fall apart," Fritz later told an interviewer. "And tears actually formed in his eyes he felt so badly, because he knew that he was going to—that he was the force that we needed to get this job. And he knew that if he couldn't make the union, we wouldn't get the job."

Actually, the nightclub did finally offer the boys the gig—but minus Bix. They declined in the end, an admirable gesture of loyalty but also an acknowledgment that Bix's horn, even then, was central to their cause.

Bix must have been inconsolable. I imagine him bursting through the front door of 1934 Grand, flopping down on the couch, and having a good cry, feeling like he'd let his chums down. Yet however much his stomach must have churned that day, it was nothing compared with how it would churn four months later, when two police officers would knock on the door and politely ask for Mr. and Mrs. Beiderbecke.

It's no wonder that Bix titled his first composition "Davenport Blues." Set to wax in January 1925 at Gennett Records in Richmond, Indiana, with a few of his friends, the performance is at times sluggish and a little glassy-eyed. It may be that they were all drunk; one biographer says as much, noting how earlier in the day they had botched multiple takes of Hoagy Carmichael's "Washboard Blues" before nailing a rendition of the Original Dixieland Jazz Band's "Toddlin' Blues," so that by the time they got around to Bix's number, "the gin bottles were considerably lighter." Add to this the fact that Bix was composing the piece more or less as he went along and maybe we're lucky to have a recording at all. His long, laid-back solo boasts nothing of the martial precision that would mark his best years, yet his grasp of melody is perfect. Even while improvising, Bix lends the tune wonderful shape and clarity, allowing it to survive, if only barely, the gelatinous mash of trombone, clarinet, and piano.

It was never my favorite, in other words. Over the years, though, I began to notice flecks of melancholy in what before had sounded like off-the-rack Dixieland, little splashes of cobalt that picked up the deepening blue in Bix's biography, and all of it brought together by that unavoidably evocative title, "Davenport Blues." I'm projecting, I know, just as I did years ago with Shostakovich, but the pianist and arranger Gil Evans caught it, too, when he recorded the tune with his orchestra in 1959. The trumpeter John Coles announces the theme with such magnificent, understated anguish—I'm not sure I've ever listened to the original with the same ears again.

Then, in 2008, an artist named Grégory Elbaz published a graphic novel in French titled, simply, *Bix*. It begins in *le printemps du Jazz Age*, when hot music is not yet very hot and the frustrated clientele of a Mississippi River excursion boat dance as best they can, with couples beating their wings, Elbaz writes, like penguins. They are eclipsed, meanwhile, by the dark shadows of Elbaz's black-and-white drawings. Everyone is dark—except for Bix, who hovers on the riverbank, horn in hand. The symbolism isn't subtle: Bix is *un spectre*, a ghost; more literally, he is a vision, something you can *see*. In Elbaz's panels, moonlight bounces off the riverboat's wake, and as Bix tramps through some real *Lord of the Rings*-looking trees, he passes in front of the moon as it hangs from the night sky, absorbing all of its light.

He keeps on going, all the way to Richmond, Indiana, and when he arrives, his bandmates appear to be impatient, even a bit annoyed. The tech guy is more than ready to go with the wax, so, without further ado—and Elbaz, like a poet employing a perfect bit of enjambment, forces us to turn the page—*Bix joue.*

Bix plays.

These days, this is what I see when I hear "Davenport Blues." And while Elbaz's remarkable book takes what I reckon to be one of the more unexpected turns in the history of comics, I'm happy for now to stop here.

Bix plays.

Even when we're not sure we want it to, even when we're overcome by the shadows, that always redeems him.

What do I mean—"even when we're not sure we want it to"?

To answer that we need to go back to April 1921, and to that knock on the door. You know what, though? That scene, with all of its thorny, uncomfortable complications, can wait.

One of the many boats that regularly chugged up the Mississippi River from New Orleans was the *Sidney*. Run by the Strekfus Steamboat Lines and catering (according to its brochures) to only "the very best class of people," it featured dance music by the Fate Marable Orchestra, an ensemble that included Louis Armstrong on cornet and Warren "Baby" Dodds on drums. In a memoir published in 1959, Dodds recalled how he and Armstrong had met Bix and some of his friends sometime in 1920. While on the boat, wrote Dodds, "Louis told Bix he didn't have a horn, so Bix said, 'Well, meet me when I go out and I'll see if I can get you a horn.' And Bix took him out afterwards and helped him pick out a horn."

As stories go, this one is enormously appealing if a bit elliptical. For instance, why didn't Louis have a horn? How could he keep his job without one? And did Bix buy him a new cornet or did he just help him find a good shop? Dodds doesn't bother with such details because, perhaps, they're not the point. The point is that two giants— only two years apart in age but representing the two poles of 1920s jazz, "the twin lines of descent," to quote the critic Terry Teachout, "from which most of today's jazz can be traced"—*should* meet there on the Mississippi; like Huck and Jim, they *should* embrace and find common ground, if for no other reason than because a good story requires it. How else to tell the Davenport yin from the New Orleans yang than to thrust the two together? Forget the cities, though. No two *people* were more yin and yang than Bix and Louis.

For starters, Bix was white and Louis black (a single and obvious difference that many have said defines all the others).

Bix was from the North and Louis the South.

Bix was (comparatively) rich; Louis was poor.

Bix was raised in a (comparatively) buttoned-up culture by a strict father; Louis was raised in a carefree culture by a whole neighborhood of women.

Bix was an aw-shucks introvert, Louis the most flamboyant of extroverts.

Bix was a man of few words, Louis a singer and prolific writer.

Bix came from Sousa and Debussy, Louis from the Sanctified Saints and blues at the Funky Butt.

Bix played it cool, keeping his horn in the middle range; Louis played forever hot and high.

Bix was self-taught, his fingerings mangled; Louis was a virtuoso.

Bix kept his instrument close, its bell pointed down, even while soloing; Louis, on the other hand, was the consummate showman.

Bix was famous only among Davenporters and fellow musicians; Louis was a State Department goodwill ambassador and one of the first truly global celebrities.

Bix drank; Louis toked.

Bix never married, while Louis took four wives, among them a prostitute, a college girl, and a dancer.

And Bix died young, while Louis, of course, lived almost to seventy, joking after a particularly severe bout of pneumonia that "Bix tried to get me up there to play first horn in Gabriel's band, but I couldn't make the gig."

So they *should* meet in Davenport . . .

But did they?

Ralph Berton, for one, thought not, writing that only "legend-mongers" believed Bix had ever heard Louis play on the riverboat. Another Bix expert, Albert Haim, agrees. A French-born, Uruguayan-raised, American-educated chemistry professor, now retired, Haim presides over an influential online discussion site about Bix, and despite being generally humorless, he occasionally refers to himself in that context—and I'm not making this up—as His Royal Majesty King Albert the First of Bixonia. On the subject of Bix and Louis, King Albert has insisted that a white man and a black man walking together like that on the street was "pure fiction" and that Armstrong's "recollection of facts was pure . . ."

Bullshit or not, this was Dodds's recollection, not Armstrong's. Still, Louis did apparently recall the encounter, albeit in considerably less detail. In his second memoir, *Satchmo: My Life in New Orleans*, published in 1954, he described his first trip up the river to Davenport:

> It was there that I met the almighty Bix Beiderbecke, the great cornet genius. Every musician in the world knew and admired Bix. He made the greatest reputation possible for himself, and we all respected him as though he had been a god. Whenever we saw him our faces shone with joy and happiness, but long periods would pass when we did not see him at all.

To which the scholar William Howland Kenney has responded by declaring the whole passage to be a "carefully orchestrated" system of coded messages meant to inform readers that Satchmo's actual views of Bix were contrary, more or less exactly, to what he was saying. "He keeps his distance by offering a vaudeville stereotype of 'our' greetings to a third-party observer," Kenney, a professor of history and American studies at Kent State University, writes, referring to Armstrong. "At the same time, he indicates that while in Beiderbecke's physical presence, 'we' treated him respectfully, but not 'seeing' him for long periods of time, 'we' were not obligated to pay him respect."

To Berton, then, Armstrong must have been a legend-monger, to Haim a bullshitter, and to Kenney a code-talker. Tallulah Bankhead was more generous, commenting in 1952 that the trumpeter "uses words like he strings notes together—artistically and vividly." And in a short biography of Armstrong, Gary Giddins calls his second memoir "justly renowned," and notes that its author's "unself-conscious candor made many people uncomfortable . . . Journalists invariably refrained from asking tough or even interesting questions, in spite of—or perhaps because of—Armstrong's willingness to respond honestly."

And yet that honesty was routinely second-guessed. When Armstrong dedicated a book to Bix—his *first* memoir, 1936's *Swing That Music*—the renowned critic Albert Murray implied that it must have been someone else giving the nod to Bix. "Not even the inscription in the book comes across as a credible approximation of either his voice on the page or his point of view," Murray wrote.

So what's going on here? Did Bix and Louis meet on a riverboat or didn't they? And why are scholars intent on discrediting Armstrong's own words about himself and his friend? In *Commentary* magazine, Terry Teachout observes that "musicologists, while recognizing and acknowledging Beiderbecke's enduring significance, have nonetheless been strangely reluctant to treat him in the same way they treat Armstrong." Why, for instance, have there been only two major biographies of Beiderbecke in forty years: Sudhalter and Evans, which is out of print, and *Bix: The Definitive Biography of a Jazz Legend* by Jean Pierre Lion, a French businessman who couldn't read music? "The most obvious reason for this difference in treatment," Teachout writes, "is that Beiderbecke is white and Armstrong is black."

Of course, objections to a statement like that come easy. For instance, wouldn't such differences in treatment have more to do with the fact that Armstrong had a long and fully formed career while Bix died a question mark? And didn't Teachout, at the time working on his own Armstrong biography, choose Louis as a subject at least in part because no treatment of him equal to Sudhalter and Evans had yet been written?

All of that may be true, but it's also perfectly beside the point. "The heart of the matter is that there is a way of looking at jazz in which blackness is the source of its authenticity. And blues is the token. And if you have that point of view, then anything else you think is of secondary interest, because that's what defines it." This is Teachout talking in the flesh, by the way. He had invited me to his art-filled Upper West Side apartment on what happened to be the weekend of Bix's 103rd birthday to chat more about Bix, Louis, and the longest-running argument in jazz—the argument over race. A short, bespectacled fifty-year-old, Teachout crossed his legs under him and sipped a cup of tea. A recent hospitalization for congestive heart failure has slowed him down only a little: his appetite for the arts remains Lieblingesque. A former dance and classical music critic, his day job is drama critic for the *Wall Street Journal* and music critic for *Commentary*; he's also a prolific blogger. He has penned a biography of H. L. Mencken and, when I met him, was close to finishing *Pops: A Life of Louis Armstrong*, which was published in 2009. Teachout later adapted it for the stage. Another biography, of Duke Ellington, was published in 2013.

On this particular Saturday, he happily and fearlessly expounded on the views of the novelist-critic Albert Murray, his acolyte Stanley

Crouch, and their arch-nemesis Amiri Baraka (né LeRoi Jones), all of whom have argued, more or less, that blacks are the real originators and innovators of jazz, while white boys like Bix were less musicians than wannabes.

"Bix is indisputably a major figure in jazz who is white," Teach-out said, choosing his words carefully. "This pushes all kinds of buttons in people." By which he means people like Murray, who, in his respected book *Stomping the Blues* (1976), called Bix and his white colleagues "intruders" into discussions of the authentic jazz greats, all of whom, Murray contended, were black. In particular, Murray directed his ire at "certain self-styled liberal jazz critics" who objected to the term "race records." "Are they truly concerned about the symbolic segregation expressed by the term 'race records,'" he asked, "or are they aiming at a redefinition of blues music that will legitimize the idiomatic authenticity of certain white musicians, whose very accents indicated that they are *not* native to the idiom but who nonetheless enjoy reputations (and earnings) as great performers?" By this way of thinking, Bix was to jazz as Elvis was to rock and roll, or as Eminem ("the Bix Beiderbecke of rap," according to the website All About Music) is to hip-hop: the Great White Thief. Black = blues, Murray has argued persistently, passionately, and eloquently, and blues = jazz; therefore, black = jazz.

"I don't understand Murray," Teachout said. "I don't understand how somebody could take such an ahistorical approach and ignore obvious and well-known facts, and obviously only a non-musician can do that kind of thing, be so blissfully ignorant of the existence of major, first-tier black players for whom blues is not part of their self-expression."

Teachout, who is white, played jazz bass in Kansas City before moving to New York. He frets that too much of jazz history and criticism is entrusted to people who know nothing about music, "well-meaning amateurs," in the words of the composer and critic Gunther Schuller.

Like Murray, Baraka was also a non-musician, but his 1963 book *Blues People: Negro Music in White America* is at first blush more sympathetic to Bix. Writing under the name LeRoi Jones, he calls Beiderbecke an "innovator" whose love of jazz led him to "a common cultural ground where black and white America seemed only day and night in the same city." And this is how Baraka thought of Bix and Louis: as day and night. "The white middle-class boy from Iowa was the product of a culture which could *place* Louis Armstrong, but could never understand him," he writes.

> Beiderbecke was also the product of a subculture that most nearly emulates the "official" or formal culture of North America. He was an instinctive intellectual who had a musical taste that included Stravinsky, Schoenberg, and Debussy, and had an emotional life that, as it turned out, was based on his conscious or unconscious disapproval of the sacraments of his culture. On the other hand, Armstrong was, in terms of emotional archetypes, an honored priest of his culture—one of the most impressive products of his society. Armstrong was not *rebelling* against anything with his music. In fact, music was one of the most beautiful refinements of Afro-American musical tradition, and it was immediately recognized as such by those Negroes who were not busy trying to pretend that they had issued from Beiderbecke's culture.

For Baraka, the bottom line is that these two men, different as they were, came together—figuratively—to create a fully American music. And Bix Beiderbecke played a critical role, maybe even *the* critical role: he took Louis's African American music and made it American.

"And that's a profoundly racist argument," Teachout snapped. "It just comes from the opposite direction of Murray's. It's utterly racist. LeRoi Jones is as reverse racist as is humanly possible."

Teachout slurped his tea.

"My interpretation of jazz is that while it started out, obviously, demonstrably black music, whatever it means to be black—remember what a complex amalgam that is—it acquired other racial admixtures from the start," Teachout said. "It's perfectly obvious from the early history of New Orleans jazz. And it acquires a major figure in Bix at the same time, and I mean literally to the month, as Louis Armstrong."

"That's when they made their first recordings," I said.

"That's right. In 1924. So what I'm saying is that it was an American music to begin with. It's the quintessential expression of what it means to be American. That's its own myth, but it's a myth that happens to be true. And that's why Orwell used to say that Dickens was the kind of writer you wanted to have on your side, a good writer to steal. Jazz is a good art form to steal. It allows you to play in so many different kinds of contexts. Jazz musicians, as opposed to jazz critics, don't have arguments about race. Except for some who are themselves extremists, and they exist on both sides of the fence. Instead, they see the music as something that's accessible to everybody, and entry to the club is simply on merit. That's what the real culture of jazz is like when you're actually a part of it. And I'm even talking about people who have racial feelings, people like Miles Davis, who was very-clear cut about this: anybody can do this. Anyone's expression of it is authentic."

Teachout's unflagging intensity seems to have been part of what put him in the hospital. No pause for tea this time—

"The whole idea that the blues is somehow a defining characteristic of jazz, in whose absence one is not playing jazz, is ahistorical," he continued. "And crazy. And of course it's at the center of the whole Albert Murray–Stanley Crouch argument about jazz. And Beiderbecke naturally makes these folks squirm because blues plays no part in his musical expression at all."

Teachout bristles at the attacks his friend Richard Sudhalter's work—especially his huge volume *Lost Chords: White Musicians and Their Contribution to Jazz*, published in 1999—has sustained from critics who wish to downplay or deny the importance of early white musicians. Actually, those critics accuse Sudhalter et al. of downplaying and denying the importance of *black* musicians. The Yale professor John F. Szwed has singled out Sudhalter for "the persistence of [his] efforts to deny African and African American contributions to world culture," while Baraka wrote that "to read Lincoln Collier or Richard Sudhalter and their bizarre *ubermenschlichkeit* is to be annoyed with a tinge of melancholy that our oppressors are, to quote poet Robert Creeley, such 'unsure egotists.'"

It's true that Baraka has always been an academic Molotov cocktail, but according to Fredrick Woodard, a bearded, bald-headed professor of African American studies at the University of Iowa, an Oklahoma native, a former resident of Davenport, the father of a jazz musician, and for a time my landlord, that's the whole point. "LeRoi Jones is always signifyin' like hell on everybody," he told me one afternoon while drinking a gin and tonic. "There it is. What was interesting is that, hey, man, belonging to the academy these days doesn't mean you can't still do the signifyin'. Like Henry Louis Gates [author of *The Signifying Monkey: A Theory of African-American Literary Criticism*, published in 1989], you create a whole way of signifyin'. You attribute it to somebody else. That's exactly what you wanna do. I maintain that Henry Louis Gates came up with signifyin' because he wanted to do some signifyin' on some muthafucka and he did it. But he attributed it to a larger culture . . . Beautiful act. Wonderful jazz movement. And in a number of ways, it was just the prescription Ralph Ellison gives [for jazz]. Unpredictable. But all of a sudden when it comes, you recognize it. *Aw, I've seen that before. How did I let it creep up on me?* You know what I mean?"

To be honest, not always, but here's what I *do* know: in this argument over Bix and race, the world turns to black and white, day and night. You're either for Sudhalter or against him; you're either for Bix or against him. Writes the critic and novelist Stanley Crouch: "Beiderbecke ceases to be a great musician and becomes a pawn in the ongoing attempt to deny the blues its primary identity as Negro-developed, introspective music, which is about coming to understand oneself and the world through contemplation. To recognize that would be to recognize the possibility of the Negro having a mind and one that could conceive an aesthetic overview that distinguished the music as a whole. Troublesome person, that Negro—especially one with an aesthetic."

"That's the big problem with Stanley Crouch," Teachout responded. "My cat knows more about music than he does. So Stanley exudes these clouds of rhetoric which sometimes are evocative, although he really needs better editing, but he does not know anything about the stuff of music."

He leaned forward on his couch: "To tell the truth about jazz is so ennobling to blacks, you know. It's enough. You don't have to pretend that nobody did anything else worthwhile. And you don't have to pretend that everything blacks did was perfect. Just tell the truth and it's the most amazing story. You tell the truth about Louis Armstrong and it's the most wonderful and inspiring story. And it's something that kids should read."

"Okay," I said. "So what's the truth about Bix and Louis? Did they meet on a riverboat in Davenport or what?"

"It seems pretty likely to me."

"You think so?"

"Armstrong is unambiguous about it, that they met. But certainly he didn't hear Bix playing then or anything like that. But we know from Baby Dodds's memoir that they met and that Beiderbecke actually got a horn for Armstrong."

"You think that's true?"

"That's unambiguous. Dodds states that explicitly in his book."

As it happens, Professor Kenney's *Jazz on the River*, published in 2005, quotes from a letter Bix wrote to his sister, Mary Louise, in which he claims to have heard the "Faite Maribores bunch" in Louisiana, Missouri. Bix conspicuously fails to mention meeting Armstrong or the band, and even compares their music to the "real jazz niggers" on the South Side of Chicago. In the end, it's Bix's precision about the location—Louisiana, Missouri—that convinces Kenney. Other historians have pointed out that the riverboat *Sidney*, at least, never actually left New Orleans and that the Strekfus brothers, as a matter of policy, prohibited band members from mingling with customers.

Still, Teachout wasn't convinced. "Well, I think that Baby Dodds locks that up," he said. "Anyway, Armstrong's memories of Bix are so specific and enthusiastic and characteristic of his own way of telling stories about musicians that the meetings obviously made a very, very big impression on him. I'm sure that one of the reasons why they did was because Beiderbecke was white. Clearly Armstrong took Beiderbecke seriously. He is a white guy playing with the Whiteman band, which Armstrong admired. You know that Armstrong's favorite band was Guy Lombardo. This is not a joke. He was extremely catholic in his appreciation of music. He admired Beiderbecke, and he would have been very impressed by the role that Beiderbecke was playing in the band. He was quite specific about that."

In fact, Louis saw Bix perform with Whiteman and wrote ecstatically about the experience. When "all of a sudden Bix stood up and took a solo. . . . I'm telling you, those pretty notes went all through me," Armstrong wrote, noting that even with all of the cannon shots, ringing bells, and howling sirens that accompanied the 1812 Overture, Bix's "pure tone . . . cut through it all."

Don't expect Kenney to budge an inch, though, either; in *Jazz on the River* he points out that when Louis calls Bix's playing "pretty," that's "not necessarily a compliment among jazz musicians." For many, the truth will always be that Louis could never have loved Bix; to think otherwise is to be blind to the evidence or perhaps just naive. In other words, whether on the streets of Davenport or in the pages of a book, it's best that these two not be seen as being too chummy.

"Incidentally, it just occurred to me—and I'm not comparing Bix to Jesus—but there are definitely some resemblances between the way he gets written about and biblical textual criticism," Teachout said. "Or biographies of Shakespeare where people don't have enough primary-source material to work with and so they engage in wild speculation. The next thing, presumably, will be someone attempting to prove that Bix was, actually, you know, a black man who made these records under another name. The Francis Bacon theory of Bix Beiderbecke."

"I'm sitting here in the flickering candlelight, the clock on the wall says three-thirty—that's three-thirty A.M., mind you—and I'm down to the last few gulps of my bottle. . . . Ruined, I tell you, I'm ruined! And all because of that infernal, bug-eyed little cornet player Bix Beiderbecke."

So begins the week-after mea culpa of *Pulse of the Twin Cities* music critic Tom Hallett, who on February 12, 2003, in honor of Black History Month, included Bix's name on a list of "Five Black Jazz Legends You Should Hear." One reader pointed out that "Bix Biederbecke [*sic*] was as white as the coke on the proverbial hooker's ass," while another suggested that he was "white as . . . well, a dead boozed-up cornet player from Iowa."

"How was I supposed to know?" Hallett asked in an article that repeatedly exclaimed, in self-flagellating capital letters, that "BIX BEIDERBECKE WAS WHITE!!" "I mean it's not like Bix's face is ubiquitous on MTV or on the sides of passing city buses, right? (Although, oddly enough, on the day I began receiving mail from incensed readers concerning Bix's skin color, I also saw a huge freight truck passing by my window with the following three letters in huge red print on the side: BIX. Unreal, man.)"

Bix Beiderbecke was not, as it turns out, the only white Iowan to have embraced 1920s black culture and to have had that embrace cause confusion about the color of his skin. Let us not forget Carl Van Vechten, of Cedar Rapids. Carlo, as he liked to be called, was a novelist, critic, and photographer who controversially installed himself as Harlem's foppish patron of the arts, leading uptown tours of downtown white people who wanted, if not to mingle with, then at least to *see* African Americans. He was a "funny-looking man," according to Mabel Dodge Luhan, with big teeth. ("Really, those teeth," Luhan wrote. "They seem to have a life of their own apart from the rest of him. They are always trying to get onto the outside of his face. If they weren't there he'd be quite a different man, but his body has to struggle against them all the time!")

In addition to those teeth, Van Vechten also had, to borrow from Teachout, propinquity, which is to say, where Carlo was, so too was the action. The nation's first modern dance critic, he attended Gershwin's premiere of *Rhapsody in Blue* and helped bring Stravinsky to the United States. He was best friends with Scott and Zelda Fitzgerald and served as Gertrude Stein's literary executor. He was one of the chief white promoters of the Harlem Renaissance and, in particular, of Langston Hughes. And on top of all that, he was an accomplished amateur portrait photographer. Approximately 1,400 of his photographs are archived at the Library of Congress—mostly of friends, black and white; everyone from Bessie Smith to Stein to Faulkner to a famous and lovely image of Zora Neale Hurston.

Van Vechten admitted to feeling "addicted" to black culture, and in his letters to Hughes he went so far as to call himself "cullud," an attitude that prompted *Vanity Fair* to accuse him of sporting a "tan" from all that time spent in Harlem. The Mexican painter Miguel Covarrubias famously caricatured him in blackface and then added a caption that read, "A Prediction." Carlo relished this kind of attention, but he offended friend and foe alike—even his own father back in Iowa—when he affixed to an otherwise banal novel the title *Nigger Heaven*, a gesture that can also be seen as an attempt to "pass": it implied, after all, that the author was not operating under the normal jurisdiction of polite, white society. On one of his more irony-free days, Van Vechten even appended a footnote to the novel explaining that while the title epithet is "freely used by Negroes among themselves, not only as a term of opprobrium, but also actually as a term of endearment, its employment by a white person is always fiercely resisted." No kidding, Carlo! (Of course, African Americans were just as worried about their own pigment. Langston Hughes famously accused W. E. B. DuBois, with the latter's promotion of the "talented tenth," of trying to turn blacks into whites. He enjoined fellow "younger Negro artists" to instead "express our dark-skinned selves without fear or shame.") So while Hurston generously dubbed Van Vechten an "honorary Negro," his legacy—when he is remembered at all—is as a symbol of white voyeurism and exploitation.

Van Vechten also was gay, his long, sometimes tempestuous marriage notwithstanding. This was just another form of passing, according to the historian Ann Douglas, who cheekily suggests that "he took literally D. H. Lawrence's injunction to strip off the 'idealistic clothes' and see 'the dusky body' beneath." And some of his more erotic photographs suggest that this may have been true. All of which is to say that Van Vechten's life—spent watching, loving, and emulating African Americans despite being welcome among them largely (if not only) because of his position as their privileged white benefactor—was as complicated personally as it was socially.

What does this have to do with Bix Beiderbecke? Most obviously, Van Vechten's experience helps us understand just how fraught a white embrace of black culture was then or, for that matter, still is today. (I'm reminded of that fact every time I host a dinner party and have to hide his novel from view.) But Carlo also helps us anticipate how critics have objected to Bix—not as a musician, or as a jazz musician, but as a *white* jazz musician. Michael Eric Dyson, for instance, has accused Bix of stealing black culture and, specifically, the music of Louis Armstrong. "A major way many white youth articulated their alienation, and affirmed their sanity, authenticity, and legitimacy, was by latching hold of the mores mediated through the artistic values of black culture as expressed in the imaginations and visions of its great artists," he writes in *Open Mike*, a collection of essays published in 2002. "What happens is predictable: Bix becomes better known than his mentor in many artistic circles and gets the opportunity to make more money than Armstrong."

The irony, of course, is that Bix is not now nor has he ever been better known than Louis Armstrong, even in "artistic circles." Nor was Louis Bix's mentor; in fact, the two, despite being friends, did not seem to influence each other musically at all. But like Louis and Carlo, Bix wore many masks: white and black; hetero and—*spoiler!*—homo; hick from the sticks, musical sophisticate. "I get around," he told his friend Eddie Condon when Condon demanded to know where he ever came across that Proust fellow. And this, according to Ralph Ellison, is what made him truly American. On the occasion of listening to Satchmo sing "Mack the Knife," Ellison calls to mind Shakespeare's Caliban in a letter to his friend Albert Murray, riffing on the "man and mask, sophistication and taste hiding behind clowning and crude manners—the American joke, man." ("Jazz is musical humor," Bix supposedly told the *Davenport Democrat* in 1929. "Some of it is obvious enough to make a dog laugh. Some is subtle, wry-mouthed, or back-handed.")

"Europeans dream of purity," Ellison continues; "*any* American who's achieved his American consciousness knows that it's a dream so he ain't never been innocent, he's been too busy figuring out his next move. It's just that the only time he ever comes out from behind that mask is when he's cornered—*that's* when you have to watch him."

This point of view hasn't prevented the popular perception of Bix as innocent, or, more properly, *the* innocent, "the innocent who," the jazz critic Scott Yanow writes, "rose and fell during the 1920s before drinking himself to death." Bix was "naive," "a trusting sort," according to his friend Bill Challis. Bix was "this big overgrown kid, who looked like he'd been snatched out of a cradle in the cornfields," Mezz Mezzrow writes in his 1946 memoir, *Really the Blues*. To Hoagy Carmichael, Bix was "he of the funny little mouth, the sad eyes that popped a little as if in surprise when those notes showered from his horn." Bix was "a lost child," according to James Lincoln Collier. Bix is "like flowing water," Fred Woodard, my old landlord, told me, his gin and tonic refilled. "He moves into a space and he takes in everything that's there." From the perspective of black musicians of the time, Bix was far from the average white boy. "I mean, he was a farm kid playing very sophisticated music," Woodard said. "The perception of the musicians he was playing with was that he caught on very quickly to the manner of style, the manner of copying, the manner of creating in the moment, and he could do that. And Satchmo could see that. And he was such a spectacle in play, and had such an effortless spontaneity in an era when white Americans, and especially white American writers, were trying to capture some of that spontaneity. To see someone like Bix Beiderbecke was to say, 'Ahh, yeah! He's genuine. He's not black.'"

So to recap: according to Dyson, Bix is not black; therefore, he's not genuine. According to Woodard, he's genuine in part *because* he's not black. And according to Ellison, he's behind a mask. *That's* how we know he's authentic!

As Bix might have said, "What the hell?"

The meaning of authentic, meanwhile, is left to the imagination.

Here's one way of looking at it: authenticity in music is a myth, like the "lithe African beauty" of Van Vechten's overwrought fiction; it's an obsession with "the primitive" and with everything black—"the negroes are rhythmic as rain, and childish as weather," writes Herbert Corby in a poem that serves as the epigraph to Wareing and Garlick's biography *Bugles for Beiderbecke*—that may have started with jazz but really got going with rock and roll. Mezz Mezzrow, a Jewish kid from Chicago, claimed to have wished he had been born black, while Lou Reed, a Jewish kid from Brooklyn, actually recorded a song called "I Wanna Be Black."

And just as the primitive was valued over the civilized, the authentic over the fake, in jazz circles the improvised, pretty much by definition, always beat the composed. "People used to ask Bix Beiderbecke to play a chorus just as he had recorded it," the cornetist Jimmy McPartland once said. "He couldn't do it. 'It's impossible,' he told me once. 'I don't feel the same way twice.'" Thelonious Monk later gave this idea a political spin: "Jazz and freedom go hand in hand," he said.

"That explains it. There isn't any more to add to it. If I do add to it, it gets complicated. There's something for you to think about. You think about it and dig it. You dig it."

Which is what Cornel West did. "I use the term 'jazz' here not so much for a musical art form," he wrote in *Race Matters* (1994), "as for a mode of being in the world, an improvisational mode of protean, fluid, and flexible dispositions toward reality suspicious of 'either/or' viewpoints."

This sense of the authentic, improvised, democratic self extended to the Beats. Jack Kerouac, for instance, aspired to a "lyric-alto" style after the jazz saxophonist Lee Konitz, hoping, in the process, to achieve "the unspeakable visions of the individual." In a similar fashion, Malcolm Lowry, author of the novel *Under the Volcano* (1947), claimed to have wanted to write like Bix played, and the editor Malcolm Cowley presumed that so did the critic Otis Ferguson. "Sometimes I think that his idea was to write as Bix Beiderbecke played the jazz cornet," Cowley writes, "with 'always this miracle of constant on-the-spot invention, never faltering or repeating, every phrase as fresh and glistening as creation itself.'" It's a powerful bit of myth, and Leon Wieseltier once tried to knock it down in the *New Republic* (ironically, the magazine for which Ferguson was an editor): "Improvisation in jazz is not a release from structure, and structure in jazz is not an experience of oppression," he wrote. "Jazz is no more democratic than any other art. It is governed, like all art, by an either/or: either you do it well or you don't."

I like his point, but the Romantic logic of primitivism and freedom is just too relentless, especially when it finds a home in music. "Music is a brilliant agent of ideology," the British poet Ruth Padel has written. "It has a unique power to make something else seem natural, seem 'just the way things are.'"

This, of course, is the real musical joke.

"You hear a song, like it, and pass it on re-stuffed with your fantasies, myths and words," Padel writes. "The whole lot is a product of history, like any artifact." African conga drummers are no less immune to it than Lou Reed. And all "authentic" ends up meaning, Padel concludes, is "sanctified by a job-lot of second-hand myths."

So drop the needle on, say, "I'm Coming Virginia." It's Bix's longest solo and one of his masterpieces, although it's true that the great African American vocalist Ethel Waters got there first. She recorded the tune in September 1926 and the following year sang it on Broadway in the revue *Africana*. As she wrote in her memoir, Waters belted it out for the "ofays" and then watched them swoon, just like they did for any "dear old mammy tune."

Bix cut his version on May 13, 1927, in New York, and it betrays pretty much no hint of what the song may have meant for Waters or her audience. In addition to getting rid of the icky Lost Cause lyrics, he eschews the gutbucket growls and half-valves that were just becoming popular with Duke Ellington and instead digs deep into the melody. In the style of an Impressionist, and with all the manly restraint of Henry James, he suggests rather than declaims the tune's dark melancholy, taking Frank Trumbauer's solo on C-melody sax—the handoff is just perfect—and gently refining it. His "correlated" phrases (Bix's term) build, one on top of the other, until Bix finally leaps up to what for him is a relatively high register and delivers what Richard Sudhalter once rather dramatically described as "Caravaggio-like shafts of light."

"Jesus Christ," my girlfriend moans when I read her that quotation. "Is it even *possible* to write about Bix without turning all purple?"

She has a point, but that's the thing about music, isn't it? It's the vessel of almost rock-pure emotion and myth.

"The world of Greek mythology was not a place of terror for the human spirit," wrote Edith Hamilton, the great scholar of classical mythology. "It is true that the gods were disconcertingly incalculable. One could never tell where Zeus's thunderbolt would strike. Nevertheless, the whole divine company, with a very few and for the most part not important exceptions, were entrancingly beautiful, with a human beauty, and nothing humanly beautiful is really terrifying."

I'm not going to parse the words of someone so distinguished as Hamilton—if not terrifying, then something else that causes men to fall to the floor shaking. You'll recall that's what Hoagy Carmichael claimed happened to him the first time he heard Bix play (more precisely, he claimed to fall onto a "davenport," a detail that, Atlas-like, hoists this otherwise-just-odd anecdote high into the thin air of myth). Louis Armstrong purportedly admitted to once having wept openly at a jam session because he "could never play as good as Bix," while the normally measured critic Gary Giddins recalled how he wept at hearing Louis for the first time: "I lifted the platter and noticed a wet spot, a drop of water on the vinyl, and realized I was crying." Elsewhere, eyes pop, gizzards jerk, feet jump: a whole jazz literature was founded at the foot of Hoagy's couch and the terrifying tip of Zeus's thunderbolt.

"There is always a poignancy to Bix's playing as if its beauty is too rare and refined, even too fragile, for this world. We almost held our breaths through his solos as we would watching a fawn running loose in the streets of New York," wrote the cornetist Randy Sandke in *Bix Beiderbecke: Observing a Genius at Work* (1996).

"No, seriously. Jesus Christ."

You might recall Fred Woodard's suggestion that LeRoi Jones, now Amiri Baraka, "is always signifyin' like hell on everybody," a statement punctuated by "There it is." In a new introduction to *Blues People*, written in 1999, Baraka appears content with this description, even likening himself to Billy the Kid, "admittedly and very openly shooting from the hip. . . . The book, from its opening words, got me high."

So I asked Baraka, ten years later and now forty-six years after *Blues People* was first published, if that's how he still felt.

"Well, first of all, I don't have that much time," the 75-year-old poet, playwright, and critic told me over the phone. I think it's fair to say he was annoyed—annoyed and impatient. I could hear the exasperated sigh, an implied bit of growl.

For several years I had been eager to connect with Baraka—ever since interviewing Teachout, in fact—and Woodard advised me that the key to winning the man's cooperation was approaching him "with sincerity." I puzzled over what this might mean, especially in the breach. I pictured myself showing up at his Newark, New Jersey, home wearing a kufi hat and being all, "Bix Beiderbecke, man. You dig?" And him being all, "Get out my fuckin' house!" Which would have been more than reasonable, all things considered. But then I thought some more about Woodard's description of him. The thing about Baraka, the professor had told me, is that he'll "go inside an idea, he'll go inside a construct, and wear it like a hat for three, four, five days, or three, four, five years. And when he's done with it, you can go through and trace and see the artistic embellishments that he's made on it, and when he abandons it, it's gone. He's got another hat, and he plays out the implications of that. . . . It's intellectual graffiti. Okay? So what? It's there."

This could be an elaborate justification for a dude who believes nothing—if Baraka can wear his hat and abandon it, why can't I slap on a kufi?—but Woodard, who was deep in conversation with himself, beat me to it. "Well, where's his commitment? *Huh? I'm committed to every single one of those. You know?* He was committed to every single one of those at the time that he was in it, so he could explore those honestly. And I would say, *he* would say, that he was authentically involved in each one of them. All right?"

All right. Woodard then goes on to describe Albert Murray as "inauthentic," and Murray's mentor, the great novelist Ralph Ellison, as a fox, a wolf, a coyote: "But when he comes at me as a coyote and tries to convince me that he's a wolf, I ain't buyin' those tickets, you know what I mean?"

All of which left me more nervous than ever about talking to Baraka, who was last in the news for his long poem about 9/11, "Somebody Blew Up America" (2001), which features a few lines—preceded by the question, "Who set the Reichstag Fire"—implying that the Israeli government knew about the attacks in advance and had evacuated its citizens from the Twin Towers. Coming as it did from New Jersey's sitting poet laureate, the poem caused such an uproar (a "detonation," to quote Baraka's own website) that the state stripped him of his title, in the process doing away with the position altogether. (The Newark public schools stepped in and named him *their* poet laureate in December 2002.)

Was this all just a hat, then? Just a construct, a bit of intellectual graffiti?

After years of avoiding such questions, I was put in touch with a colleague of Baraka who provided me with his mailing address. I typed him a letter, deciding to leave out all mention of bombs and Jews; still, he didn't reply. His colleague then provided me with Baraka's phone number, but with the understanding that he probably wouldn't appreciate a call. And that long, exasperated sigh seemed to suggest that she was right. I quickly mentioned Bix and the book, and I said that I could even take the train up to Newark to meet him in person.

"That ain't gonna happen," he said matter-of-factly, and when he finally agreed to an interview, it was only for a few minutes.

So: Billy the Kid? Signifyin' like hell? Abandoned hats?

"As far as my views on Beiderbecke, they remain pretty much the same," he told me in a raspy voice. "I think that he was a very singular kind of artist who represented a particular set of influences in the music and brought a kind of, you know, singular lyrical style to the music. There's always been excellent white players in jazz from its inception. The point is that the racist nature of society has always tried to make them the creators of it, the innovators in it, or just to leave out, you know, the *real* innovators and originators, and that's the only thing I've ever said. A lot of the critics seem to be more intent on establishing a false kind of history of the music and its development than just evaluating what exists, you know?"

I reminded Baraka of his reference to "Lincoln Collier or Richard Sudhalter and their bizarre *ubermenschlichkeit*." He chuckled.

"Sudhalter wrote a lot about Bix," I said. "Is there a way he wrote about those early white musicians that particularly bugged you?"

"Who?"

"Sudhalter."

"Sudhalter? No, no, no, no. My thing about Sudhalter is him claiming that the music rose up spontaneously within both the Afro-American and white communities post-slavery, which would either make slavery a common cultural background, or at least diminish the influence that slavery, and the Afro-American culture that developed out of that, had on the rest of the United States. You cannot make them the same because the history is not the same. And if you *try* to make them the same, well, then what's the point of that? If you're supposed to be a scholar, why are you doing that, you know?"

Which really gets to the heart of why I wanted to talk to Baraka. When I met with him in 2005, Terry Teachout energetically attacked Baraka's argument in *Blues People* (Teachout: "as reverse racist as is humanly possible"), not to mention Albert Murray's contention that the blues—as a music and as a cultural experience—is the foundation of jazz (Teachout: "ahistorical"). From everything I had read, I tended to agree with Teachout, but that was easy to do, especially over tea. I wanted to hear Baraka make his best case in order to better understand how Bix Beiderbecke fit in to the history of jazz.

"When you say that Sudhalter was trying to make the black and white musicians the same," I said, "can you help me understand what you mean by that?"

"No, he's talking about the originators. He's trying to make bands like the New Orleans Rhythm Kings and the Original Dixieland Jazz

Band—white bands—the originators of the music itself. I will say this: they might have originated what he *knows* of that kind of—I won't call it co-optation, but at least the *reflection* of original black music. He might see that as some original thing, as you could say that Bix Beiderbecke was original, you know. But what I'm saying at the same time is that it does not exist without the Afro-American origins of it. That's all. And that should be obvious to anybody. I mean, you know, unless you're gonna tell me that these white people were slaves and hence picked up the same traditions. I mean, they cannot have the same lives. It's like uh, that uh, what was that TV thing that played . . ."

Baraka paused, before continuing: "You know, there was a time when that TV thing that plays all that popular music wasn't going to let Michael Jackson on there because he was black."

This time *I* paused.

"Oh, MTV, you mean?"

"MTV, right," he said. "But it's like MTV, you know, producing a whole bunch of white singers who've been influenced not only by Michael but the whole music itself, *denying* that source and that influence, you know, or objectively denying it by refusing to admit it or to point it out. So to me, that was Sudhalter's thing. I'm reacting particularly to an essay he had in the *New York Times* where he was actually advocating this kind of common origins for the music rather than its actual history."

The article to which Baraka referred appeared on January 3, 1999, and was a condensed version of the introduction to Sudhalter's soon-to-be-published volume, *Lost Chords*. In it, Sudhalter described an "emerging orthodoxy" in jazz that

> proclaims there were no major white innovators and few white soloists of real distinction; that the best white players were little more than pale (in both senses) copies of black originals, and that in any case they affected only other white musicians. Even those black jazzmen who took inspiration from whites did so only when no other models were available, the theory goes, and by some combination of instinct, heritage, and genes were naturally more adept at the game.

The underlying assumption, now also shared by legions of fans, is that jazz is somehow more "authentic" when played by blacks.

57

Sudhalter calls this view a "Noble Lie" in the tradition of Plato's *Republic*—good motivation for inner-city black kids but a perversion of history. He cites "mounting scholarly evidence" that "documents a significant and creative white presence in 'hot music' from its inception, even in the cradle, turn-of-the-century New Orleans." He writes that early white jazzmen looked up to their black counterparts, but that the reverse was true, as well, and that these white players also influenced later generations. "The saxophonist Eddie Barefield loved to recall the expression on 17-year-old Lester Young's face when, one snowy night in Bismarck, N.D., the future 'Prez' first heard 'Singin' the Blues,' as performed by Frank Trumbauer, whose dry, witty saxophone style became Young's chief inspiration."

The only time Sudhalter mentions the origins of jazz, he's vague, referring to a white "presence" at "its inception" and "in the cradle," by which he means in "turn-of-the-century New Orleans." One could read this to mean that white players were there from the *very* beginning or almost the very beginning; he doesn't say one way or the other who invented jazz. So is Baraka battling a straw man here? Maybe not. Sudhalter is less vague and more provocative in the full introduction to *Lost Chords*, in which he writes that "research into the origins and early development of jazz" has indicated for him "that the music may not be so much a black American experience as an *American* experience," with white musicians playing a "decisive" role. This earned him a rebuke from a reviewer in the *Times*, who calls Sudhalter's book "flawed" and "a strained polemic." The reviewer further notes with approval Albert Murray's link, among African Americans, between Saturday night dancing and Sunday morning sermonizing. Sudhalter, on the other hand, "casually remarks" in *Lost Chords* that spirituals are "a tradition now known to be shared almost equally by black and white." The reviewer calls such a statement "stunning" and wonders, like Baraka, whether Sudhalter now wants to claim slavery for white folks, too.

Maybe Sudhalter is the one battling straw men. After all, who exactly forms this "emerging orthodoxy" he writes about? Murray and Baraka, who are the named villains of the piece, are hardly "emerging"; Murray was not quite eighty-three years old when Sudhalter published his essay. (He died in 2013.) It's true that by 1999 the trumpeter Wynton Marsalis, a Murray acolyte, had been artistic director of Jazz at Lincoln Center for twelve years, and that his program had been accused of systematically ignoring the contributions of white musicians to jazz. "Marsalis talks constantly about jazz as a true reflection of American democracy," Eric Nisenson complains in *Blue: The Murder of Jazz* (1997). "Yet how can he leave whites and other races out of that democracy? Is that a 'true reflection' of American life? Like it or not, there really are a rather large number of white folks in this country . . ." And yet Sudhalter doesn't mention Marsalis or judge his influence.

On the phone with Baraka, I gave the glass-half-full version of Sudhalter's argument: "I read Sudhalter and what I take him to be saying is that these early white musicians, Bix being one of them, are not always given enough credit for their importance in the early history of jazz."

Baraka just laughed.

"But you're saying—" I sputtered. "Well, you laugh. What do you think?"

"No, I mean, if you're gonna tell me that Paul Whiteman is the King of Jazz, then we have to stop talking about it."

"I didn't mention Paul Whiteman."

"No, but I'm saying that's what Sudhalter's denying. By him saying they're not getting enough credit, I mean, how does Benny Goodman get to be the King of Swing? You know the point. I'll say this: I don't resent them appropriating the music. What I resent is the fact that the black musicians don't get paid the same thing. Otherwise, they can take all they want to. Everybody learns from somebody. There's nothing wrong with that. It's the social context that makes it, you know, abusive."

I felt like Baraka had shifted on me: we had been talking about the origins of jazz; now he was complaining about the selling of jazz, and about the profits. I wanted to get back to Bix. Earlier in this book I paraphrased Baraka's argument about the importance of Bix and Louis, an argument that Teachout called "profoundly racist." I read Baraka my two sentences:

For Baraka, the bottom line is that these two men, different as they were, came together—figuratively—to create a fully American music. And Bix Beiderbecke played a critical role, maybe even *the* critical role: he took Louis's African American music and made it American.

"Did I get that right?" I asked.

"Well, see, the point is this: it's all American. Beiderbecke is recognized as a kind of avatar of a great thing. You understand what I'm saying? They're both playing American music, but Beiderbecke is *recognized* as playing American music. Louis is then made into some kind of extension of American music that ain't really American music, and that's not true. They're both American music. What distinguishes them ultimately is the social context that they created in."

By which he means the black context and the white context. And the symbol of the former, to echo Murray, is the blues. "Without the blues, I don't think you have jazz," Baraka said. "When you're listening to Duke Ellington, you're always listening to some aspect of the blues, always. Same with Cole Porter or Irving Berlin or Jerome Kern, you know. You can listen to Cole Porter all night, man. What you keep hearing is how he keeps taking the blue strain—which is not just twelve bars, which is a feeling, you know."

And Bix?

"He was influenced by it. He's an American."

Teachout and Sudhalter disagree, of course, arguing that Bix and his mates made almost no reference to the blues in their playing. But for Baraka, the blues is something deeper. Louis Armstrong grew up poor in New Orleans and he got it. Miles Davis grew up middle class outside St. Louis, but he, too, got it. Bix Beiderbecke also grew up middle class, but he didn't get it.

"You know, Beiderbecke might have amazed people to be playing, quote, *jazz* then, you know, which made him, I guess, to a lot of people unique and very interesting," Baraka said. "But Louis Armstrong was a great figure in that music from its mainstream."

Baraka seemed less impressed with Bix the more he talked. In *Blues People*, he writes that when whites like Bix and his friend Hoagy Carmichael first heard Louis, a.k.a. "the genuine article," it "must have been much like tasting real eggs after having been brought up on the powdered variety." That Carmichael expressed a preference for Bix over Louis means little. "There's no certainty that a person will like the original if he has developed a taste for the other," Baraka writes.

"You listen to Bix, you listen to what Bix knows about the world and how he does it," he said to me. "Now what they're going to do with that in American society"—Baraka chuckled—"is another thing. But you can't possibly say you like Langston Hughes but you don't like William Carlos Williams. That's not an intellectual argument, you know what I mean? But the point is, you have to acknowledge where they are coming from each to get what they got."

"I mean, to me, a more important musician, in terms of American music, is obviously Louis Armstrong," Baraka, who died in 2014, said. "But I'm not gonna deny the importance of Bix Beiderbecke. That's *crazy*."

Admittedly, I've lost the thread of our narrative a bit. The last we saw Bix, he was a student at Davenport High and perhaps even a reader of Proust. He was also something of a musical prodigy, although apparently too lazy to learn how to sight-read, thus causing Neal Buckley's Novelty Orchestra to lose out on what would have been a sweet-paying gig. Of course, we shouldn't forget that business about the controlling hands and the Tragic Temperament or—in the words of Sudhalter and Evans—his "long unconscious struggle to eradicate a sense of guilt," but for now we're still going to hold off on the cops at the door. Instead, let's just fast forward to September 1921.

That's when Bix left Davenport for Lake Forest, a school that while not a military academy was nonetheless renowned for its discipline. He lasted just nine months. The biographer Jean Pierre Lion wryly comments on "the apparent delusion of parents who, concerned about releasing their son from his musical demons, were sending him to the gates of hell: Chicago." And as you might expect, unexcused absences immediately began to pile up as Bix connected with like-minded students and locals to play jobs at nightclubs near the school; this was how he met Don Murray, the clarinetist who would become his closest friend. Bix also took the train into the city, hanging out at the Friar's Inn—a "big money" establishment, as they used to say, catering to the likes of Dion O'Banion and Al Capone—where he sat in with the New Orleans Rhythm Kings and first made the acquaintance of Hoagy Carmichael, then a law student at Indiana University. He was finally expelled from Lake Forest in May 1922, after which he joined a band full time.

If you're so inclined, you can follow this phase of Bix's life by reading, in the pages of that doorstop by Evans and Evans, his many letters home to Mom and Dad. A friend of mine has done that and it has not improved her view of Bix, whose music she otherwise adores.

"The more I read about Bix, the more I become convinced there was something fundamentally, seriously wrong with him," she once e-mailed me. "I had to give up communicating with people who think Bix's letters in Evans & Evans show us a warm, loving, light-hearted, mischievous boy (when what I saw was lies, disrespect, and a casually arrogant assumption that he, Bix, didn't really have to operate under the same social rules that governed other people's behavior), because I didn't want to hurt their feelings, and they so obviously need Bix to be all those good things."

In many of his letters, of course, Bix *is* all those good things. Here's one example from Evans and Evans, a note to Agatha dated Tuesday, February 28, 1922, in which Bix tries to finesse a recent run-in with Lake Forest's headmaster, John Wayne Richards. He begins with a couple paragraphs of sweet-talking his mom on the occasion of her birthday—"Let's see, your 42 now aren't you or is it 32 I've forgotten" (actually 52 on March 1)—before mentioning that he had been called into Mr. Richards's office, where he had learned the facts concerning academic "parole."

"We had a good talk—he sure is a peach—he told me that I had done much better in my studies and holding myself down than he had expected I would due to my handicap in being a musician," Bix writes. Mr. Richards apparently went on to admit having underestimated his charge—"he thought I'd be a girl snip and a social butterfly judging from my [high school] record"—and then asserting his hope that Bix would return in the fall. "I just thought I'd say this to convince you that I have something in me," Bix tells his mother, "which surprises me as much as it does you."

Oh, and about that parole: it was merely temporary. "Mark my word Ill get at least 4 c's & possibly 5—that's a promise. Please take this to heart mam," he concludes, "as nearly everyone is on parole that took part in the mid-winter plays."

The next few pages of Evans and Evans are full of baseball scores, tales of Bix sneaking out nights to blow his horn, even an appearance before a student disciplinary committee. There are no more letters home, however, and no official notice from Lake Forest other than this, from May 21: "By a faculty vote, Bix was asked to withdraw from Lake Forest for consistently being 'out of his room after lights out.'"

Conspicuously missing from this account is the correspondence from Mr. Richards to Mr. and Mrs. Beiderbecke. For that we must turn to Jean Pierre Lion—his biography of Bix was published in 2005—who writes that in informing Bix's parents of the school's decision, Mr. Richards noted that their son's "influence around the school has been felt to be very injurious" and "that certain parents have objected strenuously to their sons' association with him." The Beiderbeckes were quite naturally taken aback by this, and Mr. Richards, Lion writes, was himself "highly surprised" that they didn't know the full story of Bix's expulsion. "At the time he left," Mr. Richards wrote Bismark and Agatha in a letter dated May 29, "we were not absolutely dead sure as to his part with regard to liquor around the School. Since then we have definitely learned that he was drinking himself and was responsible, in part at least, in having liquor brought into the School. . . . The more we have found out concerning him since he left, the more we regret the things he did and are sorry that he was in the School at all. Bix is a very clever excuse-maker, and I think he sometimes fools even himself in a way."

It's this last line that is such a killer. Was Bix lying to his mam? Was he telling the truth? Was he a good kid, a hooligan, or something worse? Who knows?

Not even Bix!

I'm probably being melodramatic here, but recall that it was Bix's nephew who scolded me into reading Evans and Evans in the first place, who implored me to take more seriously my job of getting all the facts straight. And now here I am discovering that Evans and Evans were themselves guilty of leaving out some pretty important facts. Clearly Bix was expelled for much more than simply being "out of his room after lights out"; in fact, Mr. Richards, rather than diplomatically apologizing to the Beiderbeckes for being forced to uphold a strict set of rules, is telling them that *Bix is a bad kid*. He doesn't want Bix influencing the other boys and is sorry their son ever came to Lake Forest in the first place.

This would horrify me as a parent, while as a Bixophile it leaves me wondering: who was Bix Beiderbecke and what else don't I know about him?

It was the spring of 1924, and Hoagy Carmichael was in love. "The moon was always out," he writes in *The Stardust Road*, the first of his two published memoirs, and "the air was thick and soft and pale purple. Grass was greener . . . moon was yellower."

Sprawled out inside the Kappa Sig fraternity house in Bloomington, Indiana, he took a swig of whiskey—"like kerosene in your mouth and a blowtorch going down"—before offering the bottle to Bix. In the background, Stravinsky's *Firebird* screeched and moaned on the Victrola, casting dark shadows over the mood of the room.

Bix pushed the bottle back at Hoagy, telling him, "Wonderful. Have another slug."

"What's wonderful?"
"Music."
"Sure. Whisky too."

It goes on, with the dialogue-heavy scene written as Hollywood banter—all Hepburn and Tracy, with few attributions and spare description. Still, when Hoagy asks, "What's wonderful?" you can hear in his voice the hopefulness, but also the neediness: the greener grass and the yellower moon. When Bix answers with only "Music," a deflated Hoagy tries to cover for himself. *Sure. Music. Whoo boy, that's what I meant. And whiskey, too!* Then comes some lame joking about torts and tarts, initiated by the law student Hoagy. He persists until Bix finally snaps, "Leave that crummy joke alone; I got that crummy joke."

Carmichael plays the scene for light humor, but there's nothing light or humorous about *The Firebird*. Written in 1910 by Igor Stravinsky, the ballet tells the story of the good prince Ivan, evil Koshchei the Immortal, twelve captive princesses, and the brightly plumed firebird that helps to set things straight. Stravinsky's music is frenetic, discordant, violent, scary, sometimes hypnotic, at other times breath-takingly beautiful. It's never funny, though, a fact that casts an ironic pall over Hoagy's forced attempts at wit. What he hopes might come off as charming ends up just being uncomfortable, a point under-lined by Bix's flash of temper.

At this point, Hoagy writes, "There was a long silence," after which Bix asked—"softly"—why Hoagy didn't write music.

Hoagy protested. It was Bix who wrote the music; he did it while blowing his horn. "You write yours different every time," Hoagy said.

"What's wrong with that?" Bix asked. "I like it different."

Carmichael practically begs us to read this scene as loaded, with lines like that last one, or the talk about tarts, or Bix suddenly speak-ing "softly." Years later, Carmichael wrote into his second published memoir, *Sometimes I Wonder*, a shorter version of the same conversa-tion, in which Bix explained that yes, Stravinsky also studied law, and it was Rimsky-Korsakov who told him he should be writing music in-stead. "So he wrote this," Bix said, alluding to *The Firebird*. "The fags dance to it."

In both versions, Bix then gets up and performs a "clumsy, half-loaded" entrechat, the ballet jump in which dancers quickly interlace their legs, after which—and this is from *Sometimes I Wonder*—he "lay where he fell, moaning softly."

"The music filled us both, I sensed, with terrible longing, dreadful urges, wonderful desires," Hoagy writes. "Coupled with white mule liquor, it was strangely moving. It made us very close and it made us lonely, too, but with a feeling of release, a feeling of elation and ec-stasy. You don't forget such a mood. They only come a few times in a lifetime."

For Hoagy, anyway. Turns out that Bix liked to do this sort of thing all the time. Fred Bergin told Phil Evans, "One morning Bix and I came out of our room under the pavilion after drinking gin and lis-tening to Firebird all night (complete with a red light over the record player)." Carmichael never mentioned a red light, but it would have made the already eerie music even eerier, an already trippy scene even trippier. The mythological firebird is renowned for its glowing red plumage; is that the reason for the light bulb? I don't know, but Bix enjoyed a similar night with another bandmate, Karl Spaeth, who remembered: "When we all got high we'd go up to the room and listen to records of Stravinsky's *The Firebird* and *Petrouchka* to the glow of a dim red light. Bix, of course, was a great one to partake of any nectar that would induce an 'out of this world' feeling." Paul Mertz recalled doing the same thing up in Detroit, explaining that they also sometimes used a blue bulb, "to give atmosphere, see." Bix, he said, "certainly got a bunch of converts." Maybe Hoagy was just one in a long line of such converts, or maybe Bix, too, experienced one of those few-times-in-a-lifetime moments and sought to re-create it with Fred and Karl and Paul.

Whatever the case, Carmichael's scene barrels forward, with one especially embarrassing exchange recorded in *The Stardust Road*. Music "hurts you across the top of your nose if you can't blow it out," Bix said.

> "But you can't blow it all out."
> "You can try."
> "Bix," I said.
> "Yeah."
> "Like what . . . kind of like with a girl . . . ?"
> There was another long pause.

I'll bet there was. And if you think that I'm reading too much into this, then so is Peter B. Lowry. In a published review of a Carmichael biography written by Richard Sudhalter the folklorist worries that Hoagy's "Bix fixation borders on homo-erotic necrophilia. Come on, give us a break! Middle-class musician drinks himself to death, leaving a small trail of instances of his squandered talent and his spoor has been examined to death ever since. Get a life!" It would be kind to say that Lowry's judgment—of Bix and of Hoagy, not to mention, I suppose, of Sudhalter—is venomous. *Homo-erotic necrophilia?* He makes it sound so dirty and sick, when Hoagy seems to be telling us the opposite. *This is perhaps the central relationship of my life. Bix is why I quit the law and started to write music. Bix is why I wrote "Star Dust."* And that, I suspect, would be fine with Lowry—absent that peculiar and awkward hint of . . . sex.

Speaking of the ballet, Ralph Berton's older brother Gene was a dancer and no doubt was skilled at the entrechat. After Bix's death, he told Ralph that he blamed himself more than anyone for their friend's tragic end. Berton asked why. After all, the two of them—Bix and Gene—had had nothing in common. Even the music they loved had been different.

"We had more than you think," Gene replied. "I don't mean just because of our little fling. I mean that in a way I was *doing* with my life what he *should* have been doing—and do you know something? He knew it too. Bix knew it."

Gene went on in that vein for a bit—to a man, the Bertons loved to talk, apparently—until Ralph finally had a chance to respond.

"Wait a minute," he told his brother. "What do you mean by a 'fling'?"

We've finally reached that point in the story where Bix is now Bix—not becoming Bix or losing Bix to drink. Ironically, though, this is exactly when things turn boring. It's one band after another, one town after another; days spent on sooty trains or dusty country roads, nights spent playing the same sets of tunes in front of the same sorts of crowds. Bix hooked up with Frank Trumbauer, whom he had first met in Davenport several years earlier, and the two played an eight-month engagement at the Arcadia Ballroom in St. Louis before joining the Jean Goldkette Orchestra out of Detroit before joining Adrian Rollini's short-lived New York outfit before, finally, jumping on the Whiteman express. This is not to mention Bix's various other, shorter-lived associations—the Sioux City Six, Bromo Sulser and His Iowa Collegians, the California Ramblers, the Breeze Blowers, Nat Natoli's band, Dale Skinner's band, Bill Grimm's band, Charley Straight's band. . . . It's gruesome stuff for biographers.

"Ted Jansen band in guest appearance at the Arcadia," the time line at the end of Sudhalter and Evans reports for October 11, 1925. November 5, a Thursday, was significantly more interesting:

> Ruth spends most of the day with Bix. They have breakfast, then go to the Arcadia for rehearsal. Then dinner at the Coronado Hotel. They play indoor golf at the hotel until it is time for Bix to leave for work. After the job, Bix takes Ruth bowling.

Mostly, though, it's "In Dayton, Ohio, for General Motors Convention" (April 13, 1927) or "Band in Scranton, Pennsylvania" (May 7–8, 1927) or "Whiteman records for Victor" (January 5, 1928). That's a popular one, actually. Whiteman made a lot of money in 78s. Whiteman records for Victor on February 7, 8, 9, 10, 13, 14, 15, 16, 18, 27, 28, 29 (leap year!), and March 1, 2, 12, 13, 14, 15, 16 (Bix not present), and 17, and April 22, 24, 25. For all of May the band records for Columbia. Then to Detroit for a weeklong engagement, back to New York to make more records, then to Minnesota and Chicago, to Pennsylvania and Atlantic City, up to Old Orchard Beach, Maine, then back to New York to record again September 4, 5, 6, 15, 17, 18, 19, 21. It never stops. On days they aren't recording, they're rehearsing. Or performing. Bowling is a great event in this life; bowling and gin.

Bix and the trumpeter Sterling Bose roomed together at the Coronado Hotel in St. Louis, three blocks from the Arcadia. "One night, when Bix didn't show up," a band member later told Phil Evans, "Tram sent me to the hotel to find out why[.] I got a bellhop and a pass key. I found the two passed out under their bed with a jug of wine close, so they could reach out and hook a finger in the handle, lift it to their shoulder and let the wine trickle into their mouth."

This is what I've come to think of as the fleshy Bix, as opposed to *le Bix spectral*. This is the Bix so many writers have focused on over the years in a not unreasonable attempt at constructing an actual person out of a tedious series of dates (or a scratchy set of recordings). This is the Bix who, according to Ralph Berton, "looked like a farmboy who happened to be wearing sneakers—old greasy pants, a moth-eaten sweater several sizes too small, and tennis shoes that looked as if they had been worn while lying under an automobile, which indeed they may have been." According to the critic Otis Ferguson, who was among the first to write about Bix, he was always to be found "under the rusty tux with the soup stains, the underwear and sox you never could get off him for sending to the laundry until they fell off, and he's borrowed them from you in the first place, like as not." There's a remarkable consistency to these descriptions—Bix is always disheveled, unkempt, even smelly. "Who is this guy in the other bed sleeping in his underwear?" Hoagy Carmichael remembers asking. "It was Bix. A pale blond galoot needing a shave, sleeping in his tattered underwear with his funny little mouth open, smelling like a distillery, his crumpled clothes piled on a dirty rug, the hole showing in the sole of his right shoe." According to the one-armed trumpeter Wingy Manone, Bix always wore "raggedy old clothes," but Manone portrays this to be the result of a conscious choice that Bix has made: "If you didn't spend so much money on clothes," Bix advises his friend, "you could buy more gin."

The Bix that Eddie Condon describes is more pathetic. When Bix was hired to play some out-of-town gig, it was "the usual dilemma—no tuxedo." So Condon and his brother Jim scared up for him a pair of trousers, a shirt and jacket, studs and a tie, and even a topcoat and hat. "A few days later he returned and brought us the borrowed articles," Condon writes.

> There was a tuxedo, complete with studs, tie, and shirt. But the tuxedo was not Jim's, the shirt was not his, and the studs and tie were not mine. The topcoat and hat were also different from those we had given him.
>   "Did you have a good time?" we asked politely.
>   "I don't know," Bix said.

There seems to be an endless supply of such anecdotes, and their context generally encourages us to chuckle knowingly and not to spend much time asking questions—like what *did* happen to the Condons' clothes? And whose clothes is Bix wearing now? And why are Eddie and Jim so polite to a guy who can't take care of himself, who loses their tux, who's always unprepared, who's always drunk?

I'm often tempted to dream up a slightly different Bix, one who walks through the door, let's say, stinking of piss and mud. This Bix is cold. And sick. And when Eddie Condon asks him—politely—whether he had a good time, Bix carefully removes his hat. He rubs its felt brim with his thumb and then glares at Condon, looking him straight in the eye until Condon is forced to take a nervous swig of his gin.

This Bix says nothing and yet still has more agency than Condon's Bix. And perhaps this isn't surprising. After all, I *want* Bix to have more agency. I *want* Bix to be less pathetic—to which you might reasonably respond, *So what? That's not what happened.* Which is true, I suppose, but what actually happened is beside the point. We don't know what actually happened; all we know is the story that Eddie Condon tells, in which Bix is passive and ridiculous, or the story Wingy Manone tells, in which Bix is happily self-destructive, or the story Hoagy Carmichael tells, in which Bix appears to be passed out but is no less the butt of the joke.

So what if, when Bix walks in, Eddie Condon—who's all gin and hair grease, his Harris tweed jacket a perfect fit—laughs but then abruptly stops? Already the story is drastically different. What does that laugh mean? And why does he stop? Bix, meanwhile, keeps his hat on this time, but as he attempts to stare down his friend, he appears to be flicking his tongue against the back of his front teeth—actually, his front *tooth*, a false, or pivot, tooth that the family dentist installed after Bix years ago banged his head on the pavement while wrestling. It makes a *click-click* sound that can be heard any time he's nervous or distracted. Like now: the *glug-glug* of Eddie's gin, the *click-click* of Bix's tooth. While on the road with Goldkette, he has been known to lose it in the middle of the show so that he's forced to get down on his hands and knees to look for it. *No tooth*, he tells his bandmates, *no music*. Word leaks out about Bix and his prosthetic, and at one stop on the tour some audience members are ready with a tall painted-cardboard pivot tooth that they present to Bix before the show. Everybody laughs. *Click-click*. And Eddie—my dream Eddie, the one my story invents—asks Bix if he's okay, his brow furrowed with concern. And that's when the tooth comes dislodged and a flick of the tongue sends it on its long, arced progress across the room.

Bix was always coming apart. After a pickup game of baseball, he was "walking barefoot in his dusty tux with the pants rolled up like a kid going wading and the shirt collar off." This is according to Berton, who continues: "The nuttier he looked, the more defiant I felt. *Take a good look*, was my attitude as homeward-bound housewives and respectable Jewish CPAs stared through their glasses from across the street. *You just wish you could do what he can do, you untalented bastards.*"

What I like about Berton here is that while his Bix is more or less the same as Wingy Manone's and Eddie Condon's, he reacts to him as if he were a *real person*. Berton is embarrassed for Bix—he looks a mess, after all—and responds to that embarrassment (as an also-real person might) with belligerence, defending Bix not only against imagined enemies but also against Ralph himself. After all, it's Ralph's judgment of Bix that has prompted this outburst, not some staring housewife's.

And that's the point. Out of these various anecdotes we have constructed a "real" Bix, a fleshy Bix, who's messy, who smells, who's irresponsible. He's someone we can react to—we'll stick up for him even when we want to slug him. Or maybe sometimes we won't stick up for him. James Lincoln Collier described Bix as "almost totally ineffectual in the ordinary pursuits of life," citing exactly the behavior detailed by Manone, Condon, and Carmichael. He concluded, "Bix was, unhappily, an infantile personality." A friend of mine put it more simply: "He was, in short, an impossible little shit."

Maybe so. But coming as it does from a Bix fan, such a statement implies that Bix's character should be conceived of as being separate from Bix's music. This is an intuitive assumption, especially for those of us who happen to know a lot of writers, but it's not one that everyone makes. "I never said more than two words to [the pianist] Bill Evans. I talked to him once, but I know what he was like," the guitarist Emily Remler once told the jazz writer Gene Lees. "I know it. I'm positive. . . . I knew what [the guitarist] Joe Pass was like. He is exactly like he plays. Things come out in the playing. If the person has intelligence, and humor, and creativity, or is introverted."

You can almost hear how comforting and necessary a thought this is to Remler. *I know it. I'm positive.* And certainly there *is* comfort in the emotional logic that connects tooth and music: "At bottom the man and the artist are one," writes the Beiderbecke biographer Burnett James. "You cannot really dissociate the two in any significant way." Certainly Berton's description of Bix's "private astronomy" seems to have sufficiently inspired Geoff Muldaur's take on Beiderbecke's music that he used it as a title for the tribute album he released in 2003. In this case, personality comments on art in the manner that Remler described—although one could argue that the art on display is less Bix's than it is Muldaur's, and anyway, Muldaur himself told me the whole idea is bunk.

"Talent and character are not connected," the longtime blues and folk singer, songwriter, and arranger said. "It's a horrible realization for most people, but it's absolutely true. And it baffles people, because how could Ray Charles produce such warm and beautiful things when he wasn't this great guy, whereas [the saxophone player] Benny Carter was the greatest guy in the world. It's so random— obsessive-compulsive slob Beethoven. I mean, total slob. Kept his shitter under his writing desk. I mean, the place was disgusting, and he produces God's music."

This strikes me as closer to the truth. Like it or not, personality and art are not always simpatico, else we would have people describing "I'm Coming Virginia" as raggedy and self-destructive rather than by summoning up shooting shafts of light. In fact, James Lincoln Collier, the same one who worried over Bix's "tragic temperament," argues that "Bix's personality problems, far from giving him his musical nature, prevented him from exploring the artistic possibilities that lay before him."

There seems to be no real way to prove or disprove this. (Did Remler and Collier listen to old Bix 78s and hear, between the crackles and pops, a thwarted genius?) Regardless, what makes so challenging this mission of searching Bix's personality for clues to his music is that Bix never sits still. As portrayed by Manone, Condon, Carmichael,

FIGURE 1. *The Wolverine Orchestra poses at Doyle's Dancing Academy in Cincinnati, in January 1924. Bix Beiderbecke is seated fourth from the left. Courtesy of the Richardson-Sloane Special Collections Center of the Davenport (Iowa) Public Library.*

Mezzrow, Ferguson, and Berton et al., he is both tragic and ridiculous, a drunk and a genius. He is Everyman and One in a Million Man. The very fact that his friends found him to be odd and mysterious suggests that he wasn't much like anyone else, yet they consistently dressed him up in the garb of an average guy: the corncob from Davenport, Iowa. It helped to make Bix's genius more approachable, I suppose.

The problem with Bix's multitudes, though, is that they can sometimes cancel each other out so that, voilà! Bix disappears.

Back in January 1924, Bix and his band the Wolverines were playing an extended gig at Doyle's Dance Academy in Cincinnati, and as a routine part of their promotional efforts the band members posed for a group photo. Two of the surviving prints show all of the Wolverines (see figure 1), in their best evening wear, in front of a banner that reads:

FIGURE 2. *Bix Beiderbecke poses with cornet on knee, in Cincinnati, in January 1924. Courtesy of the Archives of Traditional Music, Indiana University, Bloomington, Indiana.*

WOLVERINE ORCHESTRA
CHICAGO

But there is a third print as well, and it features Bix by himself, "an idealized image of the young musician in a graceful moment of artistic perfection," gushes Jean Pierre Lion. (See figure 2.)

This is the Bix of my youth in Davenport, his face round, his hair perfectly parted down the middle, his tux perfectly pressed.

"His features are delicate and refined," Lion continues, "his lips turned up at the corners in a tiny smile. . . . But the true attraction of this image is his look: two shining eyes that stare at you with intensity and serenity, from which you can hardly escape."

Is this the fleshy Bix, the *real* Bix? Is he staring intensely at me or is he shyly looking down?

Lion: "This portrait would be reproduced again and again on the covers of albums of Bix Beiderbecke's records and books about him. The photograph has its own magic . . . but it probably bears little resemblance to its model."

Those eyes, "that intensity and serenity, from which you can hardly escape"—Bix is transubstantiating right before us, is he not? You might remember Grégory Elbaz, whose graphic novel we've encountered already.

Bix, *un spectre*.

Bix, a vision.

That book happens to come equipped with a slightly pompous introduction by the Belgian comics writer Thierry Smolderen that places Elbaz's story, which is to say Bix's story, in the context of "spiritual biographies" such as the famous Christian allegory *Pilgrim's Progress*. By ingeniously appropriating this 400-year-old literary genre (Smolderen argues), Elbaz transforms *Bix*, in the space of just 28 pages and 56 uniformly rectangular panels, into *une Bixographie spirituelle*.

Of course, if all you do is flip through the book, then what you'll *actually* walk away with are short, bald-headed moon men and ray guns and space machines. Also lots of light symbolism. And a deer in a dinner jacket.

Perhaps flipping through is all Albert Haim did. "The drawings are horrendous and the text that accompanies them maybe worse," he declared on his forum, although to me that sounded like an excellent excuse to look more closely.

We've already seen Bix walking through those shadowy, *Lord of the Rings*–looking trees on his way to record "Davenport Blues" in Richmond, Indiana; we've already seen how he's running a little late, how everybody's ready to go, so without making a big production of it he just raises his horn and—

Bix joue.

Smolderen might argue that such language echoes *Jésus pleure*, although in the book, Bix's horn echoes not *back* to the Bible but *up* to the moon. Literally. This is why I mentioned earlier that this story takes one of the more unexpected turns in comics history. You see, *la mélodie de Bix* seems to have activated a posse of moon men—although honestly they look like children in nothing but their underpants—and they promptly pile into their moon machine and make the quick trip down to Richmond, where, with their ray guns, they irradiate *le jeune cornettiste*.

We hardly have time to process this, and it's up again to the moon. Elbaz's next four panels stretch across two pages and combine into a single rocky sphere that seems to explode in light and shadow. It looks like a frame from Georges Méliès's *Le voyage dans la Lune*, filmed a year before Bix was born. Unlike in that story, however, our voyagers manage not to crash into the moon; instead, they perform some mysterious trick that transports our hero, now a beam of light,

down,

down,

down

to Earth again and

into *un champ de maïs*, a cornfield. Which makes sense, right? After all, this is "Bix Beiderbecke from the tall corn of Iowa." Or is it? When Bix finally pops his head up and out of the leafy shadows, he is wearing antlers and a dinner jacket.

Il a changé en bête.

He has changed into a beast—which might actually be a step up from, say, Gregor Samsa's predicament. Gregor awoke to find himself an *Ungeziefer*, a vermin, or, in many translations, an insect. Bix, on the other hand, is something nobler; instead of self-loathing he is Christlike. Think of the painting *Saint Giles and the Hind* (1500), in which the king of the Franks kneels before the holy man and his beloved hind. Saint Giles is bleeding, having taken an arrow in the hand protecting the helpless animal from its royal hunters, and now the prostrate king—on the *gauche*, or unholy, side of the picture—is asked to contemplate the awesome distance between his worldly corruption and, over there on the right side of the picture, the innocence of a deer.

So the imagery in *Bix* is older than Kafka or Méliès. Perhaps Thierry Smolderen wasn't so pompous after all for thinking about

79

it in terms of *Pilgrim's Progress*, a work whose title page promises a journey "from this world to that which is to come"—from *à gauche* to *à droite*—"delivered under the similitude of a dream." In particular what I like about the comparison is its embrace of all that mythic energy in Bix. (What is light, after all, but particles of energy?) In *Pilgrim's Progress*, Christian, as evidenced by his name, is Everyman, burdened by the weight of original sin and forced, as the church believes we all are, to confront his impending judgment. His progress, in other words, is our own. But Christian is also Anointed Man; he is different from the rest of us. When he confesses his troubles to his wife and kids, they worry "that some frenzy distemper had got into his head," and when, after a good night's sleep, he doesn't snap out of it, they "deride" him and "chide" him and "sometimes they would quite neglect him." Poor Christian! He is left to "walk solitarily in the Fields" and eventually to set out for greener, altogether holier pastures.

As we've seen, Bix contains these same multitudes. He is Everyman and Anointed Man. As a boy Bix is "perfectly normal" and endowed with "simple goodness and loyalty," in the words of Otis Ferguson, who published a remarkable pair of essays about Bix, "Young Man with a Horn" and "Young Man with a Horn Again," in 1936 and 1940. According to Ferguson, Bix is "swinging free and bold," a "kid with a prank, riding down the whole length of a chorus like a herd of mustangs." He is an archetypal American, "so generally hardy that an old sweater was all he found necessary for an Iowa winter." And yet that horn made him crucially different. "Jazz was the country where he grew up," Ferguson writes, "the fine high thing, the sun coming up to fill the world through morning."

In Elbaz, Bix becomes the moon, in Ferguson the sun. Bix's horn is his Good Book and jazz his Celestial City. He is pure narrative.

And this, I am sorry to say, completely freaks out the Bixophiles.

One poster on Albert Haim's forum called Elbaz's art "gross," while another dismissed *Bix* as "really revolting. . . . Just ugly drawings from a no-talent artist." Haim himself unleashed a fairly typical *cri de coeur*: "Poor Bix! Will there ever be an end to his desecration?" To be clear, I'm less interested in arguing matters of taste than I am in exploring the rich irony of their protest. To desecrate is to make profane something that is holy. Can one desecrate something that is not holy?

And can something be holy without, on some level, participating in the progress? Holiness, in other words, is a function of narrative.

Without fully acknowledging it, I think, Bixophiles are tangled up in exactly the same tension as mythologizers like Elbaz: Bix is a shadow, a specter, something holy; Bix is also something real. He is fleshy. Sketches can either look like him, which is good—or not, which is "horrendous." On his site, Haim uploaded an Elbaz drawing that depicts an older, fat-faced horn player nervously glancing over his right shoulder at an upright, bow-tied deer. Wrote one: "It's obvious that [Bix] didn't completely lose his good looks (the never attractive mustache notwithstanding)." "Looks more like Henry Busse to me," suggested another, referring to a different Jazz Age musician. Still another thought the drawing better favored the Whiteman trumpeter Harry Goldfield—all the while, of course, missing the deer for the horn player. In fact, no one even *mentioned* the deer!

I can't help but think about that old painting again: Albert Haim is bloody Saint Giles protecting his poor beast from the slings and arrows of vulgar men like Grégory Elbaz and Thierry Smolderen; Bix, however, is still and always the hind. And that's the rub. The "real" Bix is also the faraway, inaccessible Bix, off in his private astronomy. I suppose that this is an interesting enough thought on an intellectual level—Bix as metafiction; Bix as dream; oh, what Flann O'Brien might have done with Bix!—but on a more visceral level it's also *terrifying*. The expression on the face of the Frankish king is that of a Bix fan who has just listened to "Way Down Yonder in New Orleans." Recorded on May 13, 1927—Friday the 13th, as Evans and Evans note—it's more Caravaggio and light than even "I'm Coming Virginia." It's cheerful, down-tempo, even a bit wandering, taking its time transitioning from Tram's more languid saxophone to Bix's brighter cornet. Then, a bit more than halfway through his solo, in a moment that's as thrilling as it is unexpected, Bix scoots up to a C-sharp, the highest note he ever recorded.

Where, the king wants to know, did *that* come from?

If all of this deer business sounds familiar, that's because we've already witnessed Randy Sandke's "fawn running loose in the streets of New York." And this, as it happens, is precisely how Grégory Elbaz's book ends, with the hind running free—sans saint, sans Albert, sans any of us to protect him—into the honking traffic of New York City.

My girlfriend, Doris Day–like, shakes her head. "You people need a freaking hobby or something."

In the litany of Bix's life as a professional musician there are brief moments of actual drama—for instance, October 12, 1926. That's when Jean Goldkette's Victor Recording Orchestra, after barnstorming from Detroit all the way to the Big Apple, performed at the Roseland Ballroom opposite Fletcher Henderson. "Two of the finest—unquestionably the finest Dance Orchestras in the world—playing alternately," explained an ad in the *New York Times*, while the *New York Daily News* promised the "Battle of the Century." Up until the year before, Henderson's band had enjoyed the transformative presence of Louis Armstrong, but even after he moved back to Chicago and was replaced by the cornetist Rex Stewart, the group maintained its reputation as one of the original and finest big bands in jazz. Henderson boasted Coleman Hawkins on tenor saxophone, Buster Bailey on clarinet, and the hot but classy arrangements of Don Redman, while on the other end of the ballroom, Goldkette countered with Bix Beiderbecke, Frankie Trumbauer, and the slap-bass pioneer Steve Brown.

Spiegle Willcox, who had joined the band when Tommy Dorsey left, played trombone. He recalled that October night for the filmmaker Brigitte Berman, whose documentary, *Bix: Ain't None of Them Play Like Him Yet*, was released in 1981. Fletcher Henderson's band took the stand, he said, and opened with something fast and hot. Impressed, the crowd applauded loudly. "And then," Willcox said, "you could almost just—it was very quiet, and it was our turn . . ."

It's worth mentioning that this wasn't Bix's first stint with Goldkette. He had first joined the band two years earlier, after a good run with the Wolverines. Goldkette had recognized his talent early on, and for Bix the Detroiters represented higher pay and higher visibility. During his first recording session with the group, in November 1924, Bix lit out on the sort of solo he was already known for—"clean, fiery, and well-balanced," according to Jean Pierre Lion. Problem was, Victor's musical director, Eddie King, hated it. "You should have seen this King guy," the arranger Bill Challis told Sudhalter and Evans. "He looked like a bull, a short bull, with a bull-like head coming down to this huge can. He'd sit out in front of the band with a gripe and a grouchy look on his face." Like Roy Kautz before him, King made short work of Bix, nixing any further solos from the young cornetist. Within two months, Bix was gone.

King was "anti-jazz," Paul Mertz complained, and only interested in so-called sweet music. But the pianist also conceded that Goldkette was under contract with the Victor Talking Machine Company, and the marketplace wasn't going to support the hot music these guys were dying to play. "It seems to me," Mertz said, "that King, while having a substantial voice in the selection [of tunes], probably had to heed the wishes of others higher up in the Victor organization."

Whatever the case, Bix left Detroit for Iowa City. Intent on taking Goldkette's parting advice and learning more about music, he enrolled at my alma mater, the University of Iowa, where he pledged Beta Theta Pi and moved into the fraternity house on North Dubuque Street. He joined a band that played one night a week, and he met with a guidance counselor who forced him to add military training, physical education, and freshman lectures to his course load. He immediately started skipping classes and on a Thursday night got riotously drunk at a place called Reichart's Café, where he ended up in fisticuffs with a future Chicago Bears offensive lineman. Bix and the football player were both expelled the next day.

It is possible that no one was more upset by this turn of events than the critic Benny Green: "That a place of instruction should refuse to teach music to a brilliant natural musician like Bix, and instruct him instead in the art of cleaning a dummy rifle may look like a parody, but to Bix at the time it must have been a nasty shock. Reality is the most merciless satirist of all."

I know it's beside the point to argue with Green here, to plead that the University of Iowa shouldn't be obligated to view its top priority as recognizing and nurturing, at the expense of its curriculum, each incoming freshman's special genius—but I'm a Hawkeye and it's hard not to be a little defensive. What's important to recognize, though, is the consistency of the narrative, at least as we receive it from biographers and bystanders alike: the world is out to get Bix Beiderbecke. The harping, conservative parents, the maliciously impersonal institutions, the silly union rules, the ridiculous music directors—they all conspire to prevent him from making his art.

Which is what makes this moment at the Roseland Ballroom in October 1926 so thrilling. Here, finally, is the possibility of a real triumph. Back with Goldkette after his extended gig with Trumbauer in St. Louis, Bix is reasonably stable and reasonably sober and belting out solos—surely they're still clean, fiery, and well-balanced—in what is perhaps the hottest white band in America. As Fletcher Henderson's boys wind down their set, a crowd of musicians, here to witness the battle, begins to shift to the other side of the room, to where the Jean Goldkette Orchestra waits to begin, the band members anxiously tonguing their reeds and fingering their valves. It takes cash to dance, so the musicians in the audience keep to the sidelines; still, their presence here suggests that something more is at stake than simply which of the two bands will make the kids shimmy harder. For instance, you can think of this moment as a battle between out-of-towners and hometowners, or Midwestern boys and big-city slicks, or even white players and their black counterparts. But there's another way of looking at it, I think: tonight it's Bix against the world.

Spiegle Willcox, his hair white, his eyeglasses Harry Caray, picks up the story from there. Rather than try to follow hot with hot, he says, Goldkette's boys opened with the relatively sweet number "Valencia." "And there was a lot of smiles came up there out of the audience," Willcox recalls. "'What's this great band from the West doing, you know, playing that?'" Trumbauer, who in Goldkette's absence was leading the band, played the audience perfectly. He saved "My Pretty Girl" for next, and when they finished, says Willcox, "We just got an awful lot of applause on it. I mean, we had proven that we were pretty good. We actually creamed them!"

Rex Stewart, apparently, felt the same way; years later, he even used that same word, *creamed*. "I mean, put it this way," he said. "We were supposed to be the kings, the greatest thing in New York. We had the best men, the best arrangements. Everything. Then, suddenly, up pops this band of Johnny-come-latelies from out in the sticks—white boys on top of it—and they just *creamed* us. Stayed on for 45 minutes, instead of half an hour, and they would've stayed on forever, the way the crowd was cheering 'em on."

Stewart goes on to call the experience "pretty humiliating," and it was partly due to audience favorites like "My Pretty Girl," which Goldkette recorded a few months later (and which Pupi Avati later filmed to such great effect). (As humiliating as it may have been, Stewart didn't hold a grudge. A few months after Bix's death, he recorded a nearly note-for-note copy of his old rival's solo on the Henderson band's version of "Singin' the Blues.")

"I bumped into two of those [Henderson] musicians recently," the Goldkette pianist Irving Riskin told Phil Evans in 1962, "Benny Carter and Don Redman, who as you know are now big in their own right. When they spoke of the first night hearing us at the Roseland, Don said, 'Boy, that was great,' and Carter interpolated, 'That wasn't great, that was frightening!' Which made me feel we must have had a pretty good band. Something to be proud of.'"

Perhaps the most poignant epitaph to this moment can be found in Berman's film. She captures an elderly Willcox in his home, surrounded by books and fading band photos, a turntable, a reel-to-reel tape recorder, and a microphone on a tall stand behind which, on the wall, hangs a kitschy painting of two dogs. It's as if they're staring down at Spiegle, who has spiffed himself up for the occasion in a navy Oxford, light blue slacks, and a black belt. After telling Berman all about that night at the Roseland, he drops the needle on an old Goldkette tune and pulls out his trombone. As he listens to Bix's solo, his body sways gently to the rhythm. He flips his hair back and chuckles a bit, the look on his face one of perfect joy and concentration. In fact, for a moment he seems to disappear altogether: he's no longer trying to impress Berman; he's no longer even aware of Berman. There's only that tune. And then, when it's finally time for the trombones to play, he lifts his horn up to his lips and he blows along, as if a single year hadn't gone by.

This is the great climax of Bix Beiderbecke's story. Having managed to overcome an Odyssean host of obstacles—including but certainly not limited to the obscurity of his Iowa roots, the conservatism of his up-bringing, and the tragedy of his temperament (i.e., his refusal to learn to properly dress himself)—he waxed in the months that followed some of the most important recordings in jazz history: "Singin' the Blues" on February 4, 1927; "I'm Coming Virginia" and "Way Down Yonder in New Orleans" on May 13; and "In a Mist" on September 8. The latter tune Bix wrote himself for solo piano. According to his friends, he'd been working on it forever, and they marveled at the way he twined the herky-jerky syncopations of jazz with impression-istic flourishes reminiscent of Monet's Giverny. The piece employs whole-tone scales and a phrasing the French called *en arabesque*, both learned from listening to lots and lots of Debussy and Ravel, lis-tening carefully, as Bix was wont to do, escaping into his own Gallic astronomy perhaps. And yet, as progressive as it must have sounded then, "In a Mist" feels a bit clunky these many years later, rushed maybe. In an effort to squeeze the recording onto a three-minute 78, Bix's first take ended up too short, while the second ran long. Not until take 4—when Tram, ever the housemother, tapped him on the shoulder—did he wrap up in the allotted time.

When someone asked him what he wanted to call it, Bix shook his head. "Dunno," he supposedly replied, "I'm in a fog." Then, when someone suggested *that* for the title, Bix thought better of it— thankfully. In the end, "In a Mist" is a remarkable piece of music, especially when set against other jazz recordings of the time, but like "Davenport Blues," the only other of his compositions that Bix re-corded, it lives more fully in later interpretations than in its original form. (I've come to wonder whether this can't be said about much relating to Bix Beiderbecke.)

Anyway, it was during this time that Goldkette's Famous Fourteen disbanded, as did a subsequent ensemble in New York. Whiteman had previously approached Bix and Tram about joining his organization and they were pleased to find that the offer was still good. So at the end of October they boarded a train for Cleveland and, upon arriving, signed a contract with the number-one recording artist in the country, the self-proclaimed Calathumpic King of Jazz.

Paul Samuel Whiteman was the richest and most famous of all the dance band leaders. At 300 pounds, he was "a bladderish man . . . flabby, virile, quick, coarse, untidy, and sleek, with a hard core of shrewdness in an envelope of sentimentalism," according to a *New Yorker* profile from 1926. His shtick was to dilute the hot jazz coming out of New Orleans and Chicago into light jazz, or, in his own parlance, "jazz classique." Whiteman himself had played viola with the Denver and San Francisco symphonies; his own orchestra, formed in December 1918 after he was discharged from the Navy (and at almost exactly the same moment that Burnie Beiderbecke arrived home from the army carrying those Original Dixieland Jazz Band records), would cater to the same middle-class strivers who wanted to hear Beethoven and Enrico Caruso. From this moment on, jazz would no longer be reserved for adolescent rebels like Bix or hidden away on riverboats. "Paul got the music out of the cellars," the violinist Joe Venuti later explained to Gene Lees, and he hauled it up onto the stage at Aeolian Hall, a seventeen-story skyscraper on 42nd and 43rd streets in Manhattan. There, on February 12, 1924, at three o'clock in the afternoon, he presented "An Experiment in Modern Music," a show that premiered a piece specially commissioned by Whiteman, *Rhapsody in Blue*. Its composer, George Gershwin, sat in on the piano. (And our friend Carl Van Vechten sat in the audience.)

Whiteman's "experiment," not to mention Gershwin's, was a huge success. Before that concert, and then another one at Carnegie Hall, Whiteman was "an amusing mountebank," in the words of that same *New Yorker* piece. Afterward, he was a celebrity, a musician almost to be taken seriously. Dudded up in striped ties and smoking "incessant Chesterfields," he transformed himself the way he transformed jazz, into a bona fide sensation, and for the rest of the decade he toured the country and the world, hiring only the finest musicians and paying them royal wages (at least five times more than what they would have made in a top symphony) to gently syncopate whatever was handy—classical, popular; it hardly mattered. He only wanted his paying customers to foxtrot and feel respectable doing it.

The problem, at least where many of Bix's biographers are concerned, is that there's nothing respectable about jazz music. "Bix Beiderbecke lived very briefly and in what might be called the servants' entrance to art," Otis Ferguson wrote in "Young Man with a Horn," and for talent such as "this there were no conservatories to get stuffy in, no high-trumpet didoes to be learned doggedly, note-perfect as written." In fact, Bix Beiderbecke, whose "story is a good story," according to Ferguson, "quite humble and right," should be understood as standing for everything that is the opposite of highfalutin "Pops" Whiteman. Bix is real; Bix is authentic; and his decision to sign on with Whiteman's commercial colossus resulted in more than just bad records. It actually killed Bix Beiderbecke.

Wait a second, you ask. *Isn't the whole point of selling out to make your life easier?*

It is! And it certainly worked for Whiteman. He slyly carved out a comfortable spot for himself between populist scolds like Ferguson and their high-culture counterparts, none more vicious than Whiteman's old conductor at the San Francisco Symphony, who once told a newspaper, "A people can no more indulge in jazz without becoming demoralized than they can touch a black crock without being smutted." The cultural critic Curtis White has called this in-between-the-high-and-low, perfect-for-Terry-Gross-and-Charlie-Rose space "The Middle Mind," proclaiming it ideal for the pocketbook but a wasteland for the imagination. The *New York Times* was less judgy, describing Whiteman's approach to jazz as "a gorgeous piece of impudence."

So why wasn't what was good for the goose also good for Beiderbecke? And how does Paul Whiteman manage to kill poor old Bix merely by paying him well? Ferguson only hints at this last, rather shocking indictment, but his friend Dorothy Baker makes it explicit in her novel of the same name, published in 1938. Before we continue, though, many folks will reasonably point out that *Young Man with a Horn* was not about Bix. Baker couldn't have been more clear when she wrote that "the inspiration for the writing of this book has been the music, but not the life," of Bix Beiderbecke. Which is fine.

I'm happy to take Baker at her word, except that sometimes novelists don't get to decide how the world will receive their art, and the world has received *Young Man with a Horn* as a roman à clef. Adopting the title of Ferguson's famous essay, it gives us a Rick Martin who is Ferguson's Bix, only more so. For instance, if Bix lived in "the servants' entrance to art," then Martin—parentless and penniless—was raised in "a bed of his own in an empty storeroom." For Ferguson, Bix dying young makes for "a good story, quite humble and right"; for Baker, dying young is inevitable. "The story ends with death," she writes. "Our Mr. Martin, from the moment he began fooling around with pianos, was riding for a fall." Regardless of what Baker intended, Rick will always be Bix, and Bix will always be Rick. And the truth about Rick is that he sold out, and it killed him.

Actually, in *Young Man with a Horn*, Rick doesn't so much sell out as someone *else* sells him out. (Better to make Rick, like Bix, the perpetual victim.) He is content playing for Jack Stuart and His Collegians at the Rendez-Vous Ballroom south of Los Angeles when in swoops Mr. Lee Valentine, "the slick fellow in the white linen suit" who, over a few cocktails, buys the rights to the great trumpeter. The next morning, Rick protests, saying he doesn't want to go, but Stuart tells him he has no choice. "It had been a cash deal the night before; Jack had released his part of Rick for four hundred and seventy-five dollars in currency. The roll was in his pocket. Rick was sold whether he knew it or not. He had become, overnight, the property of Lee Valentine."

I particularly love that detail: "The roll was in his pocket." Baker—whose writing is pulpy and often just perfect—is not interested in subtlety. Rick is a slave (manhood is now money), while his buddy Smoke Jordan, who long ago had tutored Rick in the mysteries of jazz, is free. When he arrives in New York, Rick finds his mentor playing a club, and there "looked at Smoke Jordan's black face shining above that magnificent collection of white-skinned drums, and he saw how much the same he was." Or, put another way, the primitive has stayed true to his music; what else could he do? Rick "was at home now, natural and right, and this was homecoming. The only home he'd ever known was this kind of music, and here it was, changeless and abiding."

Rick later joins an even fancier outfit, the Whitemanesque Phil

Morrison Orchestra, and the contrast with Smoke's band couldn't be any sharper. "It was an organization," Baker writes, "and almost as businesslike as an insurance company. They rehearsed three afternoons a week and Morrison drove them"—yes—"like slaves. . . . But it wouldn't do to call it a great orchestra," Baker argues, "because it pandered to all tastes and there was always that grandiose ending. It was just a good big orchestra, playing out its nightly schedule at one big hotel or another, working for money, drawing a crowd, getting people out on the floor."

Meanwhile, Rick Martin's self-awareness is remarkable. He astutely recognizes the artistic chasm that separates Smoke and Phil, and concludes that to achieve anything meaningful he must quit the latter and rejoin the former. (That Smoke and his crew don't themselves recognize the chasm—"Boy, you must have got good getting a job like that," one of them tells Rick—is precisely what makes them all "natural and right" and, of course, black.) Passive Rick finally makes a decision, and more than anything it contributes to his premature death. Ironically, what kills Rick isn't joining Morrison but leaving him, which sets him free to chase, like all Romantic heroes from Quixote on, after something that can't be caught. "I don't know what the hell that boy thinks a trumpet will do," worries one of Smoke's men toward the end. "That note he was going for, that thing he was trying for—there isn't any such thing. Not on a horn."

If Rick had never met Smoke, then he might have enjoyed, like Phil Morrison and the rest, the relative fame and fortune of the dance-band circuit. Perhaps that's why Baker begins her novel by awkwardly asserting, "In the first place maybe he shouldn't have got himself mixed up with negroes. It gave him a funny slant on things and he never got over it." But if Rick hadn't gotten himself mixed up with Smoke, then he never would have been the sort of soloist Morrison would seek to tame and so destroy.

Bixophiles who complain that Rick should never be confused for Bix, need to reread Burnett James, the Englishman whose short biography appeared in 1959. A nearly straight line can be drawn from Otis Ferguson, through Dorothy Baker, to James, whose Bix is the capital-A Artist adrift in the land of Commerce: Whiteman "knew Bix's worth. . . . But nothing can alter the fact that in his band Bix was a solitary figure—lonely and often frustrated, his life not a part of the life around him, his art private and personal." What's worse, Bix had been duped. As James would have it, Whiteman lured the cornetist with his reputation for

> playing a lot of music with a conscious jazz background. As time went on, however, and he became more and more involved in commercial entertainment . . . [Whiteman's] musical ideals [became] more and more subservient to his business sense. In these circumstances, Bix found his situation growing less and less sympathetic until in the end it became next door to intolerable. He was constantly frustrated, unable to fulfill himself, and in the end it destroyed him.

Remember that none of this is Bix's fault. The world is out to get him: Mom and Pop, Roy Kautz, Eddie King, and now Paul Whiteman. And, like Rick, he did not choose to join Whiteman; according to James, he was guided there by destiny: "If his destiny had led him to where he could have found associates playing music with which he could have absolutely identified himself, he might conceivably have found the moral and intellectual strength to prosper as man and musician. But that wasn't to be."

Sounding angry and disappointed, Burnett James comes awfully close here to calling Bix a coward. He's like a parent sadly shaking his head, or maybe like the folkies who crowded the stage at Newport in 1965, expecting their hero Bob Dylan to come out strumming his acoustic and blowing his harp. Instead, he plugged in and the kids nearly rioted. In many respects, Bix and his biographers anticipated this distinctively 1960s obsession with selling out, which became such a fixture of the rock and roll myth that The Who parodied it with their 1967 album *The Who Sell Out*. (On the cover, Pete Townshend hawks deodorant and Roger Daltrey literally bathes in baked beans.) Like Bix, the rock star has been "swindled," to borrow from the title of a Sex Pistols song. To be great, he must be an artist, but to be heard— and what's the point of being great if you're not heard?—he must be a businessman; he must compromise his art. The rocker who gives in to this injustice sells out. In the rock critic Robert Pattison's memorable description, he buys a nice house in suburbia for his mom, and "for himself he gets a chateau, a Porsche, a kilo of cocaine, and a lifetime supply of Jack Daniels. He becomes the creature of his managers," exhausting himself on cheap sex and busting up hotel rooms, until, "when the cash men have extracted the last drop of vitality from his fast-graying pulp, the sellout wakes from his stupor to discover he is a sodden has-been." Next up: bad cologne, gold chains, and a farewell tour of the Middle East. "The sold-out rocker never dies," Pattison notes; "death is too noble."

For Bix the proto-rocker, selling out is different only in that he never stops being the Artist. In Baker he suicidally unsells himself, while in James he surrenders to the moral angst of it all. Checking in with Benny Green, I find that he disagrees on only one point: rather than understand, as Rick did, that Whiteman meant compromise, Green's Bix actually admires the King of Jazz. "So far from being a moral coward who sold out to the highest bidder, Bix was the blind unreasoning artist who followed his advancing sensibilities as only a blind unreasoning artist can," Green writes, "completely oblivious of the consequences." And the consequences, of course, can be heard on record. To Green, a musician himself, Whiteman is nothing more than "a mediocre vaudeville act," and Bix's looking to him "for pearls of wisdom was like Tarzan at a Keep Fit Class." Poor Bix! He couldn't see what his playing so clearly evinced: "the pitiful gulf between his own mind and the minds which conceived the holocaust preceding and following [his] solo."

I'd like to say more about "calathumpic" in a moment; I don't mind admitting I've fallen in love with that word. But first, here is Ralph Berton, who on page 367 of *Remembering Bix* takes a deep breath and then really lets fly:

> The records Bix made with Paul Whiteman must remain for all time as one of the most peculiar series of bastardized, hybrid concoctions ever perpetrated in the whole history of the very peculiar, hybrid art of jazz. To understand them, fully to penetrate them in all their unbelievable panoply of bad taste, barefaced pretentiousness, stupefying, monstrous, limitless vulgarity, and portentous triviality, is to understand some profound and ugly truths about the curious uses to which art and beauty may find themselves put in our curious, fucked-up society—and some equally profound and beautiful truths about the blind persistence and tenacity of the human animal in general, and Bix's creative instinct in particular.

In *Lost Chords*, Richard Sudhalter admirably pushes back against this sort of invective—"admirably" because I think Sudhalter has history on his side. As for Berton, he has this paragraph, which is perfectly paced and just gorgeously angry. Read it aloud, and you'll hear the way it builds, the first sentence a comparatively short foreword to the second, the second as furious as it is syntactically eccentric, until the whole bit finally crescendos into that climactic, and pinprickingly vulgar, "fucked-up"—before exhaling again with a hopeful little coda on the dignity of man. It's one of Bix's solos, only in words.

Anyway, gorgeous or not, Sudhalter pushes back on Berton by citing unnamed Beiderbecke "colleagues" who observed "that, far from feeling bound or stifled by the Whiteman orchestra, as Green and others have suggested, Bix felt a sense of exhilaration." It was like going to school, they said—and not the University of Iowa! Years earlier, when saying so was a bit more risky, the critic and composer Gunther Schuller had labeled Whiteman's music "admirable" and noted that "there is no question it was admired (and envied) by many musicians, both black and white." In a book on popular music, the musician and critic Elijah Wald takes Schuller's point a step further, reminding his readers that even Duke Ellington loved Whiteman, and that if you're going to hail Ellington as a composer of "America's classical music," as Grover Sales has done, then it helps to admit that the person who invented that paradigm for right jazz-thinking is the same person who came up with "jazz classique."

This all may be true—about Whiteman and about Bix—and it certainly would render Berton's rant a mere instance of apoplexy, except that I keep focusing on the particular language he uses to describe Whiteman: *bastardized, hybrid, bad taste, limitless vulgarity.* Apparently, these are supposed to be bad things, and it reminds me again of that word "calathumpic." I first encountered it in Don Rayno's massive and defensively adoring biography of Whiteman, volume 1 of which was published in 2003. Rayno's book immediately called to mind the Evanses' gargantuan *Leon Bix Beiderbecke Story*, perhaps because Norman Gentieu is right there at the beginning, as he was in Evans and Evans (q.v., "the error-ridden glut has now been rendered kaput"), contributing prefatory remarks that reveal him to be, again, righteously perturbed with the state of the jazz universe: "It is an irony of fate that much of the literature of jazz has been written by opinionated dilettantes in music and purblind ideologues. Thanks to such self-appointed arbiters of taste, historical and musical verities have been trashed as irrelevant impediments to their reckless rhetoric, and nowhere has this been more dismayingly demonstrated than in the case of Paul Whiteman—who sinned unforgivingly in being proclaimed by the public as the King of Jazz." Except that according to the book that follows, this is not true. The ones doing the "proclaiming" were not members of the public, Rayno writes, but Whiteman's own publicity team, in particular a woman named Estella Karn, who had previously shilled for the circus and "tended toward ballyhoo." In fact, she had tried to gussy up the "King of Jazz" into "The Calathumpic King of Jazz," but, according to Rayno, "that fictitious superlative"—anchoring an attractive and metrically indisputable line of iambic tetrameter—"didn't stick."

Which is too bad. It sure stuck with me, and I wanted to know whether it really was fictitious. Turns out: no. Or at least not exactly. This is from *Elson's Music Dictionary* (1905):

> Calathumpian music. A discordant combination of sounds. A vulgar and grotesque performance upon instruments unmusical and out of tune.

As in, for instance, Thomas Pynchon's *Mason & Dixon*, which bears witness to "an assortment of Calathumpians . . . with a full Battery of cowbells tun'd to the Pentatonick Scale, Drums with 'Possumskin Heads, Whistles and Gongs and a Military Bugle found in the woods after Braddock's defeat." This, perhaps, is the vulgarity against which Ralph Berton rails, except that it hardly fits into the traditional "sellout" narrative, in which our hero lives at "the servants' entrance to art" and not in some stuffy conservatory where all the bugles and cowbells ring perfectly in tune. Whiteman, meanwhile, is supposed to be the opposite of calathumpic. After all, jazz—*real* jazz—is vulgar, and Whiteman's great triumph, as well as his great crime, was that he *de*-vulgarized it.

If I have Berton right, then what he's doing is pointing out the irony of a situation where Whiteman's respectable music was, in fact, vulgar, and the crock-smutted noise that Bix played—profound and beautiful and blindly persistent—was capital-A Art. The problem is, such distinctions are never quite that easy—just ask Whiteman, whose whole enterprise depended upon them. Back in 1924, when he hauled jazz up and out of the cellars, he hoped to give his audience a whiff of just how musty and gross things had gotten down there. So he called for "Livery Stable Blues," a tune popularized by Bix's beloved Original Dixieland Jazz Band, and instructed his boys to give it the full calathumpian treatment. "The man with the clarinet wore a battered top hat that had ostensibly seen better days," the *New York Times* reported. "Sometimes he wore it, and sometimes he played into it. The man with the trombone played it as is, but also, on occasion, picked up a bath tub or something of the kind from the floor and blew into that. The instruments made odd, unseemly, bushman sounds."

The *Times* got the joke, and perfectly understood Whiteman's point concerning the evolution of jazz from bushman to LaRocca to the ever-elegant Gershwin. But what about the hoi polloi? In his book *Jazz*, published two years after the concert, Whiteman describes their reaction: "When [the audience] laughed and seemed pleased with 'Livery Stable Blues,' the crude jazz of the past, I had for a moment the panicky feeling that they hadn't realized the attempt at burlesque— that they were ignorantly applauding the thing on its merits."

How dare the masses not understand the distinction between high and low, capital and lowercase, uplifting and just plain god-awful?

Whiteman, in other words, had completely missed the irony but also the sheer brilliance of his almost-title: the Calathumpic King of Jazz. It weds royalty with vulgarity in a *bastardized hybrid* that pays perfect tribute to the bewildering mash-up that is, and always has been, American popular culture. Take minstrelsy, which began with white performers donning blackface to parody black culture. Blacks soon became minstrels themselves, but as the historian Ann Douglas points out, because their audience was white, they were not at liberty to adjust the form's conventions to provide a more realistic version of themselves. Instead, they were bound by the new rules of minstrelsy, which put them in the position of being black people imitating white people imitating black people. Men became women: white men transformed into black women, black men into white men as black women. Masks, parody, sexual transgression, racial shifting— it's the American joke, man! And when Whiteman's band performed "Livery Stable Blues," it participated in this same tradition, with classically trained symphony players pretending to be unschooled New Orleans white men pretending (if we are to accept Baraka and reject Sudhalter) to be the music's black originators who, in turn, copied, learned from, and goofed on all sorts of high European idioms. In the end, what's vulgar and what isn't gets lost in the jumble, and at Aeolian Hall the audience forgot what they were supposed to cheer for and instead just cheered for what they liked. No wonder Whiteman panicked.

While attempting to make a clean run from lowbrow to highbrow, he instead got mucked up in the Middle Mind, trapped between the seemingly irreconcilable myths of primitive and civilized, black and white, jazz and classical, circus and concert hall. Ironically, Bix and Louis, Nick LaRocca, and all the other jazzmen were already right there, had always been there. "Livery Stable Blues" as the Original

Dixieland Jazz Band played it—with chokes and gargles, and even horse whinnies—was no more pure (or primitive or authentic) than the same tune at Aeolian Hall. And to say that Bix sold out when he joined Whiteman, that he compromised the perfect vision of his art so that he wasted away like poor John Keats on the Spanish Steps, would be to say that early black jazzmen sold out when they imitated the oompahs of the German brass bands or turned a reel into a cake-walk. The Calathumpic King of Jazz was just a different, slightly more mainstream face on a job-lot culture, same as it had ever been.

I once interviewed Geoff Muldaur, a folk and blues musician who in 2003 released a tribute album to Bix's music, *Private Astronomy*. "Whiteman just agonizingly does not swing," he insisted. "And he gets a lot of credit for bringing certain things to the American public, and Gershwin and the whole bit, but it ain't like the Trumbauer stuff. It just kills. It just swings so hard. And early Bix groups, Bix and Our Gang, the Wolverines—they swing like crazy!"

I happen to agree with Muldaur—but our yen for swing says nothing about Bix and everything about our conception of jazz and what it's supposed to mean 80, 90, 100 years later.

And that, I suppose, is the point. However much I try to be fair to the history, on some level that is personal but also mythical and at least *feels* primal, I need Bix to kill. I need him to just swing so hard.

There is Bix and there is What Bix Means.

However much you parse and complicate Bix and Whiteman, however much you turn them into real people, you still yearn for the symbols. Bix is the saint and Whiteman the villain. It makes sense and smacks of justice. It's not enough to love the heart-stopping, hard-swinging "Sorry," waxed just days before Bix joined Whiteman—the way its opening, grenade-burst staccato ignites Don Murray's 32-bar clarinet solo, or the way that Bix pushes against the beat, rides above it, and then, finally, hangs back with a brilliant five-note off-the-beat run that defies notation. Jean Pierre Lion twice uses the word "astonishing" to describe "Sorry," and Bix himself boasted, "I have never felt better on any recording date." And it *is* astonishing, but that's not enough. I inevitably compare it to, say, "(What Are You Waiting For?) Mary," recorded a month later and hopelessly muddled with mutes and those diabetic violins, so that not even Bing Crosby can rescue it, let alone Bix. In this instance, Whiteman conveniently explains both what I loathe and what I love; or, put another way, my love of "Sorry" *needs* my hatred of "Mary." 99

In his book *The Birth (and Death) of the Cool*, published in 2009, the music historian Ted Gioia writes that the jazz of the 1920s was often described as being "hot," so much so that fans sometimes left out the "jazz" and just called it "hot music." Gioia then wonders how hot music could also be so cool. "There was a surface level, all fire and energy, a sound and fury so direct and unapologetic, so in your face, that all other styles of music performance of that era seemed restrained by comparison," Gioia writes. "Yet below this loomed a hidden level, an interior landscape, a reserve behind the hot that imparted an aura of mystery, of cool aloofness to the whole proceedings." He notes that paradoxes such as these are at the heart of the cool aesthetic and then, a page later, crowns Bix, in whom "we encounter all the inner contradictions," as the "founding father of cool jazz" and "cool personified."

In Bix Beiderbecke, hot and cool are resolved. He is "the most fascinating case study" of the early white jazz musicians who were, Gioia argues, "the forerunners of the personality type that became dominant among the baby boom generation in the late sixties": the cool cat. James Dean, Elvis Presley, Marlon Brando. As white musicians playing music associated with blacks, Bix and his gang were "outsiders among outsiders." They were children of privilege who lived spontaneously, dabbling in drugs, hoarding experience, and using their art and lifestyles to stick it to their bourgeois parents. It makes sense, in this context, that a reviewer in the *Washington Post* once described Bix as "the Kurt Cobain of the 1920s: a tortured musical genius who in a short and sadly besotted bohemian life seemed to encapsulate something essential about his times. If he didn't exist, it would have been necessary to invent him."

What finally made Bix so cool, Gioia writes, was "the malleability of his life," the way in which he overcame the cornfields, the Teutons, and the lack of lessons and "reinvented his life in stylish, sometimes outrageous ways on the largest stage imaginable."

My only argument with Gioia is that he conflates Bix the man and Bix the symbol. Did Bix *really* use his art to stick it to his parents, or was he, per Benny Green, the "blind unreasoning artist who followed his advancing sensibilities"? I don't know, and for the moment I don't care, because Gioia's Bix is Otis Ferguson's Bix or the critic Robert S. Greene's Bix—a Bix who "approximates a feeling," in Greene's words. This is What Bix Means, and it's enormously attractive, enormously seductive.

"Bix was never actually a person," Eddie Condon writes; "he was a living legend. . . . Without effort he personified jazz."

As such, Bix's story isn't *a* story; it's *the* story. In a *New York Times* essay, "In and Out of Storyville" (1987), the writer Vance Bourjaily takes a predictable swipe at *Young Man with a Horn*—"the best thing about it is the title"—before claiming that Dorothy Baker's novel is American culture's first iteration of what he calls The Story, which "goes like this: a musician of genius, frustrated by the discrepancy between what he can achieve and the crummy life musicians lead . . . goes mad, or destroys himself with alcohol and drugs. The Story might be a romance, but it is a valid one. Beiderbecke's was far from the only life that followed that pattern." Among jazz musicians, you can easily count off Bunny Berigan, Charlie Parker, Chet Baker, Billie Holiday, Dinah Washington, Bud Powell. The Story is implied in Robert Johnson's deal with the devil, and it's the foundation for the mythology that sprung up around rock and roll. And yes, of course, it's true that without Dorothy Baker Elvis still would have wandered into Sun Studios itching to make a record about his mama; he still would have swiveled his hips, still would have grown fat and tacky. And in the end, he still would have died that same pathetic death on his bathroom floor. But without Bix, Baker, and The Story, without the Calathumpic King of Jazz foreshadowing Vegas shows and purple jumpsuits, our understanding of Elvis Presley would be completely different.

In 2005, the Bix 7 road race in Davenport actually put Elvis on its annual poster and hired an Elvis impersonator to unveil it while shaking his hips and singing, "A whole lotta running goin' on." Albert Haim's online forum erupted in outrage, with Haim objecting that "there is absolutely no connection between the music of Bix" and that of Presley or other early rockers and that making such a connection was an "abomination." Another Bixophile offered that "Bix could have kicked Elvis' ass in a race anyday" [*sic*]—a playground taunt that seems to confirm, rather than rebut, the cultural connection between Bix and the essentially adolescent energy of rock and roll.

There is Bix—Haim is right: his music is nothing like Elvis's—and there is What Bix Means. There is also what *jazz* means. It is "the symbol, or the byword, for a great many elements in the spirit of the times," the art critic Gilbert Seldes wrote in his 1924 book *The Seven Lively Arts*, continuing that "as far as America is concerned, it is actually our characteristic American expression." The conductor Leopold Stokowski, also writing in the 1920s, further explained that "jazz has come to stay because it is an expression of the times, of the breathless, energetic, superactive times in which we are living, it is useless to fight against it. . . . America's contribution to the music of the past will have the same revivifying effect as the injection of new, and in the larger sense, vulgar blood into dying aristocracy."

This is familiar by now: jazz represents the primitive versus the civilized, except that here it's at once primitive *and* modern. And if jazz is an expression of a culture obsessed with looking ahead and with what's new, then it's certain that the culture will quickly abandon jazz. When Stokowski, in a Duke Ellington sort of way, says that jazz is here to stay, what he really means is that jazz is holding a place for rock and roll, which is holding a place for hip-hop, which is holding a place for whatever else is breathless, energetic, next. Jazz isn't here to stay; it's here to disappear.

Which is why I think it's the perfect music for Bix.

F. Scott Fitzgerald, like Bix, knew a thing or two about Prohibition liquor, and although a writer and not a musician, he fits The Story as well as anyone. But Bourjaily comments that he finds it odd that a "writer who'd given the word 'jazz' its currency . . . seemed to have known nothing much about it; outside of an occasional reference to party music in the stories and in 'The Great Gatsby,' and a scene or two of people dancing to the gramophone, he wrote little enough about music of any kind." Another critic, Mitchell Breitwieser, actually turns to that scene in *The Great Gatsby*, and arrives at a very different conclusion. A society jazz orchestra performs for partygoers "Mr. Vladimir Tostoff's latest work which attracted so much attention at Carnegie Hall last May," a piece titled "Vladimir Tostoff's Jazz History of the World." Breitwieser argues that this is likely a veiled reference to Whiteman's famous "Experiment in Modern Music," before noting that Fitzgerald cut from his manuscript any real description of the music. Nick Carraway is left only to comment: "The nature of Mr. Tostoff's composition eluded me . . ."

Rather than knowing nothing about jazz, Breitwieser argues, Fitzgerald seemed to intuitively understand its very essence. Jazz is spontaneity, improvisation. "One of the things I like about jazz, kid," Bix told Jimmy McPartland, "is I don't know what's going to happen next. Do you?" As a result, "an aesthetics of jazz would almost be a type of non-aesthetics," Gioia has written, noting the way that a jazz soloist strikes out on his own, refusing the premeditation of form, symmetry, and balance. The tension of jazz is located not in the knowing but in Bix's world of not knowing. Jazz, by its nature, is meant to elude. Breitwieser, meanwhile, contrasts "Emerson's 'Representative Man,' who *has* something, some mystical X that he bestows, and Gatsby, who has only desire, that is, who *lacks* rather than has, bestowing only a sharply focused version of others' more diffuse lacking."

I'm not normally a huge fan of academic papers, but I love this one, because Breitwieser then argues that this absence echoes the French philosopher Claude Lefort's conception of democracy, as opposed to a nation. In a nation, Lefort writes, "power was embodied in the prince, and it therefore gave society a body. And because of this, a latent but effective knowledge of what *one* meant to *the other* existed throughout the social." In a democracy, however, with its branches of government, its checks and balances, its resistance to the trappings of the prince, "the locus of power becomes an *empty place*."

What happens next is just such an empty place and What Bix Means is a kind of silence.

I'm reminded of the end of *The Beiderbecke Connection*, a 1988 British comedy-mystery television series about two schoolteachers, Trevor and Jill. A devoted Bixophile and unfailing optimist, Trevor finds in Bix mystical power, pure feeling. In the show's final scene, Jill, Trevor, and their new baby, First Born, relax on a hillside overlooking a scarred West Yorkshire landscape, and Jill bemoans the state of the world. Trevor responds by explaining exactly what went wrong:

> TREVOR: People don't hear the music.
> JILL: Back to music.
> TREVOR: Certainly. What else is there? (*Looking at First Born.*)
>   He can hear it.
> JILL: Bix?
> TREVOR: And Duke and Bird and Prez.
> JILL: The Beiderbecke connection.
> TREVOR: That's the sanity clause. You only have to listen.

But instead of Bix's music, there is only the wind.

Anyway, none of this Bix-as-sellout criticism takes into account "In a Mist" or the fact that Bix's musical sensibilities seemed to be leading him slowly away from jazz. In 1925 he had taken a lesson from a classical trumpeter, and while in Whiteman's employ he toyed with the idea of writing a jazz symphony. It may have been Whiteman's proximity to the classical world—personally, in the men he employed, and in the music he played—that drew Bix to him in the first place.

When Maurice Ravel unexpectedly dropped by a New York recording session on March 12, 1928, just a few months before his ballet *Boléro* premiered, Bix apparently fluttered with nerves. The band performed a few numbers for the famous composer, and according to the vocalist Al Rinker the Frenchman was "extremely interested in what Bix was playing." Later that night Bix screwed up the courage to approach his idol in a speakeasy and the two enjoyed a long conversation, the details of which have been lost.

Whatever we think about Bix's supposed aesthetic degradation, what can't be denied is his *physical* degradation. His drinking—which like his music seems to have no clear beginning or end—dated back at least to high school and appears to have significantly increased after he joined Whiteman. According to his bandmates, Bix even drank onstage. "He's got to sit up there with his trumpet," the arranger Bill Challis remembered, "and what's more natural than maybe have a drink, or something like that." In Bix's defense, his limited ability to sight-read meant that he was stuck with third and fourth trumpet parts, which in practice amounted to him waiting around until he could blow one of his now legendary solos.

Drunken-Bix stories began to pile up like empty whiskey and gin bottles. There were late nights out, trashed hotel rooms, and the time he missed his train and found a pilot to fly him to his next gig. When a few of Whiteman's boys met him on the airfield, Bix fell into their arms, drunk. Somehow he still managed solos like the one on "From Monday On," a pleasantly upbeat tune written by Bing Crosby and Harry Barris and recorded by a small combo on February 28, 1928. Bix waxed three extant takes over two sessions, and each of his performances is distinctive and memorable. The song features tight, swinging harmonies from Crosby, Al Rinker, and others—hardly a mediocre vaudeville act—but Bix cuts through them like a swinging scythe.

"In a Mist," meanwhile, was becoming popular with audiences. In April 1928, the Davenport paper ran a feature describing a midnight radio broadcast of a Whiteman performance that featured Bix playing his piano composition. Among those tuning in was "a little family group in the B. H. Beiderbecke home, 1934 Grand Avenue." The article summarizes Bix's life and career—"displayed his jazz tendencies since earliest youth . . . went to the local schools . . . veered away from the labor of learning . . . cornetist with the Jean Goldkette orchestra"—before concluding with a few words from his mother. "We can always tell when Bix's horn comes in," she says. "We know every time Paul Whiteman's orchestra is on the air and Leon knows we'll be listening in. The air [i.e., tune] is carried by the other cornetist but the sudden perky blare and the unexpected trills—those are the jazz parts and they are Leon's."

The following October Bix even performed "In a Mist" at Carnegie Hall with Sergey Rachmaninoff in attendance. It was, according to Jean Pierre Lion, "a peak in Bix's professional career." "Generous applause greeted the end of the number," the biographer writes, and "Paul Whiteman had to stop Bix from returning too quickly to his chair; nervous and embarrassed, Bix bowed awkwardly before retreating behind his music stand."

The next few months were disastrous. In November 1928 Bix suffered a severe nervous breakdown in a hotel room in Cleveland. "He cracked up, that's all," the trombonist Bill Rank explained. "Just went to pieces; broke up a roomful of furniture in the hotel." Then, in February 1929, his friends found him in his New York hotel room lying in a pool of his own blood. Shocked and concerned, they immediately began to gossip. "The 'inside story,' according to Paul Mertz, was that "Bix and another friend were badly beaten up and worked over one night in a strange speakeasy. A broken bottle used as a weapon by one of the assailants gashed his thigh (or kindred part) to the extent that he was never able to walk without limping." They were "a couple of sailors," Roy Bargy confirmed, "or at least low-type characters," and Bix was rushed to the hospital, after which Whiteman personally saw that he was put on a train home to Davenport. And kept on full salary.

While Bix was resting at his parents' place on Grand Avenue, a reporter from the *Democrat and Leader* approached him for an interview. The newspaper couldn't get enough of him, and the Carnegie Hall gig, plus the opportunity to speak to the young star in person, provided the hook for another story. And when it ran on Sunday, February 10, 1929, the feature appeared prominently on the front of the paper's third section with a photograph identifying Bix as a "noted trumpeter." (See figure 3.) This is the only known interview of the jazz legend and for that reason ought to be an invaluable resource for insights into Bix's character, what he sounded like when he talked, and especially what he thought about jazz and other types of music, too.

And yet there's always been something a little off about the article, something that jazz scholars have struggled to clearly articulate. I decided to take a closer look and, like so much else related to Bix, what I found at first delighted and then shocked me.

Days of Real Sport Here Recalled by John Witt's Birthday

'Jazz Is Musical Humor,' Says Davenport Composer and Cornetist of Whiteman's Band

Believes Humor of Jazz is Many-Sided; Classifies Catch-as-Catch-Can Music as "Sweet" and "Hot," but Prefers the "Hot" More Than Purring Respectability of the "Sweet."

PLINKY-PLANK! Bluesy moans! Crooning tones! Ear-tickling, toe-inciting, soul-wrenching melodies —that's jazz!

Put them all together and what have you?

"Musical humor," says the world's hottest cornetist of Paul Whiteman's orchestra, Leon "Bix" Beiderbecke, who is convalescing from a recent illness at the home of his parents, Mr. and Mrs. B. H. Beiderbecke, 1934 Grand avenue.

Noted Trumpeter

LEON "BIX" BEIDERBECKE

CUPID SELECTS FAST TACTICS FOR CAMPAIGN

Modern Darts to Speed Over Telegraph Wires on Valentine's Day.

The bachelor's club will be no more! Whether true love is swift and the mail's too slow—that is the question! At any rate, love will brook no obstacles this year, judging from fancy Cupid Valentine campaign tactics for 1929.

WATER COLOR ART REVEALS OLD TRADITION

Medium Expressed by Johnson's Work Adapted to American Mind.

By HERMON MORE

Remember Way Back In 1885 When the Ol' Witt Swimmin' House Looked Like This?

The old bathhouse at the foot of Front street which was abuzz with comings and goings of prominent Tri-city dudes and belles 44 years ago. Background shows old bridge and arsenal.

At Age of 3, Rode 40 Miles on Horseback to See Lincoln; Later Wrecked Fence Rail-Splitter Built

John Clayton Bliff and Replica of Lincoln's Log Cabin He Fashioned.

Was Proprietor of Bathhouse in Period When Steam-Heated Natatorium Was Yet a Dream

You Took a Swim for a Nickle or a Dime, Depending on Your Size and Your Pocketbook and There Were Row Boats, too, for Love-Sick Swains to "Squander" Two-bits an Hour On.

REMEMBER the old swimmin' house? The old Witt bath house at the foot of Rock Island street where you took a kid could take a swim in the little hole for a nickel or in the big hole for a dime?

Those were the days of real sport! The days when Judge James Bollinger, Attorney Louis Block, and Dr. William L. Allen outstunted each other in high dives. The days when the rotund proprietor, John Witt, smiled and joked with the "boys" and gave ten or twenty or a good at the office if he were suffering from a bad taste of extra dry times.

OBSERVES 94TH BIRTHDAY TODAY

JOHN WITT

Lived "Side by Side" with Abraham Lincoln in Early Boyhood Days

W. C. ATKINSON

To begin with the former, and speaking as a longtime editor, the lead is wonderful:

> Plinky-plank! Blooey moans! Crooning tones! Ear-tickling, toe-inciting, soul-wrenching melodies—that's jazz!
>
> Put them all together and what have you?
>
> "Musical humor," says the world's hottest cornetist of Paul Whiteman's orchestra. Leon "Bix" Beiderbecke, who is convalencing [*sic*] from a recent illness at the home of his parents, Mr. and Mrs. B. H. Beiderbecke, 1934 Grand Avenue.

The writer goes on to fill out Bix's quote. "Jazz is musical humor," he said. "The noun jazz describes a modern American technique for the playing of any music, accompanied by noise called harmony, and interpolated instrumental effects. It also describes music exhibiting influence of that technique which has as its traditional object to secure the effects of surprise, or in the broadest sense, humor."

I'm hooked already. Bix is a journalist's dream of pithiness: "Jazz is musical humor," he says, while mixing a dash of slang ("noise called harmony") with the more buttoned-up language of a certified expert: *Interpolated instrumental effects. Exhibiting influence. Traditional object. Secure the effects.* Whew! This is hardly, to quote Ralph Berton, a "wordless" Bix, the kid for whom, seven years earlier, four Cs would have constituted significant scholastic improvement. This is more the sort to read Proust and then lecture about it, in perfectly puckered French, to a gymnasium full of bored undergraduates.

Anyway, the article continues with a paraphrase of Bix outlining the "negrotic" origins of jazz, when the music was full of "'barrelhouse' tones" and saxophones blown into "jugs and lengths of gaspipe." Bix argues that Whiteman's famous Aeolian Hall concert changed everything, suggesting that its "cacophonic combinations" demonstrated "what a change came over the face of Melusina and Terpsichore in a decade." Then comes another direct quote from Bix:

> "The jazz band's chief stimulus, of course, was the rise of the negro 'blues' and their exploitation by the negro song-writer, W. C. Handy," the cornetist stated.
>
> "They at once were melancholic and humorous, and dealt exclusively with the singer's own emotion and philosophy. Their ex-

periments were convert [covert]. In today's jazz they are open. The visual effect of comic instruments and bodily contortions of the musicians is, tho dispensable, a part of jazz itself."

Again in paraphrase, Bix goes on to distinguish between "hot" and "sweet" jazz, declaring his preference for the former, "which slightly modifies the original pandemonium of the 'Livery Stable Blues,' more than the purring respectability of the 'sweet,' whose hush and muffled throb is heard behind the balustrade of potted palms at debutante dances."

I'm struck by the reporter's language. It positively leaps off the page and begins to fox-trot. *Purring respectability! Cacophonic combinations! Over the face of Melusina and Terpsichore!* I love it, but *Melu*-who? A quick bit of research tells me that Melusina (or Melusine) is a European folk character usually depicted as a mermaid (c.f. Mendelssohn's *Zum Märchen von der Schönen Melusine*), while Terpsichore is one of ancient Greece's Nine Muses and rules over dance and song. Which makes sense, I suppose, but is the reporter here really paraphrasing Bix Beiderbecke or is he paraphrasing . . . well, H. O. Osgood?

If Paul Whiteman, bandleader, wrote the first full-length book on jazz in 1926, then Henry Osgood, critic, wrote the *other* first full-length book on jazz in 1926: *So This Is Jazz.* And in its introduction Osgood vividly describes the music's "ear-tickling," "nerve-harrowing, soul-wrenching noise" before making mention of the "cacophonic combinations" responsible for its earliest iterations. Now turn to chapter 12, and you'll find that Osgood has reprinted his original 1924 rave of Whiteman's "Experiment in Modern Music" wherein the music is "nerve-tickling, toe-inciting," and he argues that Whiteman's famous concert "proved what a change has come over the face of Melusina and Terpsichore in a decade."

What a "change," indeed.

And as long as we're dumping key phrases into Google, it seems that the *Democrat*'s anonymous reporter relied on at least one other bit of Whiteman-related research: the *Bookman* magazine, April 1928, in which he found Abbe Niles's regular popular-music column "Ballads, Songs and Snatches." Niles declares that "there is better popular music today than in the Golden 'Nineties, the Elegant 'Eighties, and so on down, but its quantity is embarrassing. However—*Début-dance fox-trots*, recalling the hush and the deep muffled throb of the full Whiteman band behind a forest of potted palms."

This is all nearly word for word what we find in the *Democrat*, although the Davenport paper's slight variation offers a bit tighter rhythm and what a great word, *balustrade*! Except that Osgood also happens to use that word in describing a similar scene, just as he also employs the wonderful adjective *blooey*. The examples of borrowings and plagiarism are beginning to accumulate, but let's be clear—they're only interesting up to a point. I want to know what, if anything, they *mean*. In this case they suggest that at a minimum there are four voices banging around in this article: one belonging to its anonymous author, one to Bix, one to Henry Osgood, and one to Abbe Niles. The very fact of these multiple voices also, I think, urges caution with respect to where one starts and another stops. If, as seems to be the case, the *Democrat*'s reporter had a copy of *So This Is Jazz* right there on his desk as he (or she) wrote, then it would be fair to wonder what else he took from the book beyond just the occasional verbatim phrase. Did he, for instance, put any of Osgood's words into Bix's mouth?

The next section of the article, affixed with the subhead "Humor 'As You Like It,'" recapitulates the theme of musical humor. "The humor of jazz is rich and many-sided," Bix tells the reporter. "Some of it is obvious enough to make a dog laugh. Some is subtle, wry-mouthed, or back-handed. It is by turns bitter, agonized, and grotesque. Even in the hands of white composers it involuntarily reflects the half-forgotten suffering of the negro. Jazz has both white and black elements, and each in some respects has influenced the other. It's [*sic*] recent phase seems to throw the light of the white race's sophistication upon the anguish of the black."

This is the stuff that scholars, if they bother to take notice of the interview at all, love to quote. It presents a Bix Beiderbecke who is miles away from the one depicted by Albert Murray, Stanley Crouch, and Amiri Baraka, someone who at best was an "intruder" in discussions of jazz and who at worst outright stole the birthright of African Americans. That's why Geoffrey C. Ward, in a history of jazz that accompanied the Ken Burns documentary, highlights Bix's nod to "the half-forgotten suffering of the negro," and why Stephan Talty, in *Mu-*

latto America: At the Crossroads of Black and White Culture (2003), uses these same words to suggest that "white musicians did understand that they had tapped into an understanding of life as a dare with consequences that was, at its root, black."

And Talty, like me, can't help but be drawn to this idea of musical humor. He writes: "For humor, Beiderbecke meant something more than the harmless spoofs that 'nut' jazz, with its costumes, its stunts and gags, worked in; he described jazz's humor as 'bitter, agonized and grotesque.' It was a response to pain." Talty says this in part because of the "anguished" context, but also, I would guess, because stunts and gags weren't Bix's style. Still, Ward scoffs at all this, claiming that to Bix, "jazz itself was 'musical humor,' nothing more."

Which is fine. The point is that Bix's words suggest a reading of jazz that is interesting enough, and complex enough, for scholars to disagree about. But the question lingers: are these really Bix's words at all? Sudhalter and Evans dismiss the whole affair as reflecting "little more than the convoluted view of jazz and its practitioners taken by American journalism of 1929," which doesn't speak to the question at hand, except that the biographers also tellingly refer to the reporter as "interviewing" Bix, placing the word in scare quotes. Jean Pierre Lion, meanwhile, is equally ambiguous. In describing the article, he writes that "Bix is quoted as saying . . ." and "Bix then supposedly emphasized . . ." as if to signal to his readers his doubts regarding the quotations' authenticity, but without forcing himself to declare outright that the article is a fraud. "This long interview gives, at the end, a faithful image of the young musician," Lion writes: "once again, the mirror is empty. Bix has managed to limit his words to general considerations, shying away from any personal or intimate question."

In other words, the article may not, in fact, reflect Bix Beiderbecke, but that's not because he didn't say the things he's quoted as saying; rather, it's because he didn't answer the questions with more personal details.

I imagine an exasperated Bix responding: *What do you want from me, man? I give you musical humor. I give you the half-forgotten suffering of the negro, and that's not enough? What the hell!*

And it *is* frustrating because I terribly want this to be Bix's voice. "Bix Sounds Off on Jazz," promises the headline of a July 12, 2005, article (about the article) in Davenport's *Quad-City Times*. "He was a star, but Leon Bix Beiderbecke still had time to talk about the music that had made him so." That's right. Bix the excuse-maker, Bix the wordless, but also Bix the star. What did he have to say about race and jazz, this star who was friends with the great Louis Armstrong? What did he have to say about the future of jazz, this star who was pushing the music into the avant-garde with his impressionistic piano pieces?

I want to know!

And yet . . . why the Shakespeare allusion in the subhead? Is it because Osgood, on page 6 of *So This Is Jazz*, quotes *Merchant of Venice*? And this business of humor. Osgood has something to say about that, too, writing about "serious jazz" that is also "funny." Of course, such references are hardly definitive of anything, and I'll admit that it's plenty easy to get carried away. This is especially true when one is accustomed to treating Bix less like a person than like a code: something to be studied and, with luck, broken. So let's just relax a bit and continue with the article.

A new section bids "Goodbye Grieg and Lizst!" (misspelling the latter composer's name). That's what Bix did once he quit his piano lessons and "taught the cornet to laugh by unexpected thrills, to moan by sudden perky blares, to do stunts, and to hold its head up high." After graduating from Lake Forest (which, of course, he did not), he went to the University of Iowa, where "he droned 'one, two, three, four' on the piano while he transposed and translated notes and melodies into orchestral scores." From there he found the Wolverines and, later, Jean Goldkette.

As it turns out, the chronology here—it should read the Wolverines, Goldkette, *then* Iowa, *then* Goldkette again—is the least of problems. We must now add to the chorus of voices one Agatha Beiderbecke. As the musician Brad Kay pointed out to me, that earlier story in the *Democrat* in 1928 about Whiteman's midnight broadcast contained this quotation from Bix's mother: "The air is carried out by the other cornetist but the sudden perky blare and the unexpected trills—those are the jazz parts, and they are Leon's." It would make sense to imagine that our anonymous reporter had dug that earlier article out of the archives and borrowed from it—poorly, I might add; how can Bix's sound both "moan" and be "perky"?—just as he borrowed from Osgood and Abbe Niles in the *Bookman*.

In fact, looking back at the earlier article, I notice how different a portrait of Bix it paints. "He was known as a jazz artist in every school he attended," the again-anonymous reporter writes, "but beyond that school had little appeal and he had no inclination to go on to college." Music lessons are described as "a grind," and he took "not more than a score in all" (this last phrase was transferred verbatim to the 1929 article). "He had wonderful promise, his teachers said, but he veered away from the labor of learning. What was the use of droning 'one, two, three, four' when you could rattle off the latest jazz tune thru a magic sense entirely apart from mathematics. So ran his youthful reasoning."

So in 1928 droning "one, two, three, four" was of no use, while in 1929, it's word for word what he did at university, a place that according to the 1928 piece he never even attended.

Now that we've added another voice to the chorus I'm becoming suspicious of everything. Did Aggie really say what she's quoted as saying, or did those words, as Kay believes, come from "the head of this journeyman news reporter, this purple prose slinger"? And if they did, why couldn't that same (or some similarly inclined) purple prose slinger put words into Bix's mouth?

I want to be hopeful in the fashion of a Bixophile named Peter Curry, who declared on Albert Haim's online forum in 2002—back when there were doubts about the interview's veracity but nothing more—that he accepted Bix's words exactly as they were presented. "I'm going to assume that the reporter was no fool," Curry wrote, "that he/she knew how to take shorthand as accurately as if Bix's words, his syntax, what he said, how he spoke, had been incontestably encrypted by Dictaphone." As for Bix, "I assume he's pouring coffee, sucking on his pipe, maybe nervously swapping around his personas, from 'just one of the boys' to 'man of the world' to vaguely bohemian scholar, spokesman and historian of ultra modern music. He's not yet 27; he's survived a personal crisis; he's turned his life around; he's beaten the bottle for good; his Whiteman chair awaits him; his consciousness simmers with countless as yet unwritten compositions; the decades stretch before him; he savours this touch of home-town recognition."

How poignant. But is it true?

The article's final section is headed, appropriately, "We Want More!" Here Bix elaborates on his life with Whiteman. "We have great times traveling about," he says. "The 'boys' are airplane crazy and movie-shy. We have a new Travelair plane and several are learning to pilot."

"Might come in handy sometimes," he laughs, "in case we oversleep and miss the train, but we're generally on time. In fact, one time we were a bit ahead of the Uptown theatre in Chicago and the curtain went up without warning. 'Be nonchalant!' was employed and we picked up our instruments and started to play."

It's funny, but only here at the end—the part of the article generally ignored by scholars because, honestly, who cares about your "great times traveling about"?—do I get the sense that I'm finally hearing Leon Bix Beiderbecke speak to me. It comes as a bit of a surprise, and as a great relief. This is Bix, oversleeping and missing the train. This is Bix, movie-shy (whatever that means) and airplane crazy. This is a person I recognize, and his appearance, however belated, offers me some hope that it might have been him all along.

And thus he spoke, I think. *Finally.*

Except that then it happened. Convinced I had identified all the voices in the article, all the various cacophonic combinations, I was only offhandedly googling a few more phrases when up popped something I hadn't seen before. It was a newspaper article published on September 1, 1928, in the *Evening Independent* of St. Petersburg, Florida: "The Official How and Why of Jazz—From a Lawyer" by Louise Garwood for the NEA Service, a national newspaper syndicate. The lawyer, it turns out, was none other than Mr. Bookman himself, Edward Abbe Niles, "a Rhodes scholar, the grandson of a Yankee bishop, a graduate of Harvard Law school," and an associate at the Wall Street firm of Cadwalader, Wickersham, and Taft, who is "described by his wife as the 'world's worst dancer.'" He also happened to be the author of *Encyclopaedia Britannica*'s entry on jazz.

"Jazz is musical humor," Niles told Garwood. "The noun jazz describes a modern American technique for the playing of any music, embracing tricks of accent and rhythm, characteristic interpolated melodic figures and instrumental effects. It also describes music exhibiting influence of that technique which has as its traditional object to secure the effects of surprise and in the broadest sense, humor."

I might as well admit that at first I was so excited by my find that I ran around in my slippers yelping, *I knew it! I just knew it!* This, after all, was something completely new. Along with Osgood, it was the key to the whole article and proof, once and for all, that none of these words actually belonged to Bix—except maybe for the "great times traveling about." That totally sounds like Bix.

After a while, though, the rush of discovery wore off and my heart choked. What kind of con man—and make no mistake, the reporter who wrote the 1929 article is the con man here, not Bix—pickpockets an entire interview like that? Was he that convinced that no one in Davenport had read a nationally syndicated piece that had run just a few months prior? Or perhaps I'm being unfair. Perhaps Bix was just that terrible of an interview, that inarticulate. Maybe his "great times traveling about" was the best quote this reporter could wring out of him, while the whole time lying there on his desk and tempting him was this Niles fellow, a Rhodes scholar and an interviewer's dream: pithy *and* learned. The man quoted Psalms, for crying out loud, although the Davenport reporter was smart enough to leave that part out.

What he didn't leave out included Niles explaining how Negro jazz musicians once "blew into jugs and lengths of gas-pipe." The rest of that particular sentence was also stolen, as was the stuff about W. C. Handy: Niles was a Handy scholar and knew the songwriter well, even called him "Bill."

Of course Niles also wrote that column for the *Bookman*. According to Garwood, he classified jazz as either "sweet" or "hot," but it was Garwood, not Niles, who wrote of the "original pandemonium of the old 'Livery Stable Blues'" and the "hush and muffled throb" and "potted palms." Which means that, for those still bothering to keep track, our anonymous reporter plagiarized Garwood, who plagiarized Niles.

At this point it goes without saying that Niles believed "the humor of jazz" to be "rich and many-sided." *Dog laugh, wry-mouthed, half-forgotten suffering*, and *the anguish of the black*—they're all there. So, too, are Grieg and the misspelled Liszt.

I'm reminded of Lion's mirror metaphor, and how the words from these various sources keep reflecting back at each other, like two mirrors set up to create infinity. With every new image, Bix grows smaller and smaller, until eventually he disappears.

Hans Eekhoff, a prominent Dutch record collector and sound engineer who lives in England, sees it differently. For him, Bix is right there in front of us, just as he's always been. After I revealed my discovery on my personal blog, Eekhoff used the comments section to hail it as "important" and "very interesting indeed." But he dismissed the likely scenario I had laid out, in which a reporter interviewed Bix, came away with little worth quoting, and so plagiarized his story from Osgood, Niles, and Garwood. "There is another possibility," said Eekhoff: Bix wrote (and therefore plagiarized) the article himself.

"Did Bix have so little to say that the interviewer thought it was necessary to borrow from other sources?" Eekhoff wanted to know. "I am sceptical about that. . . . I think it is more likely that Bix himself copied these statements to add some depth and seriousness to his 'interview.'"

The theory strikes me as highly suspect. Why is it "likely," as Eekhoff would have us believe, that Bix had not only read the Niles interview and Osgood's *So This Is Jazz*, but happened to have copies with him on his impromptu visit to Davenport? Why must we "doubt that a provincial interviewer from a local paper" would have found and read these sources? After all, Davenport, as we've seen, was hardly a backwater. And why would Bix, disinclined to do much besides blow his horn, suddenly be motivated to tackle a reporter's job for him?

When I posed these questions to Eekhoff, he again was dismissive. "Would [Bix] have accepted the invitation to be featured in an article and not have anything to say?" Eekhoff wrote. "Nonsense. I am pretty sure that he put his heart and soul in it."

Almost willfully, Eekhoff seems to have missed the contradiction at the heart of his argument. Rather than be satisfied that Bix Beiderbecke had little to say, he instead insists that Bix wrote an article in which virtually none of the words are his own. He put his heart and soul into plagiarism.

"These quotations no doubt reflected his own opinions," Eekhoff wrote, "but Bix realised that they were rather better put than he could do it." In other words, what had once been proof that Bix had little if anything to do with the article—its words sound nothing like him—now becomes evidence that he himself was the author.

As I continued to engage Eekhoff he only became more certain. "I am convinced that [the reporter] didn't write the article," he told me. "Bix did." And elsewhere: "I will never believe that Bix just wasn't interested, had nothing to say and simply let somebody at the *Davenport Democrat* do the ghost-writing and put these highly esoteric quotes in Bix's mouth."

At this point I backed away from the debate, but what fascinates me about Eekhoff—who stands in here for so many of Bix's friends and admirers, then and now—is his growling and persistent refusal to let go of *his* Bix: a good kid who may not have been much of a writer but who had "heart and soul."

I'm certain.

I will never accept.

"I'm almost done writing a book about the guy, and I don't feel I know him nearly well enough to be so certain," I wrote to Eekhoff at one point. "And now something I thought I knew to be true is not true. That provokes in me *less* certainty, not more."

A snatch of newsreel from May 1928 provides us our only glimpse on film of Bix Beiderbecke performing. Wanting to publicize his move from Victor to Columbia, Whiteman opens the Fox Movietone session by dramatically ripping up his contract. He then launches the band into "My Ohio Home," which, while not exactly a holocaust, is perhaps a bit too *Leave It to Beaver*-y for my taste. Still, plump and polished Whiteman leads his boys with all the earnest gravity of a funeral parlor director until, about a minute in, the brass section rises and there—tucked way on the far left of the black-and-white frame stands Bix. Even when you've looked at the clip a hundred times, as I have, you can't help but gasp a little.

Talk about the *fleshy* Bix! Although it's only four and half years since the most famous photograph of him was taken—face round, hair perfectly parted, his tux perfectly pressed—he looks surprisingly different. He's gained weight, grown a mustache. The hair is still greased down, the ears sticking out, but he wears only a loose, button-down shirt and no jacket. He looks solid, confident, the opposite of spectral. And perhaps that's why I keep replaying this video: while Bix blows nothing of interest musically, he nevertheless feels irresistibly present.

What does that even mean, though—for Bix to be present? In trying to find Bix, what is it that I'm looking for?

My girlfriend suggests, cleverly, that I must go back to that first encounter with Bix, on the set of Pupi Avati's biopic. "You sat on the same bandstand then," she explained, "and everything since has been an attempt to recover that proximity."

I don't know if she said it quite in that manner, sounding like Freud with his legs crossed, but you get the idea. From the very beginning, Bix for me was a construct, a character. The actor Bryant Weeks was nothing like the historical Bix; he was hot, for crying out loud, with perfectly normal ears, and he couldn't at all play that horn they gave him. He stood in for Bix but never inhabited him.

The newsreel, though, shows me someone I might have actually known. I went to high school in Davenport with guys who looked just like him. We bowled on Friday nights and slurped Mountain Dew with vodka. We ran from the cops and told our parents we'd been studying. Some of us were even musicians, dragging ourselves to Youth Symphony on Saturday afternoons to rehearse Prokofiev and Dvořák. (Sadly, I never got to play Shostakovich.) During the summer we worked in the cornfields and swam in the river. We spoke with flat Midwestern vowels and rarely if ever raised our voices to authority. Lonely and itching to leave, we also felt perfectly at home.

We grew up on Bix and we grew up *like* him, too. In this there is a certain kind of intimacy. But of course there's more to it than that. Whatever unified sense of Bix I may have once held, it has since been shattered into a thousand tiny pieces, each a possibility, an intellectual temptation: Bix the innovator, the intruder, the Proustian, the innocent; Bix the funky, the genius, the artist, the drunk; Bix the sellout; Bix the impossible little shit.

The exercise of finding Bix involves, if not putting these pieces back together again, then at least identifying them, mapping them out as best I can. Although to see him standing there, those big hands of his curled around that cornet, is to be reminded of the fact that few of us make such perfect sense. We all have our mysteries, our secrets. Bix may look easygoing behind the soundtrack of "My Ohio Home," but remember: he was only six months away from that breakdown in Cleveland.

After returning to Whiteman in the spring of 1929, Bix joined the band on a summer-long excursion to Los Angeles, where Universal Studios hoped to produce a movie revue called *The King of Jazz*. Production delays created ample time for partying, however. "Bix was drinking pretty heavily again," his fellow cornetist Andy Secrest recalled. "We really thought he'd taken the cure at home, but he'd apparently just rested or something, because it didn't slow him down." By September 1929 he was back in Davenport, and Mr. and Mrs. Beiderbecke checked him in to the Keeley Institute in Dwight, Illinois, about 180 miles east of Davenport, and he spent October and most of November discreetly sobering up—after which he promptly started drinking again. His solos, such as the few bars he took to wrap up Hoagy Carmichael's "Georgia on My Mind," noticeably flagged. His genius for invention waned, and, in the words of Benny Green, "the golden door was being slammed in his face." Black Thursday, meanwhile, had wiped out most of his savings, and after collapsing during a live radio performance of the *Camel Pleasure Hour*, he was finally out of a job. Come the end of 1930, diagnosed with alcoholic polyneuritis, suffering from the DTs, and fighting a pulmonary infection, Bix Beiderbecke was dying. And yet again he was back in Davenport.

The days at home must have been long. Friends like Esten Spurrier were around and there were always gigs to be had, but Bix was in no shape to play, let alone live up to his sporadic press. Then one day he went poking around in one of the closets at 1934 Grand. Who knows what he was looking for, but according to Spurrier what he found was a tall stack of his own 78s—"My Pretty Girl," "Davenport Blues," "In a Mist," "Singin' the Blues," "I'm Coming Virginia"—records he had faithfully mailed his parents over the years. "We can only try to conceive what his feelings must have been," Ralph Berton writes in *Remembering Bix*, "on coming home during his final convalescence

. . . full of love and guilt, ready to try again to become their son, on discovering that not one of them—*not even his mother*—had even so much as bothered to listen to one of them. Every record was still in its original envelope, unopened—gathering dust on the top shelf of a closet. They were ashamed of them."

In Berton's view, which has become widespread, Bismark and Agatha had failed to love and support their son, to accept his calling, or to recognize his genius. Bix was the "jazz cornet player exiled by shame / from the classic Victorian house in Davenport," writes the poet Rod Jellema. And his parents' failure can be summed up neatly in this single anecdote. It's a singular failure and perhaps one that is not all that uncommon, but for Berton, it transcends the Beiderbeckes and becomes also a collective failure: these are all the parents of all the tortured artists—they're the *reason* the artists are tortured—and Berton turns on them with prose that is exasperated, sarcastic, and prosecutorial. "Had Bix been the tough renegade such a family deserved," he writes, "this excommunication might have had small effect; his reaction would have been a healthy *Fuck you too, Jack*! But Bix was too 'good' a boy for that, too guilty about the pain and humiliation he had supposedly caused them by his defection."

This is a weird reading of the historical record, though, isn't it? After all, Agatha seemed to be attentive and supportive when it came to her son's career. When the Whiteman Orchestra stopped in Chicago in November 1927, she paid Bix a surprise visit. "His mother was very pleased he had—in her own words—made it to the top," Bix's colleague, the trumpet player Charlie Margulis, said. "She felt her son had reached the height of his career." Five months later, Whiteman played that live radio program, the one about which the paper quoted Agatha as saying, "We can always tell when Bix's horn comes in. We know every time Paul Whiteman's orchestra is on the air, and Leon knows we'll be listening in." Does that sound like a mother who had banished her son, who cared not whether he lived or died? Of course, this was the same interview in which Agatha supposedly described "the sudden perky blare and the unexpected trills" of Bix's cornet, words that may not even have been hers. Still, a few months later, in July 1928, Bix's brother, Burnie, actually joined him in a Chicago studio for a recording of "Ol' Man River." And then in November 1928, Bix's parents saw him play in person with Whiteman when the orchestra stopped in Clinton, Iowa, north of Davenport. Bix cut way back on his drinking to prepare for the visit, and he sweated his way through the evening without incident. After the show, Bismark and Agatha even got to shake the hand of the great Paul Whiteman and hear him talk up their son's talent.

Just a week later, though, came the breakdown in Cleveland. Those who knew him speculated that Bix was hell-bent on destroying himself, though they dared not speculate why. Hoagy Carmichael was typical: "I respected him and loved him at his best—and I leave the enigma of the inner Bix Beiderbecke for others to figure out if they can. But I don't think the searchers will find much more." Ralph Berton was atypical. He was determined to crawl into Bix's head, to poke around his psyche no matter how ugly it got. He wanted to do this out of contempt for the Great Bix Myth, especially as he encountered it in Baker's *Young Man with a Horn* and the subsequent Kirk Douglas film adaptation. He wanted to do this out of his belief "that the real Bix was a far more interesting and dramatic character than either of the invented ones." Which is why he zeroed in on those supposedly unopened records and why he dared speculate that Bix was a martyr for jazz. But mere disapproval . . . does that really lead Bix to drink himself to death?

It should be said that towering disapproval is something the Germans have traditionally excelled at, which is why, at this point, the German philosopher Theodor W. Adorno leaps to mind. His essay "Perennial Fashion—Jazz" was published in 1967, just two years before his death, and it heaps scorn on all things syncopated. More interesting, though, is the fact that Adorno frames his objections in familial terms, arguing that the music's "rebellious gestures are accompanied by the tendency to blind obeisance," mirroring the sort of person "who chafes against the father-figure while secretly admiring him, who seeks to emulate him and in turn derives enjoyment from the subordination he detests." In other words, says Adorno, it's not Mom and Pop we should be worried about, but just Pop.

This is where the biographer Richard Sudhalter picks up the thread. "Even given a certain amount of Teutonic rigidity, Bismarck [*sic*] Beiderbecke's obvious and growing coldness toward his younger son seems curious," he wonders aloud in a long and highly dramatic endnote in his controversial book *Lost Chords*. (A friend of mine has wryly dubbed this the Ominous Endnote.) "It is certainly out of pro-portion to any imagined chagrin at the boy's failure to do well at school or at his having become a dance band musician." A few years back, when Bix told his dad about making it into Whiteman's orchestra, there was no way the father could have misunderstood what an important accomplishment that was. "Yet his reported response was cool, distant," Sudhalter writes. "What, too, could have made him sufficiently bitter to have refused to open or play his son's records when they arrived, regularly, in the mail—and even prevented other family members from doing so?"

To answer that question—to the degree to which it *can* be answered—we must return, finally, to April 1921 and that knock on the door.

This, I presume, is how Mr. and Mrs. Beiderbecke came to learn of an incident involving their son that took place earlier in the day. What happened continues to be the subject of fierce debate and many of the details, despite our best scholarly efforts, remain ultimately unknowable. Nevertheless, we *do* know that some members of the Beiderbecke family and those close to them, including, quite possibly, the biographers Phil Evans and Richard Sudhalter, worked to keep the following events secret for nearly eight decades. Their conspicuous silence, combined with that puffed-up pronouncement from Sudhalter and Evans—that Bix's "adult life may be viewed as a long unconscious struggle to eradicate a sense of guilt"—suggest that this may be a critical, in some respects even *the* critical, moment in our story.

Best, then, to begin with the police blotter and arrest report, which were recorded on April 22, 1921, a Friday. Officers Len and Halligan charged Leon Beiderbecke with a "lewd & lascivious act with child" and listed his age as eighteen, his height as five-seven, and his complexion—referring not to his skin but to his eye- and hair-color—as "dark." According to the officers' account of what happened, a five-year-old girl who lived at 1703 Iowa Street accused Bix of taking her out of the rain and into Goddard's garage at the corner of Locust Street and Grand Avenue. The two climbed into an automobile and Bix shut the door, after which, according to the report, he allegedly put "his hands on her person outside of her dress." When she "hollered," two men came running: James L. Duncan and Mahlon Bailey, both of whom worked across the street. Write the officers: "They went over and the girl went home"—a curious ending to the scene, as it neglects to say what they saw; whether they, the girl, or her father reported the incident to the police; and what Bix said or did at the moment the men intervened. The report only tells us that Bix "waived preliminary hearing before Judge Scott" and was held on a bond of $1,500.

The year before, Bix had been picked up for speeding on West Fourth Street in downtown Davenport, and the incident, which resulted in a twenty-five-dollar fine, was reported in both the *Davenport Democrat and Leader* and the *Davenport Times*. Although Bix paid his fine "almost cheerfully," according to the *Democrat*, the *Times* noted that "the court informed the defendant that [only] his age had saved him from jail." Now other forces seemed to be working on behalf of young Beiderbecke—luck? family influence?—because neither paper reported this latest and far more serious run-in with the law. In fact, the *State of Iowa v. Beiderbecke* dropped from view entirely until September 26—Bix was away at Lake Forest—when the county attorney officially dropped the case. By then, however, one other piece of paperwork had been submitted and filed: the affidavit of the girl's father, Preston R. Ivens. It provides the only other primary-source narrative of the day's events.

"I live at 3030 Grand Ave. Davenport, Scott County, Iowa. I am a student at the Palmer School," Ivens begins, referencing the Palmer School of Chiropractic, the first college of chiropractic medicine in the world, founded in Davenport in 1897 by D. D. Palmer. His son, B. J. Palmer, had run the school since 1906. Ivens continues:

> On April 22, 1921 my little girl came home, told me that a man took her in the garage, said some awful things to her. I ran up to the garage, then called up the police but could get no clue. Next day I saw 2 boys whom I had seen when I went to the garage. I asked if they saw a man take a little girl into the garage the day before. They said yes & told me it was the Dft. My little girl told her story to me & later to the chief of police & the County Attorney. She said he asked her to show herself. The little girl is 5 years old. In consideration of the child[']s age & the harm that would result to her in going over with this case I would request that no action be taken by the grand jury. I consulted with Dr. Eliot & Dr. B. J. Palmer & Dr. Craven & they all besides with Mr. C. H. Murphy thought it best to drop the case for the betterment of the child.

Not surprisingly, the language of Ivens's account betrays the emotion of a father attempting to protect his daughter. (The girl's name, we now know, was Sarah "Sally" Ivens, and she was sight-impaired.) Mr. Ivens's concern about the "awful things" Bix allegedly said strikes me as genuine, as does the frantic nature of his dash to the garage where, to his dismay, he "could get no clue" about what had happened. Upon cutting to the quick of the accusation—"She said he asked her to show herself"—you can feel the stomach-turning disgust as he adds, "The little girl is 5 years old." You can also feel the weight of the community on his back: B. J. Palmer directed the Palmer School of Chiropractic, Frank W. Elliott was the school's business manager, and John H. Craven a professor. Cornelius H. Murphy was a local hotshot attorney who had once successfully prosecuted Palmer's father and who may have been representing the Beiderbeckes' interests. These were unquestionably Davenport's elite, and collectively they put their hands on poor Pres Ivens's shoulder and said, "Son, you've got to let this go . . ."

The police report and Ivens's affidavit make for compelling, even disturbing, reading, but they also leave open a number of questions. Why did Sally and her father live at different addresses? Or had they moved in the subsequent months? Who were the two boys Preston Ivens saw at Goddard's the next day? Were they Duncan and Bailey, the men from the police report? There also is a potential problem with Mr. Ivens's chronology of events. As Rich Johnson points out— you remember Rich Johnson: "Well, his name wasn't Bix, it was Bismark, and I have so much proof, it's unbelievable"—Ivens seems to say that he could "get no clue" about what had happened until the day after the incident, when the two boys identified Bix. But according to the police report, Bix was arrested on the same day—in other words, the day *before* Ivens finally got a clue. Is this apparent discrepancy the result of sloppy writing; does it reveal that Bix was a suspect even before witnesses could be found to testify against him; or does it simply mean that the police were satisfied that Bix was their man even before Ivens was? In the end, the facts are a muddle. The available documents leave us still wondering whether Bix did what he was accused of doing, and whether there could have been enough evidence to convict him. It's also unclear whether anyone pressured Ivens to drop the charges and what role, if any, Mr. and Mrs. Beiderbecke played.

Inevitably complicating many reactions to Bix's arrest is Ralph Berton's bombshell claim that Bix had had a "fling" with Berton's brother Gene. As you might imagine, this was vehemently denied by many Bixophiles, for whom the claim appeared to cause significant angst. And anyway, I realize that to discuss Bix's arrest—which is to consider the possibility of pedophilia—in the same breath as Bix's sexuality is to commit a relational error. Gay men are no more likely than straight men to be child molesters. Whether Bix was gay, straight, bi-, or anything else should be irrelevant to the facts of April 22, 1921—and yet it never has been.

The connection was first hinted at publicly in the Ominous Endnote, the context for which was the possibility that Bix had been gay.

In it, Sudhalter suggests that "it is useful to consider a few abiding Beiderbecke mysteries." Among these are the seemingly inexplicable "wrath" Bismark directed at his son, Bix's "banishment" from Davenport combined with his habit of regularly sending money home, the "protective, almost defensive, quality" of later remembrances of Bix by his friends and colleagues, and a previously mentioned incident in which Bix may been attacked in the groin by a sailor wielding a broken bottle.

Something's definitely up, Sudhalter writes, but what?

> In the absence of information, speculation has remained unresolved, firmly in the realm of hypothesis. But some documentation indeed exists: carefully husbanded, withheld from public view, it records an event deemed serious enough, at least in the context of the early '20s, to have kindled Bismarck [sic] Beiderbecke's indignation; prompted the family to ship the boy off to Lake Forest in disgrace; driven friends to circle the wagons when historical inquiry began to get too close; kept Bix, even as a grown man, desperately seeking parental approbation and forgiveness . . . Will the specifics ever be made public? Perhaps not: the facts remain closely guarded and cannot be discussed here without betrayal of confidences. But information exists, and knowledge of its existence begins to make sense of the contradictions surrounding Bix Beiderbecke's short life.

Sudhalter never explains how this context might shed light on whether Bix was gay, but it's not difficult to connect the dots: *There was something different about Little Bickie, something that angered his father, rallied his friends, and led him to be viciously attacked. He must have been gay . . . or something worse.* With the caveat that we'll never really know—and really, it shouldn't even matter—Terry Teachout told me "it sure all fits."

I interviewed Sudhalter in 2003, five years before his death, and he confirmed that the mysterious and "carefully husbanded" documentation was indeed related to Bix's arrest for a "lewd & lascivious act," but he didn't reveal what confidences prevented him from writing the truth. It's at least possible that he and Phil Evans had made an arrangement with the Beiderbecke family to keep the incident a secret in exchange for access to Bix's papers. For fans, scholars, and Beiderbeckes alike, according to the biographer Jean Pierre Lion, Berton's book only vindicated that long-held silence. "Phil Evans knew of this story," Lion wrote to me in an e-mail, "as did all people who had worked on Bix and who lived in Davenport. When Ralph Berton's book was published, the 'homosexual' story was a big shock for the Bix fans (Phil Evans included). Berton said that he had been questioned all his life about these few lines [in his book] . . . I guess that when he learned about this arrest, Phil Evans thought it was better to keep it secret, in order not to add any possible confirmation to Berton's story."

And the secret held until 2000, a year after the appearance of Sudhalter's *Lost Chords* and its Ominous Endnote. That's when Geoffrey C. Ward published the first-ever account of Bix's arrest in *Jazz: A History of America's Music*: "At nineteen, he was arrested for what the Davenport police blotter called a 'lewd and lascivious act with a child'—apparently just a fellow teenager, a girl from down the street. The case never reached court but the scandal must have been humiliating to him and his family." There are problems with this account, however. Bix was not nineteen at the time; he was eighteen. And the victim was not "just a fellow teenager," but a five-year-old girl. One might question whether Ward had even seen the records, which are clear about these facts—except that he quotes from them.

Ward's revelation sparked Bixophiles to find the original arrest records and Albert Haim to post them on his online forum. This, in turn, led Lion to the documents, which he published in his 2005 biography. In his own book, Rich Johnson presented still more information about the arrest, including a theory that Johnson seemed to think finally absolved Bix of any guilt.

I asked Lion, a French textile manufacturer, his opinion. "Bix had probably drunk a bit too much, one more time . . . and that was it," he wrote in an e-mail. "Nothing really 'horrible,' and I can hardly see [that] there [was] any significant 'sexual' content. But, as we say in French, this new story—added to so many previous ones—was for Bix's father 'the drop of water with which the cup overflows': that was the last straw!"

I pressed Lion, who died in 2010, on how he could so easily dismiss such a serious charge. What wasn't horrible about asking a five-year-old girl to show herself? "I believe Bix was a bit 'hot' and half-drunk when this happened, and that it was a kind of silly game that turned out the wrong way," he told me after confessing that he regretted ever publishing the documents in the first place. "Nobody knows what may cross a little girl's mind. . . . I'm convinced Bix was a kind fellow and not a pervert . . . [which] the rest of his life does confirm (as far as we know)."

Lion, in other words, was convinced that (a) Bix more or less did what he was accused of doing; (b) he didn't do anything wrong; and (c) Sally Ivens may have misunderstood, exaggerated, or perhaps even lied about the incident. For his part, Rich Johnson runs with the latter theory—that someone lied. In his posthumous *Bix: The Davenport Album* (2009), completed with the help of Jim Arpy and Gerri Bowers, he includes a four-page primer on the plight of Davenport's Germans during and just after World War I. As we've already seen, there was a book burning at Davenport High, there were efforts to stamp out any language except for English, and there were mass arrests, including, as it happens, the arrest of a congressman and former mayor's brother. The man was charged and sent to jail under the Espionage Act for attending an anti-draft rally.

"The Espionage Act expired at war's end," Johnson writes. "Ethnic bigotry did not."

Johnson then turns to William H. Roba, the same Davenport historian I had interviewed several years earlier: "According to Bill Roba, a professor at Scott Community College, Mr. Ivens had lost a brother in the war. That and Ivens['s] staunch advocacy for the *One-Hundred*

Percent Americanism policy is what Roba believes may have led to an accusation in 1921 against Bix Beiderbecke for the vilest of crimes."

"One Hundred Percent Americanism" was a postwar nativist movement (never a policy) that cast suspicion on any manifestations of Old World identity—language, clothing, music, dress. It's plausible that Ivens could have been so enraged by the death of his brother that he took it out on a kid with a funny name like Bix Beiderbecke. But Johnson doesn't provide any evidence for such a theory—he doesn't name the brother or explain how he knows that Ivens was a bigot. (I've found no evidence of such a brother myself.) Remembering that when I had interviewed him Roba had been working on an academic essay about Bix and his German American roots, I asked him to send me a copy, and he did. In the article, Roba takes up the story of Bix's arrest in some detail; however, those details raise more questions than they answer.

According to Roba, the incident happened on April 21, not the twenty-second; Bix at the time was hanging out with two friends, one of whom was Fritz Putzier, and "Ivens apparently became incensed when he learned [that Bix's] last name was German." Although Roba never mentions One Hundred Percent Americanism, he does argue that the private Davenport Outing Club, of which the Beiderbeckes were dues-paying members, was "a stronghold of anti-chiropractic belief," which may have put B. J. Palmer in a tough spot. With a large new class entering the Palmer School in the fall, Palmer likely was anxious about the prospect of bad publicity and may have wanted the case to go away as much as the Beiderbeckes did. Finally, Roba implies that the money Sudhalter, in his Ominous Endnote, mentioned Bix sending home each week during his professional career may have gone to repay his parents for a settlement with the Ivenses. Unfortunately, Roba doesn't cite sources for any of these claims, or develop any of these arguments, and when I asked him to elaborate, he responded that he would need to check a few things. I never heard from him again.

So where did Roba's version of events come from? It's impossible to say. And did the Beiderbeckes and the Palmers lean on Ivens? I asked Christopher Bix Beiderbecke—Richard Bix's son and brother Burnie's grandson—that very question. (You remember R. Bix Beiderbecke: "Brendan Wolfe's article . . . was interesting reading but contained numerous errors and, as Clinton's spin doctors would say, frequently gives a 'false impression.'") He told me that Bix's father and grandfather both were far too principled to have intervened in the case and would have found "the idea of trying to exert influence to get any authorities to back off the case as too distasteful to even attempt." Absent any proof to the contrary, Beiderbecke believes that Bix's parents would have been 100 percent supportive of their boy and convinced of his innocence.

In fact, he believes they were supportive despite deciding, in the months after his arrest, to pull Bix out of Davenport High School and enroll him in the more discipline-minded Lake Forest Academy. Or perhaps this is *how* they were supportive. Sudhalter and Berton label it banishment, but others might describe it as simple, by-the-books parenting, an attempt by the Beiderbeckes to separate their son from the destructive influences of jazz and alcohol and to shield him from gossips and bigots.

That this decision turned out to be a disaster, setting their Little Bickie on a terrible, twin course to musical stardom and self-destruction—well, who can blame them for that?

The biographies mostly avoid the subject of Bix's sexuality, although Jean Pierre Lion mentions Berton's notorious claim and, in a footnote, even offers additional support for it. Apparently Berton, who died in 1993, was interviewed in 1989 and reiterated what he had written fifteen years earlier in *Remembering Bix*, with the added and irresistible detail of a drag party that Ralph, Gene, and Bix had all attended.

Bix in drag.

The mind reels.

Or maybe not, actually. According to an online drag-queen name generator, he would perform as Monica Intervention (or Fretty Betty or Holly Wood). And according to the 2005 novel *Hudson Lake* by Laura Mazzuca Toops—in which Bix, I should just tell you, has great sex—Bix already boasts the "incongruous features of a baby doll— small red mouth, snub nose, and eyes that seemed to be laughing at something." Only thing left is a cute little flapper dress—nothing frilly—and maybe to shave those legs.

In the meantime, though, it's worth emphasizing this idea of incongruity. It's at the heart of being a drag queen, and it's no less at the heart of being Bix. He was the great American mutt, "a farmboy who happened to be wearing sneakers," as Berton remembered, or, per Eddie Condon, a kid who arrived home from a gig wearing a top hat—but whose top hat was it? As we've seen, he was an unexpected, sometimes incongruous mixture—of black and white, farm and city, classical and jazz, high culture and low, rebel and mama's boy. So why not of male and female? "The great American icons are racial, ethnic, and sexual hybrids, hybridity being an American purity," the critic Lee Siegel writes. "Brando had a woman's face buried in his features (Elvis idolized him)—so did Miles Davis and James Dean.

The macho Pollock's gossamer skeins of color have a feminine delicacy."

And Bix Beiderbecke, all baby-dolled up and off to a party with his friend the ballet dancer, isn't a girl and isn't not a girl . . .

While Lion seems to give credence to Berton, he does not corroborate another controversial anecdote, this one from Sudhalter and Evans and regarding Bix's girlfriend Ruth Shaffner. Nineteen, farm-raised, and "cute as a bug's ear," Ruth earned nine dollars per week in St. Louis working the front desk for a podiatrist. And when she wasn't working, she was hanging out at the Arcadia Ballroom, which is where she met Bix. "Words can't express how wonderful he seemed to me," Ruth later recalled. "He was so handsome, and had a smile that was just out of this world." The two started to date, and it's clear that Ruth was badly smitten. "I found him a kindly, fun-loving person," she said, "with a great sense of humor and a personality plus— and a handsome man." She added that he was always well groomed. "I never saw Bix when he wasn't clean. Always clean-shaven, fingernails, not a hair out of place, teeth brushed. Even his shoes were always shined, and I might add that if his tie wasn't just right, he'd buy a new one." Seems that Bix was love-bit, too, although Sudhalter and Evans don't seem convinced by this talk of hygiene, moving on from her aside with a terse "Whatever the case . . ."

Anyway, one thing led to another and Ruth got pregnant. After thinking on it a spell, she informed Bix of her decision not to have the baby. Her parents were churchgoing types, after all. It would be impossible. Bix angrily objected before cooling down a bit and trying to sweet-talk her. "A baby's a wonderful thing," he said. "It's ours. We made it. Together. Nobody's going to hold that against you."

"He was smiling at her," Sudhalter and Evans write, "that damnable smile that always made her melt . . ."

In the end, she got the abortion.

"If only I could relive my life," Ruth later said. "I was so young, and didn't know what the outcome of it all would be. Bix tried so hard to persuade me, but all I could see was how impossible it was because of my family and everything."

This episode is remarkable for a number of reasons. For one, Ruth comes across as pleasingly complicated. Her love of Bix and her unself-conscious idealization of him seems sincere, as does her insistence that everything in their relationship was "mutual." But her decision to abort their child was anything but mutual. Depending upon your perspective, it can be seen as unfair, courageous, hypocritical, justified, or immoral. It was certainly independent. And the fact that she appeared to have regretted her decision years later only makes her all the more human. But Bix—while he shows flickering signs of life here, briefly getting his Irish up over Ruth's decision and at one point blurting out, "Impossible is a ridiculous word"—remains his usual enigmatic self.

Perhaps what's most remarkable, however, is that if Lion is to be believed the abortion episode never even happened. "In December [of 1926] she had noticed an abnormal delay in her monthly cycle," Lion reports. "Days went by with increasing anxiety, but nature was kind, and to the couple's great relief, Ruth was soon 'freed' . . . and still very much in love."

Had Ruth Shaffner changed her story over the years? Had she lied and was now telling the truth? Or had she been telling the truth before? Did Richard Sudhalter just make the whole story up, along with her quotations? If that was the case, does that mean his coauthor, Philip Evans, never saw the manuscript before publication? These questions have been given the full ad-hominem treatment over the years, but to no definitive conclusion.

In the context of Berton, Shaffner, et al., Bix Beiderbecke's sexuality is reduced to a series of he said–she saids, his identity left to flirt with s/he. (*Somebody fetch Miss Intervention another gin!*) But maybe we've got the equation all wrong. Rather than Bix on one side and girls on the other, or men, or whatever, how about this: there's Bix and there's us. Bix doesn't seduce Ruth or Gene, but from the grave, his horn in hand, his mug bent into that damnable grin, he seduces us.

Softly, as Hoagy Carmichael might have put it.

Regardless of what happened back in the Kappa Sig house while listening to Stravinsky's *Firebird*, there is no doubt that Hoagy woke up the next morning a changed man. Where before he had been a law student with pretensions, he was now a composer, and within a couple of years would pen "Star Dust," a song developed around a snatch of improvisation he'd once heard from Bix. It would go on to become one of the most recorded tunes in popular music history. On a particularly lovely recording from 1942, Carmichael plays the piano, sings (the lyrics are by Mitchell Parish), and even whistles, his broad Indiana accent communicating what, for the time, was an unusual emotional directness. "The melody haunts my reverie," he croons, and the wide-eyed, sad-eyed yearning you see welling up on the face of the singer in Roy Lichtenstein's 1965 painting of the same name— that yearning originally belonged to Hoagy Carmichael.

"Finally Beiderbecke took out a silver cornet," Eddie Condon writes. "He put it to his lips and blew a phrase. The sound came out like a girl saying yes."

And yet at this point, you have to go back to the arrest, don't you? I mean, how can you imagine Bix *seducing* you, let alone you saying "yes," while at the same time acknowledging at least the possibility of his having fooled around with a five-year-old girl? A familiar complaint about Bix and other artists is that their work sometimes gets lost in our obsession over biography. So what if Beethoven was a slob or T. S. Eliot an anti-Semite? Personal lives shouldn't matter. It's the art that should consume us.

On an intellectual level I get that. But right here, right now, with Bix—it's tough.

Of course, the whole problem can easily be avoided by taking either of two approaches. One, declare Bix's personal life strictly off-limits. Or two, refuse to acknowledge *even the possibility* of his having done what he was accused of doing. Albert Haim, for his part, has opted for both, advocating on his forum for "the sacredness of privacy"—meaning that, from his point of view, Evans and Evans shouldn't even have published Bix's letters to his parents. However, Haim has also written, in the context of Bix's arrest, that "the presumption of innocence is not just a legal phrase, but a living principle. To me, an individual who is not proven guilty is innocent, not only in the legal sense, but also in fact." A Swiss lawyer named Emrah Erken agreed with him. "Bix is not guilty and this means he didn't do it," he wrote on the forum.

Such claims—existentially, ethically, and legally dubious at best—only make sense in the context of that awful shudder I experience every time I think of Bix in Goddard's garage with that little girl. Or when I recall the words of Lake Forest's headmaster, John Wayne Richards: "Bix is a very clever excuse-maker, and I think he sometimes fools even himself in a way."

Whatever happened in 1921, the priority has been not only to protect ourselves and our ability to fully enjoy the music, but also to protect Bix. In fact, my friend Barb Wascher, whom I met through Haim's forum, has cleverly suggested that there must be what she calls the Secret Society for the Protection of Bix Beiderbecke's Reputation, arguing that the existence of said society is implied in Sudhalter's Ominous Endnote—the part where he describes Bix's "protective, almost defensive" friends and relatives. She goes even further and names Hoagy Carmichael as one of the Society's founding members. In both of his published memoirs, *The Stardust Road* and *Sometimes I Wonder*, Carmichael tells the story of getting expelled from Bloomington High School for having "said something to a little girl in braids." She was "a blue-eyed blonde with a baby stare, brain to match—and a body she didn't fully admit to yet." She sat in front of Carmichael in study hall and he "said something that had been said to girls millions of times." But this time "she ran screaming in outrage and told." After being sent to the office, Carmichael faced a principal who "acted like a movie version of a First World War German sergeant" and accused him of "the vices of . . . Oscar Wilde."

"Did this really happen?" Wascher wondered in an e-mail to me. "Or is it a fabrication, like so much of Hoagy's tale-telling? Either way, what is he trying to tell us? The language is furious, his outrage over the girl tattling, and the punishment meted out by the principal, palpable. It's possible that he and Bix shared a history of getting into trouble for saying 'dirty' things to girls in high school, but the coincidence is hard to believe. Hoagy is beginning to look like Bix's sin-eater, concocting a story complete with censure from a silent, imposing Teutonic father figure."

Wascher went on to ask whether this is the sort of protection to which Sudhalter alluded. Perhaps some vestigial version of this story, intended as a grand diversion, even made its way into the historian Geoffrey Ward's faulty description of Bix and his "fellow teenager." "And what," Wascher asked finally, "does Oscar Wilde, he of the love that dare not speak its name, have to do" with anything?

Besides maybe *The Firebird* . . .

Bix and Tram | A Hot Jazz Classic · Set C-144

FIGURE 4.
*In 1947
Columbia
Records
released* Bix
and Tram: Bix
Beiderbecke
with Frankie
Trumbauer's
Orchestra,
*featuring cover
art by Jim
Flora. © The
Heirs of James
Flora, courtesy
JimFlora.com.*

In 1947 Columbia Records released *Bix and Tram: Bix Beiderbecke with Frankie Trumbauer's Orchestra*, a 78-rpm record that was, according to its cover, "#20 in a series that made jazz history." About that cover: it's twelve-and-a-quarter-inch square with a parchment-colored background and all-cap, serif letters that look to have been crayoned in black, red, and a pale, lizardy green. (See figure 4.) Bix is blowing his cornet, Trumbauer his C-melody sax, but their heads (Bix's topped with a tiny fedora, Tram's a bowler) are more or less bean-shaped with great hooked noses, coffee-cup-handle ears, and bulbous, birdlike eyes. Bix's arms and head are bright red, Tram's that lizardy green, and their shirts the reverse—finally, race is no longer an issue for these two—with everything attached to everything else collage-style (think Matisse, Stuart Davis, or Picasso's *Guitar, Sheet*

Music, and Glass). And out of their horns: two Christmas-tree-ready strings of beads, notes "spun out . . . from a silver spool," as the trumpeter Max Kaminsky once described Bix's sound, a sound that this modernist bit of nonsense suggests must have been, to swipe a word from the jazz historian Richard Hadlock, "architectonically" perfect.

The first time I saw this album cover it was attached to its creator Jim Flora's *New York Times* obituary. In the notice, the *Times* explains that until late in the 1930s, records were covered only with heavy art paper, a title embossed on the front and spine but no more. Flora, a jazz fan who worked in advertising, sold Columbia Records on his vision for something better, was hired, and quickly advanced to the position of art director. From there, he used his "lighthearted blend of surrealism and cartoon notable for its comic juxtapositions of physically exaggerated characters" to revolutionize the way that record albums were produced and marketed in the United States.

Jim Flora, in other words, was a father of album cover art, and what I've always loved about this particular cover were those beads. Looking more closely recently, I saw that Beiderbecke and Trumbauer's red and lizardy green heads were tied together by a piece of string, and the string was knotted in a bow and ornamented with a lovely valentine-shaped heart. *Bix and Tram*, I realized, was more than mere nonsense; it was a study in collaboration and perhaps even friendship. I relayed this observation to a friend, and she encouraged me to look closer still: Bix's heart beats firmly in his lizardy green chest, but where is Tram's? His must be the heart on a string—a tiny detail that suddenly transforms *Bix and Tram* into something much more fraught and more complicated than first meets the eye.

Tram, not Bix, was the vulnerable one, at least according to Flora, and perhaps unsurprisingly he was the one who first pursued the partnership. "I had heard Bix in the old Wolverines Band," he later wrote, "and I said to myself, if I ever had my own band again, that's my boy!" Then, in 1925, he did get his own band—for the gig at the Arcadia Ballroom in St. Louis—but not everyone thought that he and Bix would be such a heavenly match. "When I tried to locate Bix, by asking around, I always got the same answer, 'Look out, he's trouble. He drinks and you'll have a hard time handling him.'" Tram, though, was undeterred. "That didn't stop me," he wrote. "I was determined."

And so he was. When Bix got so loaded he couldn't find his embouchure, Tram looked the other way. Or when Bix just didn't show up for work one day, Tram dispatched someone to look for him. Once, Bix forgot to bring his cornet to a gig in Trumbauer's hometown of Carbondale, Illinois, and Frank managed to borrow one from a family friend whose son played in school. Tram built his band around Bix's sound—it was the "catalyst" that brought everything together, Goldkette pianist Irving Riskin claimed; his fellow musicians "merely travelled the road that Bix built," remembered the saxophonist (and former symphony violinist) Bud Hassler—yet Tram was forced to take Bix aside and teach him how to read the parts.

"Bix had a screwy way of picking out notes from a violin part, playing them in the key of 'C' on a 'B flat' cornet," Trumbauer wrote. "It was confusing to everyone, even Bix! We fixed up a book of regular trumpet parts and for hours on end, I would work with Bix. I would teach him a tune, note for note, and then hand him the part and we would follow it. Bix was a brilliant boy and it wasn't long before he could follow new parts."

Bix was a brilliant boy, Tram says, and he sounds not like a chum but like a public-school teacher. Only two years older than Bix, Tram was so much more the grownup, and the one with grownup responsibilities. He was married. He was a father. Bix, meanwhile, was up all night with a jug of corn whiskey during a summer stint at Hudson Lake, Indiana, so that Frank and his wife, Mitzi, felt the need to show up in the morning with a bag of burgers lest he not eat and be unable to play. Tram actually warned Mitzi not to mix with Bix and his cohorts—he "didn't even want her to meet with us on a harmless, social level," Riskin told Phil Evans—and who can blame him? Bix's cottage was littered with half-filled cans of food and weeks-old dirty laundry, one of his bandmates recalled. And when someone asked what Bix did with all the garbage, he replied, "We just kick it around until it disappears."

Bix was a brilliant boy, Tram says, and when the call came from Jean Goldkette in Detroit, Frank insisted that Bix be hired, too. Goldkette's people weren't so sure. "I admit that Bix is a great cornet player," the drummer Charlie Horvath told Trumbauer, "but I don't know if Jean will take a chance on him." Horvath reminded Tram of Bix's first stint with Goldkette, during which the kid had had trouble reading music and once nearly missed a train out of sheer cluelessness. As the train

pulled out, Bix was just sitting there on the depot bench until someone finally yanked him aboard. And when that someone inquired as
to what in the hell Bix thought he was doing, Bix replied that he *had*
been on the train and had loved the inside so much he wanted to see
it from the outside.

My reaction almost certainly would have been, *What a corncob!*
But Tram defended his charge. "Bix has changed," he told Horvath.
"He has matured. . . . Tell you what! Bix will be my responsibility and
I won't accept the job without him!"

Off to Detroit, then, where taking responsibility for Bix meant, as
usual, putting a roof over his head, grub on his plate, and plenty of
corn down his gullet. "Fortunately we had a Greek restaurant near the
office called the Elite," a band member told Phil Evans. "We arranged
for his meals there. There was a speakeasy in the Graystone building (upstairs in front), he drank on the tab and we took care of his
room at the Billinghurst Hotel." To repay the favor, Bix "continued to
put the balance of his money into slot machines in the [Graystone's]
speakeasy."

Bix was a brilliant boy, Tram says, and you can't help but hear the
soft ring of condescension in his voice. For his part, Pupi Avati just
plain infantilizes Bix in a scene from *Bix: An Interpretation of a Legend*
where, new to the band, he joins Frank and Mitzi at their farmhouse.
Trumbauer, like the actor who portrays him, was tall, slim, and wore
a dashing Ronald Colman mustache; if he also padded around his
place in a ridiculous-looking red silk robe with Chinese prints on it,
then more power to the Avatis. He looms over Bix, having just given
the boy a music lesson, and evidently he sniffs something awry.

TRAM: And who washes your stuff for you?
BIX: I manage by myself.
TRAM: Well, that's obvious. You've been wearing the
     same shirt for a week!
BIX: [*Blank stare.*]

It's that stare—what is it, incomprehension? autism?—that provokes Tram to march Little Bickie down the hall and into the wash-
room, where he runs a hot bath. "I want you to stay in here at least
an hour, okay?" he says. "And scrub hard!" Bix and Tram, meet Felix
and Oscar.

"Tram had an adult and therefore complex love for Bix," a friend of mine wrote in an e-mail, and I take her to mean that there was probably a certain amount of anger mixed in with all the *He's changed*! and *Gee, what a swell guy*! Still, the payoff for both of them was the music, obviously, and my favorite example has always been "Borneo," a novelty tune they recorded in New York in April 1928. After a short intro and some business involving a bamboo horn-eo, Bix and Tram launch into one of their famous chase choruses, trading licks back and forth, one declaiming, the other responding. It's as if they're talking to one another. The intimacy of it is almost startling.

Geoff Muldaur, whose first group, Jim Kweskin's Jug Band, covered "Borneo" in 1963 after hearing the Bix and Tram version, told me that this is how Bix blew all the time, with or without Trumbauer. "There's something conversational about the way that Bix plays," he said to me. "He comments. He'll make an opening statement, and the next statement is an answer to it. There's a logic to it, much more than with Louis Armstrong going up and hitting a blasting note to thrill everybody viscerally. It's like somebody talking." Here, Muldaur hummed a Bixian solo. "Whereas Louis is"—then he hummed again—"and you're like, woo! And you're elated, but it's not like someone is talking to you as much. I think that got to me in some way."

You want and need Bix talking to you, and when he's talking to you, you want and need to keep up with him. And maybe that's the thrill of the chase chorus: the drama of listening to Frank Trumbauer— the older and wiser of the pair, Obi-wan to Bix's Luke, let's say— struggling to keep up with his protégé.

"Tram told of his trepidation recording chase choruses, trying to follow Bix's phrasing," Esten Spurrier told Phil Evans.

Tram admitted he rose to the challenge and came up with things he didn't know were in him. Bix said, "I tried for some terrific things as a challenge to Frank. I really got such a kick out of Frank's replies." Bix thought some of the best licks Frank ever played were on chases and he could have been more extemporaneous. What a shame Frank became overshadowed by Bix. Having heard him from the start of his career, I felt he certainly was the father of lyrical playing.

Bix was a brilliant boy, and sometimes his brilliance eclipsed poor Tram. But not on "Borneo," or at least I don't think so. They trade their licks and you can feel the high wattage of their relationship, the tension but also the joy, until, at the end, their instruments converge in a single moment of dissonance that feels both humorous and wryly appropriate.

Anyway, we all know what happens next. The bamboo babies stop at the break of dawn-eo, and not even Tram, with his Chinese robe and bag of burgers, can keep Bix in line. "Bix was now getting out of hand," Trumbauer wrote after one of his buddy's many benders, "and Paul [Whiteman] asked me to try to straighten him out. I promised that I would do my best, but that wasn't enough. What influence I ever had with Bix was now gone!"

True to form, Pupi Avati takes the poignant end of a complicated friendship and reduces it to a confrontation between schoolmarmish Tram and the petulant jughead slumping in the back of the rehearsal. "Listen, you little asshole," Tram growls when Bix doesn't play what's written. "You're going to do what I say. Otherwise, you can just go back where you came from."

Bix mumbles, "All right"—and there's that expression on his face again. Or is it the *lack* of an expression?

"I guess I am a minus quality," Bix wrote in a letter to Tram while back in Davenport rehabilitating. He complained of pneumonia that had flared into a lung infection. He complained of pain in his knees and of the difficulties posed by sobriety. He complained of not having a cornet to play. And then he begged for money: "Tram, you probably know better tha[n] anyone my financial status after going through a grand of my own and I am really broke and now is when I need money the most. So I wonder if you could see fit to send me some money. Try like hell, boy."

Try like hell, boy, even as he simultaneously carped to Spurrier about "Frank Trumbauer's foibles and little persnickety introductions, interludes and endings. Soup to nuts." (Is it me, or is Esten Spurrier some kind of trickster character, unleashing mischief wherever he goes?) Regardless, nobody seems to know whether Tram ever sent the money. My friend e-mailed to say that her husband votes he didn't. "He says Mitzi would've said no. I say Tram probably did, whether Mitzi said no or not. But I'm a sentimental slob, and I like Tram. I can't help it."

That's how I feel, too, which is why the end of this story is so heartbreaking. While performing with Whiteman at the Edgewater Beach Hotel in Chicago, Tram gets word that Bix is in bad shape, and he's the one who phones Mr. and Mrs. Beiderbecke in Davenport.

Andy Secrest—a Bix soundalike—had taken Bix's spot in the Whiteman Orchestra, and when news came that the boy had died, he remembered that "Tram went out back. I didn't know whether to leave him alone, or whether he needed comfort, but I elected to go out and see if he was all right. All Tram could do was ask, 'Andy, why didn't Bix call? I've always been there for him. Why didn't he call?' Of course, I did not have an answer. No one did."

In Avati's film, Tram basically disappears after calling Bix an asshole. From here on out, the friends who have Bix's back are Don Murray, Hoagy Carmichael—portrayed, unexpectedly, as a swarthy Italian—and the violinist Joe Venuti. In fact, the film is framed by Venuti's train journey from New York to Davenport, where presumably he hopes to pay his last respects. The actor Emile Levisetti, whose beautiful, made-for-soft-porn eyes foreshadow his professional future . . . he's the *man* here, not that skinny dude in the Chinese robe. In the end I can't tell if the movie wants to say that Tram's was "an adult love and therefore complex," or that Tram was just a giant wuss who didn't really care about Bix. Maybe that's everybody's dilemma. I mean, what are you supposed to do when you're lizardy green—the color of Venus, the goddess of love, but also, in China, the color of the cuckold—and you're chasing after a minus quality, your poor heart out there dangling from a string?

In 2009 I interviewed a jazz pianist and Bixophile named Brad Kay, whom I first had encountered on Albert Haim's online forum. This is an excerpt of our conversation:

BRAD KAY: Then when I was about fourteen I had these friends who thought I was a very amusing character. They said, "You play that old music on the piano. You should be collecting the old records. My dad has a bunch in the garage. Maybe he'll give you some." So I went over to the house, and there was Mr. Ball.

BRENDAN WOLFE: This is in California?

KAY: Yes. I've lived my whole life in Los Angeles. And Mr. Ball said [*in a cranky-old-man voice*], "Yes, I have records in the garage, but I'm not giving these away. I paid seventy-five cents apiece for these records and I'm gonna charge you the same."

And I said, "Okay," and I went in there. Well, I mean, little did I know. I pulled out, let's see, a King Oliver Vocalion, two Lonnie Johnson Okehs, some Benny Goodman–Tommy Dorsey "scroll" Victors, and these were all in brand-new condition in their original sleeves.

WOLFE: So these are old 78s?

KAY: Oh, yes. So Mr. Ball looked at my haul and he says [*in that same old man's voice*], "You've selected some very nice things. That'll be six dollars and seventy-five cents. Now I want to ask you a question. Have you ever heard of Bix Beiderbeck-ee?"

And I said, "No, who's that?"

And he said, "Well, he was the greatest cornet player in the history of jazz." This guy was from the Midwest, see.

WOLFE: We protect our own.

KAY: Yeah. So we went in the house, and he sat me down at his elaborate hi-fi system. This was 1965 or '66. And he played me several Bix records and it sounded wonderful. I was only halfway paying attention because I really wanted to get home and listen to my haul, you know? But it was like he lit a fuse, and three days later the bomb went off. It was like I had the longest delayed reaction in human history. *What the fuck was that?! What was that record?* And I made a beeline for Mr. Ball and begged him to play me those records again. That was my introduction to Bix.

WOLFE: You were fourteen?

KAY: That's right. And that began two things: one was my search for jazz 78s, especially Bix. The other was this insatiable desire to learn the cornet. Because I had to find out how you made a sound like that. That was the beginning of my long, sorry odyssey in music, really.

WOLFE: And so you've studied Bix ever since, and even idolized him.

KAY: I think *everybody* idolized Bix because he was the best around, but [*long sigh*] he had no hooks, no handles, no sharp edges. He was indefinable. Unless you were also a musical genius and could run with him, there wasn't really much to go on. He spent most of his life just trying to be a regular guy, which he was anything but.

    You know, the question that comes to mind is what can I tell you about Bix that hasn't been endlessly written about before. How can I help you?

WOLFE: You're asking me?

KAY: Well . . .

WOLFE: It's a fair question. The reason I'm talking to you is that sure, to some extent this stuff has been endlessly written about. But when you take the biographies of Bix, from Wareing and Garlick, Burnett James, Sudhalter and Evans—

KAY: I'm wearing some garlic right now.

WOLFE: —and Ralph Berton right up to Jean Pierre Lion, what I've found, especially in *Man & Legend*, is this contempt for the legendary Bix.

KAY: What they try to do is define him by citing the facts, what he actually did, where he went, and so forth. They try to pin him down with circumstantial evidence. I think the reason why Bix Beiderbecke is the most punctiliously documented jazz musician is precisely because he was so slippery and indefinable as a person. Because people keep trying to define the guy and they couldn't.

WOLFE: Bix the empty vessel.

KAY: Right. And now everybody wants to be his pal! Everybody wants to be his best bud. And they all think they know him, see. And to me it's all bullshit. I mean, I've been to Davenport, Iowa, but you know, I never cared about any of that stuff. I don't care to look at any old dance halls that he played in. It's like the barn after the horse has run out. Because everything you need to know about Bix that's for real is contained on his records. It's what he actually played on the records, it's the sounds that he made that mattered. That's all, you know? Who he was doesn't really matter a bit as far as I'm concerned. I mean, he was a poor, confused guy who was in the grip of a demon somehow. I know the feeling.

WOLFE: What do you mean?

KAY: What I mean is that he absolutely should *not* have had the career that he had. He should have been a bank president or a lawyer or a senator. He should have taken over the family business and turned it into a coal and lumber empire. And today we'd all be buying Beiderbecke coal and lumber. But no. He was simply possessed by the music. It dwelled in him. It was an entity. It was above and beyond, separate from and not connected to any real human life. Again, I'm well aware of this because I have a similar problem.

In his memoir, Eddie Condon says that Bix, even at the end, sat at the piano and played the same incredible, marvelous, inventive, original stuff, and then Condon looked at his face and he saw the *absence* there, the dead eyes. There's something Faustian about this. And it's easy to see why legends accrue to him because you know he was definitely in the grip of something. He was staring into space. The music was just coursing through him and volition, desire, a definable goal—none of this had anything to do with that.

I've always felt that Bix, like Robert Johnson, had a

hellhound on his trail. He was not a happy camper. Not at all. His drinking is proof of that. Bix could drink like a Trojan and yet he never appeared to be intoxicated. It just tamped him down a little. It took the edge off. That's all it ever did. He didn't drink for kicks or to get high; he drank to stay sober. So he could navigate a little, so somehow he could have a little space to himself. There's a haunted quality about the man. And I feel terribly sorry for him. He never could find any relief for this. And he spent his whole life, in his letters, his communications, especially to his folks, trying to prove how *normal* he was!

WOLFE: He was anything but.

KAY: He was relentlessly on the move. He was heavily invested in things constantly changing, as you can hear anytime you listen to the alternate takes of his recordings. I mean, he relentlessly turned his back on his own work and wouldn't countenance it, wouldn't reference it. There was the story about an old chum who was also a cornet player, who played note for note his "Jazz Me Blues" solo from Gennett and he just winced and grimaced, and said, "What on earth are you playing *that* for?" See. He had gone beyond, he was going beyond. And to me the terrible thing is there was nothing and no one that could stop his rush of self-immolation. I think that if he had lived longer, he was well on his way to inventing the music that twenty years later would be known as bebop. See, because he was employing all the harmonic tricks, and some of the rhythmic tricks that people like Charlie Parker were hitting on years later.

WOLFE: I'm wondering if you can help me understand the self-immolation.

KAY: Okay, well, when you listen to his records, what you hear, especially when there are alternate takes, is Bix just burning his way through his musical options. He doesn't just vary his improvisation when he approaches the same tune another time. He doesn't just vary what he did before; he completely alters it, reconceives it. He reinvents it. It's like he's gone to the trouble of building this house of cards and it's a beautiful thing, like he's built this Chartres Cathedral out of a deck of cards, you know, but that's not good enough. He has to tear it down and build the Chrysler Building next. This is what he does in every alternate take. He utterly reconceives what he did to the point that when you combine the two takes so that they're synchronous, you hear that he harmonizes and counterpoints what he had previously done.

WOLFE: So you can put one on top of the other?

KAY: You superimpose them and they sound like they were two parts of a duet.

WOLFE: What would be an example of that?

KAY: Well, my favorite example is the Whiteman record of "Changes." Because it just, oh my gosh, it sounds like King Oliver and Louis Armstrong, like two cornets just blazing away there. And among all of the great jazzmen of the 1920s who left alternate takes of their work, Bix Beiderbecke is unique in possessing this quality. Nobody else does this.

WOLFE: And how do we bring that back to self-immolation?

KAY: Because all this comes at a price. To me it sounds like the cat was just burning and churning his way through everything. He was constantly using up his options musically and I'm sure in life, as well. *This is no good, throw that out. This is no good, throw that out.* Couldn't stand to listen to his own old records. I think he was constantly seeking. There was something that constantly eluded him. He couldn't manage himself. If he could have, he would have been a big name in music after 1928, and not just amongst his fellow sidemen. He published "In a Mist" and performed it at Carnegie with Whiteman. He was becoming a force! He could have said, "I'm on to something pretty good here. I think I'm going to capitalize on it. I think I'm gonna write more music like 'In a Mist.'" But he couldn't see any possibilities. He was too deep into his pain. So that's what I mean by self-immolation.

WOLFE: I think you've put your finger on what is at the heart of the Romantic legend of Bix, which is connecting this idea of the searching quality of his art with the fact of his early death. And it seems to leave behind this big question mark of why did it have to end that way.

KAY: Well, I don't think it's such a big mystery. Bix isn't the only artist whose life was a relentless search. If you look at other alcoholic geniuses, there's a pattern; it's rare but it happens. It's just that the results are always unique and different with each person. They put the pedal to the metal and they just burn out! I have insights because I came dangerously close to that myself. Not that I'm comparing myself to some kind of genius.

WOLFE: But you've lived the life.

KAY: Yeah. I understand how this works.

WOLFE: I'm curious to know how the alcohol fits into that. You talked about drinking to stay sober, but I'm still not sure what you mean by that.

KAY: Okay, well, when you're in the grip of such a powerful inspiration, a lifetime of it, it's like you're never alone. You never have time to yourself. You're always being prodded and assaulted by this other, this thing. It's a very fine line between this kind of genius and the paranoid schizophrenic who hears voices. I was hospitalized once. I was in a mental ward when I was twenty-eight. I had a total breakdown around the same age that Bix died. And I remember being incarcerated on the fourth floor with all the crazies, and the doctor interviewed me one day—a nurse with a clipboard was taking notes—and he says, "So Mr. Kay, do you *hear* things in your head?"

And I said, "Of course!" And he looked at the nurse, and the nurse looked at him, and she started writing. And I went, "Hey, wait a minute! I'm a musician; we're *supposed* to hear things!"

And there happened to be a piano there, and I ran to the piano and started playing, and I'm sure she wrote something like, *Patient exhibits piano-playing mania.*

Well, okay. I think maybe I *do* have a piano-playing mania, and I think Bix had one too. And he had a cornet-playing mania and he had just a *music* mania. The music called him at every moment of his life. And this is a very hard thing to live with because it precludes anything like normality. I mean, what could be more normal than growing up on Grand Avenue in Davenport, Iowa? Okay? I was there. I was in that house. I saw that cute tree-lined nice neighborhood, that *Leave It to*

Beaver picket fence, middle-class neighborhood that looks like Norman Rockwell created it.

I feel like Bix and I have that in common. I came from a similar background, from a nice, comfy middle-class family where they all expected me to go into business, and to this day it's like I can't relate. I can't have a real conversation with my family. They don't understand me. I can say, "Hi, how are you?" and "I'm doing fine."

"Are you making money?"

"Yeah, I'm making money."

"Oh good!"

You know, but I can't begin to talk to them about what drives me. They don't have the slightest comprehension or interest. And personally I feel close to nobody. I don't have a girlfriend. I don't have a wife. I don't have a family. Why? Because I've been fucking obsessed with music all my life! Like everybody who approaches Bix, I feel like I have a personal connection with him. Well *fuck*. But I've walked the walk.

On August 6, 1931, Bix Beiderbecke was living in Sunnyside, Queens, on 46th Street. His apartment was a mess. According to Ralph Berton—who, it's worth reminding ourselves, was not actually present—there was "dust everywhere, empty bottles and full ashtrays, in the refrigerator a half bottle of milk blue with mold, half a can of dried-up sardines." Bix was a mess, too, "lying there in a suit of dirty BVDS, half covered by a dirty sheet, dirty socks under the bed and on the chair, a general look to the place as if no one was living there."

The temperature had reached ninety-two degrees that day, 58 percent humidity. For relief, "Bix had fixed up an electric fan on a chair next to the bed to blow directly upon his pillow, which was soaked in sweat," Berton writes. This primitive form of air conditioning—common among New Yorkers, who sometimes dipped their bedding in ice water before turning on the fan—worried his watchful landlady. She scolded her tenant, saying he would "catch his death," but Bix just stared back at her, his "swollen eyes half glued shut." He declined her offer to call a doctor, saying he had everything he needed, "including a half-full bottle of what she took to be gin, and the electric fan going back and forth with a low hum."

According to Berton she called for an ambulance anyway.

"He seldom went out, except to buy gin," Bix's rental agent, George Kraslow, told Phil Evans. (In all accounts except for Berton's, Bix's landlady is actually a landlord.) "He seemed to be struggling with himself and drank almost continuously." He also played piano, often late into the night. The music simultaneously disturbed and entranced his neighbors, who complained to Kraslow, but only "half-heartedly." In Frederick Turner's novel *1929*, published in 2003 and based closely on Bix's life, a woman across the hall lies in bed, listening to "the most private recital possible, one in which the mysterious, unseen artist dreams aloud."

"The tenants explained that they really enjoyed the piano playing and didn't want to get anyone in trouble," Kraslow said, "but [they] had to get up in the morning. I became friendly with him and tried to stop him drinking so heavily, but it seemed to be an obsession with him. He just couldn't stop."

Bix had entertained few visitors over the past weeks. One or two musician friends had stopped by, also Dr. and Mrs. Haberski, who lived in the building. Some biographers identify the couple as both being physicians; others say that Mrs. Haberski served as her husband's nurse. Either way, they checked in on their neighbor from time to time, doing their best to convince him to seek care in a hospital. He had pneumonia, they told him, but he stubbornly refused all treatment.

Babe Ruth also visited, apparently. Although he hit forty-six home runs that summer, the future Hall of Famer was so overweight that, according to one historian, he was forced to remove doors from their hinges to move from room to room in Bix's apartment. Musicians explained to Phil Evans that the two were longtime friends and loved to chat about baseball and jazz in equal measure. Another friend from way back, the cornetist Jimmy McPartland, remembered the last night he saw Bix. "He had a very bad cold, and he was broke besides," McPartland said. "I told him to go home and stay there until he got over the cold, and [I] lent him some money."

"Thanks, kid," Bix said. "I'll be all right. I've got a job at Princeton in a couple of days."

Princeton University was putting on a dance and had hired a band with the understanding that the famous Bix Beiderbecke would be on the stand. No Bix, no band. That was the deal. Problem was, as McPartland had noticed, Bix had taken sick. Bix tried to interest the dance committee in another cornetist—McPartland possibly?—but they wouldn't bite. "When he learnt that his absence would cost his colleagues their jobs he defied common sense, put aside the advice of his friends, and went abroad in the cold night air," the biographer Burnett James writes. "The result was fatal." At least one other biography tells nearly the same story, and Berton admits that it "sounded a lot like Bix, and for years that story circulated in magazines and in biographical books, until someone thought to look up the date of his death, and started wondering what college boys would be doing running a dance in the middle of summer, and how it happened to snow in August." Of course, the story's literal truth wasn't the point. (And anyway, Bix did play at Princeton, with Benny Goodman and the Dorsey brothers, but on May 1 and 2.) As Burnett James understands, the point was to demonstrate "Bix's characteristic courtesy and loyalty to his friends which precipitated his end."

"His last act was, as I say, characteristic," James writes. "He would not willingly disappoint his colleagues, and it proved his undoing. His end was in keeping with the rest of his life, in that it was directly brought about by an action and impulse at once generous and foolish."

In his memoir *Really the Blues*, the musician Mezz Mezzrow describes an afternoon's adventure with Bix and the clarinetist Pee Wee Russell. "Bix nearly got run over by a locomotive," Mezzrow begins, and then tells of how he and Russell followed their friend in search of buried liquor. They crossed fields, a railroad track, and even a barbed-wire fence until Bix "dug out a jug, handed it to Pee Wee, and started back." On the return journey, however, Russell got caught on the wire and "just hung there, squealing for help and hugging the jug for dear life." If he had relinquished his grip on the liquor, Mezzrow explains, he might have freed himself more easily, but he refused. After all, "what's a guy's hide compared to a gallon of corn?"

By this point, Bix had "staggered down to the railroad tracks," where he plopped down, pulled off his shoes, and proceeded to empty them of sand. That's when his friends noticed the train. "All of us began screaming at Bix to get the hell out of there," Mezzrow writes, "but he thought we were just kidding him and he threw stones at us." When he finally "woke up" to the danger, he rolled off the track and down the bank, leaving his shoes behind: "Those funky Oxfords got clipped in half as neatly as if they'd been chopped with a meat cleaver."

The anecdote concludes with Bix telling his friends: "That just goes to show you, it's dangerous for a man to take his shoes off. First time I took those things off in weeks and you see what the hell happens. It just ain't safe to undress."

There is a kind of terrible poignancy to this story. "All of us began screaming at Bix to get the hell out of there"—his obliviousness has never been in sharper relief—"but he thought we were just kidding him and he threw stones at us." The Bix that Mezzrow gives us is a familiar one—drunken, obviously, but also mischievous, remote, unconcerned. His clothes, as usual, are a mess. But now these traits are beginning to turn on him. They're dangerous. They're putting him in harm's way. Still, even in the lazy summer of 1926, his friends are concerned about him. That seems to be one of the points to this story, that Bix's friends have his back, even if it's clear that their yelling didn't do much to alert him to the train. (He just "woke up," after all.) So what, then, does one make of Mezzrow's rhetorical question: "What's a guy's hide compared to a gallon of corn?" Am I a scold for thinking this kind of throwaway line is more than a bit callous? Pee Wee Russell was an alcoholic and a notoriously unhappy man. "He drank so much for so long that he almost died," the *New Yorker* jazz critic Whitney Balliett writes, "and when he miraculously recov-

ered, he began drinking again." Bix, at the end of his life, was guzzling straight alcohol flavored with lemon juice drops.

What's a guy's hide worth? Not enough, perhaps.

That was Red Nichols's perspective. In a 1937 article in *Down Beat* magazine, the "carrot-topped" band leader and old friend of Bix had this outburst: "Gin and weed? Hell! They didn't kill him. MUSICIANS KILLED BIX BEIDERBECKE! Some of those same musicians living today know what I mean. Bix died of a broken heart. And it was broken by the professional jealousy of musicians who couldn't stand to be outplayed by him so easily."

Nichols went on to charge Bix's friends with appreciating their boy's greatness only after he was safely dead. (This was exactly Berton's claim, only about Bix's parents.)

"Yes, Bix was appreciated after he was dead," he said. "But when he needed a lift, they wouldn't give it. Many a night they got him drunk and if he slipped or didn't play up to his best, they would pan the hell out of him."

Nichols's accusations are, for lack of a better word, weird. How does one kill another person with jealousy? How does one die of a broken heart? According to the *Down Beat* reporter, Nichols was "sober as a grim-pussed judge on election day" while being interviewed—this despite his being in a club, chain smoking at the bar, a glass of beer in front of him. "He didn't touch it," the reporter assures us. In this case, sobriety translates to a kind of seriousness, and Nichols is quite serious about wresting Bix away from the idea that he had anything to do with his own death. The *real* Bix, Nichols argues, was a god so delicate that he could be snuffed out by his own admirers.

Et tu, Mezzrow?

No doubt many of his friends bristled at such comments. When Bix was playing the *Camel Pleasure Hour* radio show in 1930, three of his bandmates took turns running by his apartment every day on their way to the studio—making sure he was up and dressed, making sure he had his horn, making sure he was in his chair and ready to play when the "On Air" light flashed red. But Bix kept at the bottle anyway, and that's when he began making excuses for himself. Sudhalter and Evans quote a fellow named Pat Ciricillo: "He told me that every time he tried to go [on] the wagon, friends came up [to his room] and visited him with gin bottles, and that tempted him."

Is it possible that the "his friends killed him" story actually originated with Bix himself? "People came around, sure," Sudhalter and Evans write, but what they found was Bix feeling sorry for himself. He complained that "life has passed me by" and that his many flatterers had ripped off his music in order to make a quick buck. (Bix didn't steal black musicians' stuff. Others stole *his* stuff. The irony is exquisite.) "What about all those guys who aren't ever around when you really need them?" Sudhalter and Evans imagine Bix thinking. "They wouldn't give me a quarter now. Hell, there are only two musicians I'd go across a street to hear now. That's Louis and LaRocca."

Louis Armstrong himself told the same story. "[Bix] had a lot of admirers," he once told an interviewer. "In fact, that's what mostly killed him. He wasn't the type of lad who had his own strong mind. When he felt bad and wanted to say good night to the gang he ran with, they would always say, 'Aw, man, stay a little longer . . . and have another drink.' Poor Bix would force himself against his will. And so he kept this up, until the gang just didn't believe him when he said, 'Fellers, I don't feel well.' When he finally did get home, he died."

In Mezzrow's anecdote, Bix disregards his friends; in Armstrong's, he's in their thrall, so much so that he seems to have misplaced his free will. Poor Bix, indeed. He didn't want to drink; he just wasn't the type "who had his own strong mind." According to the arranger Bill Challis, "he was still a kid—naive, not childish, but a trusting sort." He was a mark, in other words, killed, according to Pee Wee Russell, because he "couldn't say no to anybody."

Bix begins to look more and more like a Christ figure—betrayed by his friends, fated to die. But he also comes across, in the hands of those around him, as a rather poorly drawn fictional character. The stories his friends tell slickly mythologize him and, by extension, themselves. That these stories might also implicate these same friends or their kind in his death is merely an accident; what's important is that they absolve Bix. Never once, though, did any of his friends stand up and ask, "Could we have done better?"

Ralph Berton comes the closest. After one of his trademark, blistering attacks against Bix's parents, Berton lightens up a bit. "In defense of their fumbling," he writes in *Remembering Bix*, "let us note that no one else ever did much better, including his best friends and loudest admirers. Not once in Bix's lifetime would any of us offer any clear coherent view of what our confused hero was all about, or how he was to steer a rational course toward a rational goal. As one of them sadly remarked long afterward, none of us ever really knew who Bix was—least of all, of course, himself."

Berton's is an indictment of his and others' actions, sure—"we all failed him," he writes at one point, "as he failed himself"—but it's also an indictment of their imagination, of our imagination. If Bix were a three-dimensional human being, rather than some cardboard-cutout messiah, would we be so quick to rob him of his agency? If we *knew* Bix, as opposed to just admiring his music, would we not be forced to ask ourselves more pointedly and honestly how and why he died?

Look at Hoagy Carmichael. In multiple memoirs, both published and unpublished, he describes Bix as his closest friend and his greatest musical influence. His terms are never less than rhapsodic—"He had completely ruined me," he wrote upon first hearing Bix play—so that when Bix died, the loss, according to his biographer Richard Sudhalter, was "bitter and lasting." Carmichael's flair for the self-dramatic was sometimes poignant: he claimed to carry in his pocket, for the rest of his life, Bix's mouthpiece. He even named his son after Bix. But just as often his tales were sized a shade tall. Exaggeration was a function of the genre, of course, and Carmichael was driven both by his taste for sentimentality and his love for Bix. As a result, the critic Benny Green was not inclined to take Carmichael's "anecdotage" seriously. "The only time I ever met Carmichael," Green writes, "he had half a dozen Bix stories at his fingertips, stories I had never heard before, and I confess I found myself wondering whether Carmichael had either."

As the years went by, Bix seemed to disappear into these stories. In fact, one of Carmichael's recurring themes has to do with never knowing who his friend really was. In *The Stardust Road*, he writes of trying to describe Bix to his oddball surrealist friend William "Monk" Moenkhaus. "I remember trying to explain Bix to Monk," he writes. "I remember trying to put Bix together for Monk, so that he would see him and hear him and feel him the way I did. It was like the telling of a vivid dream and knowing that it wasn't making sense."

Green points to another passage from *The Stardust Road* in which Bix, near the end of his life, brings a girl to Carmichael's apartment. "We didn't have a drink," Carmichael writes, "we didn't talk music, and it soon became apparent that the girl had no idea who Bix was. And then the terrible thought struck me. I didn't know either." Green hoots at this last sentence, calling it "maddening." One presumes he finds it aesthetically unnecessary, but it's more than that. It raises a question that Carmichael refuses to address: what are the consequences of not knowing your own best friend?

In 1950 Carmichael starred with Kirk Douglas, Doris Day, and Lauren Bacall in the Hollywood adaptation of Dorothy Baker's *Young Man with a Horn*. Baker's novel showcased Bix in the guise of trumpeter Rick Martin and gave him an irresistibly romantic sheen. The movie went one better and upgraded Bix's story with a happy ending. Its closing lines come straight from Carmichael's lips:

> He learned that you can't say everything through the end of a trumpet, and a man doesn't destroy himself just because he can't hit some high note that he dreamed up. Maybe that's why Rick went on to be a success as a human being first—and an artist second. And what an artist.

Sudhalter makes the case that Carmichael, not the screenwriter, wrote these words, but he also ignores the heartbreaking irony. Bix did indeed destroy himself, and while Carmichael certainly felt the loss, he responded by drowning himself in parties, alcohol, and all of that anecdotage. Did he feel torn and guilty about Bix's death? Did these feelings of guilt drive him to forget his friend for the legend? Sudhalter doesn't speculate and neither, over the years, has anyone else.

Instead, we allow Bix to suffer, we encourage it even, because it serves our mythic needs. The literary critic Sven Birkerts wrote about this phenomenon in 2003 after the overdose death of the writer Lucy Grealy, an outsized character who had battled disfiguring cancer all her life. "Reading Lucy's work we realize how vigorously we cling to the myth of inwardness, the idea that personal suffering can become a source of strength," Birkerts wrote in the *Boston Globe*. "When she died, we lost, along with the person, some of the consolation of that myth, though of course most of us will renew it elsewhere and in others. It is that essential."

Birkerts then noted Grealy's love of attention and wondered, cautiously, whether it had made her a coconspirator in her growing legend. "It was all the more sad, then, in recent years, to catch glimpses of what was happening in her hidden life," he wrote. "For the hopeless side of Lucy had found its way first to painkillers, then to heroin, and through heroin came the downward pull of oblivion. That her decline was as gradual as it was suggests to me that there were rallying surges of resolve, and renewals of faith in the possibility of transformation, if not outward then inward. Certainly there was the care and attention of her many friends."

Notice how Lucy, like Bix, isn't to blame for her addiction—the action belongs to "the hopeless side of Lucy," an "it," not a "she." Notice, too, the way Birkerts imagines her pain in the feel-good terms of "resolve," "renewal," and "transformation." Initially, he had seemed skeptical of fetishizing other people's suffering, but not anymore.

And then there are the friends. When it first appeared, I e-mailed the Birkerts essay to a buddy of mine, a recovering alcoholic who had once met Grealy. His reply was quick and fierce. He said it was "appalling" that her friends were not more angry at her and at themselves. How, he asked, did they not notice her "slow downward spiral," before acknowledging that, of course, it does happen. We fail to notice even while we allow our loved ones "the luxury of such a spiral."

"I'll suggest that suicides tend to come when people view their lives as a sequence of diminished returns," he wrote. "They remove 'the shock of possibility' from their lives, supplant real risk with drama, and in cahoots with 'friends and family,' they begin to live their own fictions."

There is little evidence that Bix *consciously* lived his own myth, but stories have a way of looping back into our reality, controlling what they once only described or explained. His friends saw Bix as a boy genius destined to die, a hapless victim of fate, a kid without "his own strong mind." Even Bix seemed to believe that ("Life has passed me by," etc.), so that when he did finally die, his death was both the culmination of all the stories about him and the cause of still more. Bix himself, meanwhile, drifted further and further away. Who was he? Like Hoagy Carmichael, we will always wonder. What seems clear is that Bix's friends didn't kill him. In the face of alcohol and addiction, friends are powerless. Lucy Grealy's friend, the novelist Ann Patchett, discovered as much. "What she was suffering from was beyond me to fix," she wrote in a 2003 essay for *New York* magazine, an essay that was later expanded into the memoir *Truth & Beauty* (2004), "so I did what I knew how to do for Lucy: I made her happy for a little while."

It wasn't enough.

While he was still alive, Bix's friends tried to save him. Or they didn't try to save him. He died either way, and their gift to him, which was also a kind of apology, was Rick Martin.

He deserved better.

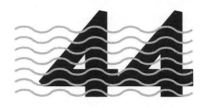

"Dearest Mom & Dad," Bix wrote in a letter home dated June 16, 1931.

Although it was less than two months before his death, things had been going better for him lately. He had stopped drinking, at least for the time being, and his friends had noticed that he was taking care of himself, paying attention to his appearance for the first time in months. What better time for a big announcement?

"I hope you are all well—& now about my *future* wife."

Her name was Alice and she was a born and bred New Yorker—"you should hear her accent—sounds like Aunt Blanch"—with red hair and blue eyes. Her mother's name was Weiss, Bix said, and her dad's O'Connell: German-Irish, just like Bix. "Here is something that I've been dreading to say because of mother—she's a staunch catholic[;] she has dragged me to her mass 3 or 4 times trying to convert me, and I've taken her to the 5th Ave. pres. Church—she says she likes it but her 2 brothers & 3 sisters would squeak." No worries, though, Bix wrote. "They all like me."

Here, you can almost picture Bix picturing himself in front of Mom and Pop Beiderbecke back at 1934 Grand. He knows what's coming: "Bickie, how on *earth* are you going to get married? You don't have a job. You don't have any money."

And he's got an answer.

"I told Alice that I wouldn't get married until I had a couple thousand," he explained, noting that she then "winked at me and said 'you've got it' and showed me a bank book—I almost swooned." The girl had bonds, bank stocks, the works, he told his parents. "I promise you that I fell in love with her before I knew that."

Her parents were wealthy, Bix went on to say, but they died when Alice, now twenty years old, was "quite young," after which she spent nine years in a convent. After dividing the estate with her siblings, she was worth about $10,000, according to Bix's best estimates.

"I'm sending a picture of her—what do you think of her?" he wrote, offering that he had had to drag her into a Photomators on Broadway "and for a buck we got this picture—Alice didn't want me to send it to you until she got a good one made. This will give you an idea of her."

In a postscript, Bix mentions that he had not one, but two job offers pending, both outside of New York City. Until he made a decision and moved, he could be reached at an address on Long Island. He left this part out, but it was the home of a musician friend, Rex Gavitte, and his wife. (A few days earlier, Bix, cornet in hand, had tried to sit in with Gavitte's band, then playing at Saltzman's Restaurant on East 42nd Street, but he was deemed fit only to play piano.)

Bix's girl, meanwhile, is almost too good to be true—nine years in a convent and worth a cool ten grand. "I'm certain that I never met her," Hoagy Carmichael told Phil Evans years later. "I can recall two girls in Bix's life: Cornelia Marshall in Indianapolis, December 1924; and Helen Weiss who lived in Sunnyside near Jackson Heights." But couldn't this Helen Weiss and Bix's Alice Weiss O'Connell be the same girl? Or did he make them both up? For years no one knew for sure. "About Helen Weiss, I don't know her whereabouts," another of Bix's friends, Stephen Ickes, told Evans, "but I gathered that she knew Bix in 1930 when he played on the Camel Hour and knew someone who was living in the building where Bix [eventually] moved. She was able to find him an apartment there (Apt. #1-G) and visited with him. She was connected with the entertainment field. I understand she was dark-haired, blue eyed, and very beautiful."

And so she was, at least judging by the photograph Bix sent home, which is almost certainly the product of a studio and not, as Bix claimed, a Photomators on Broadway.

Bix wrote his old friend Esten Spurrier in these last days, telling him that he was noodling on the piano again and thought he might produce something important before long. "Also that he thought that, at last, he had fallen in love, and his new outlook and demeanor," Spurrier recalled, "had undergone a change." He continued: "Bix knew, always, that his danger was in the first drink and that if he could take one and refuse the next, he had conquered. In writing, he remembered this, and seemed proud to say he was able to do so. His class and pride of being rebelled against being an alcoholic. Poor man—because of his great name and personality, he just had to be tempted so often and severely in comparison to us 'little people.' But I firmly and with all honesty believe with all my heart that a new Bix was abornin' in 1931."

Hoagy Carmichael also had noticed a change. He and his girl-friend invited Bix and Helen—Alice?—over for dinner and, according to Sudhalter and Evans, he "was stunned at how good Bix looked. The girl struck him as 'a bit mothery, maybe lost herself, but neat,' and willing to adapt to Bix and his needs." Table talk was small and the evening uneventful, but on the way out the door, Carmichael pulled Helen aside. "I told the girl to please call me immediately if anything happens," he remembered. "When he got sick, she failed to do so. Otherwise Bix might be alive today, meaning I would have seen that he quickly got the best."

For Bix, the Weiss girl was a convenient means to convince his anxious parents and concerned friends that he was finally back on his feet—that he was rich even, despite his having hit up Jimmy McPart-land for money—and that a new Bix was abornin'. For Carmichael, she was nothing more than a scapegoat. And for the rest of us, Helen Weiss/Alice O'Connell has remained a ghost.

Or at least she had until 2012. That's when a determined Bix scholar named Chris Barry, in pursuit of the piano on which Bix had so memorably "dreamed aloud," rearranged some names, supplied more than a pinch of shoe leather, and, to his surprise, discovered Alice Regina Weiss, daughter of Theodore Weiss and Helen O'Con-nell. (Her father, not her mother, was a Weiss.) I'll be the first to admit that I had become convinced that Alice resided only in Bix's some-times foggy head—this despite the photograph he had sent home and despite the fact that the names "Alice O'Connell" and "Weiss Family," both from New York, had been mysteriously noted in the register at Bix's funeral as having sent flowers. But wait. If her name were actu-ally Alice Weiss, then why did she send her condolences under the name Alice O'Connell? For that matter, why did she years later apply for a marriage certificate using an entirely new middle name, Claire?

Other questions present themselves. Why was her age different from what Bix told his parents (she was twenty-four, not twenty), not to mention the number of her siblings (she had three brothers, not two) and the relative wealth of her parents (her father had been a waiter)? Here's the real kicker, though: Alice Weiss was married. And not only that, she was married to Bix's friend, the bassist Rex Gavitte, with whom he was living at the time he penned Mr. and Mrs. Beider-becke his letter.

There's some reason to believe the romance was not imaginary. Alice Weiss divorced Gavitte a year after Bix's death; he, too, drank too much, and died a year later. She saved original photos that likely had belonged to Bix and apparently she took possession of his piano, too. And Bix's sister recalled having received her own letter from Bix in which he also declared his intention to marry. But what kind of declaration was that, exactly, when the girl was already spoken for and Bix was living on her and her husband's couch? For the time being, these questions remain unanswered, leaving the whole affair to serve as one last what-might-have-been before death finally re-asserts itself in our story.

Which it does when one day Bix suggested to his friend, the trombonist Jack Teagarden, that they "go down to the Bellevue morgue and have a look at the stiffs." Teagarden, a tall, imposing Texan, arched his eyebrows a little. "I told him, well, if I had a pint of gin first, I might be able to go. So I had my gin and off we went."

Bix came up with the idea when his brother, Burnie, wrote to say that he had gone to work at Oakdale Cemetery in Davenport. The death business, Bix thought, might be worth investigating.

"It must be the most gruesome morgue in the world, that place," Teagarden remembered. "There we were, and Bix slipped the night caretaker a five-dollar bill to let us through, and in we went. By then I was doing pretty good and it didn't bother me, but after a while Bix started to get sick. So we left."

Teagarden thought the whole episode might have been some kind of creepy premonition, like Bix was seeing *himself* as a ghost. He later asked Burnie about it. "Nope," the brother said. "I was in the business and he wanted to see the best in the world. That's all there was to it."

On May 7, 2005, Scott Black, a cornetist who for many years had played with Leon Redbone, posted about Bix's alcoholism on Albert Haim's online forum. (You remember Scott Black: Bix "got more ass than a toilet seat.") "He would have his slips at times and go on a real bender," Black wrote, "but would get it back together again."

> And those slips became the legendary stories told over and over, giving the impression that the last few years were nothing but a drunken haze. And nothing could be further from the truth. What was the big problem in 1930–31, was lack of sleep. Thanks to one S.O.B. mostly, who enjoyed getting Bix trashed, and making fun of him. I believe that he did as much to kill Bix Beiderbecke as the alcohol did. It was at his urging that Bix took that first drink in 1931, after being sober for many months. All so he could have a big laugh and tell the "boys" another "drunken Bix" story.
>
> May he rot in hell.

I called Black because I wanted to learn more about this S.O.B.—Judas to Bix's Christ—and when we finally hooked up, he was in Bakersfield, California, at the home of Linda Evans. Phil Evans's widow was herself dying of cancer and Black was in the process of taking possession of the couple's fifty years' worth of research. He was packing boxes into Linda's Plymouth Voyager, which he planned to drive back to New York.

"I hope I have enough room," he said in a voice that sounded tired with worry. Black has said many times that Phil had been like a father to him, and he has been a tireless advocate on his late friend's behalf in what has amounted to a running war over Bix's legacy. It began in 1974, with the publication of *Bix: Man & Legend*, a book that Sudhalter wrote and Evans researched. When Evans objected to the final product—for instance, the imaginary dialogue, the abortion episode, and the speculation about Bix's relationship with his father—there was a spectacular falling-out, and the book has long remained out of print.

"How much stuff is there?" I asked Black.

"Oh, six or eight thousand letters," he said. "Hundreds of hours of taped interviews. It's just so much information. People ask me how much is there and I tell them that J. Edgar Hoover didn't have this much information on Martin Luther King. That's how massive it is."

"And these letters—"

"They're from everybody, everybody who knew Bix that was alive from 1954 on. You name it, every sideman from George Johnson of the Wolverines, to letters from Hoagy and Louis, Teagarden, and geez, Bill Rank and Roy Bargy. It just goes on and on and on and on. There's a 1954 letter from Louis talking about when he first met Bix, and how much they enjoyed each other. They were really close, much closer than people realize."

"That's in the letter?"

"From the letters, from different interviews with Louis, and just, you know, from other people mentioning them being around each other a lot. Louis spent some time with Bix in '30, '31, telling him to take care of himself. Supposedly, Bix played on one of Louis's recordings, in the horn section. Bix was in the studio and just joined the band; he didn't solo or anything. Louis asked him to play, but nobody can remember what side it was."

I chuckled in a way that I hoped sounded skeptical.

"Bix actually heard the record from one of his Davenport friends who went over to Bix's place to visit. They were listening to some new records and they found this one by Louis, and Bix just started laughing. 'What's so funny?' And Bix said, 'I'm on this.' But this guy from Davenport didn't remember anything else about it. He told Phil, 'I didn't think Bix'd be dead in six months.' It was a shock, you know? But one hell of a story."

That story, presumably, would have been in the book that Black was then creating out of his Hooveresque pile of information. (He has since abandoned the project and gifted the Evans material to the nascent Bix Beiderbecke Museum and Archive, in Davenport.) "It's over 500 pages so far," he said, "all in the first person. No theories. No b.s. from other people. Nothing from anybody that didn't know Bix personally. And that's what it should be. An entirely different picture of the guy comes out. Completely different."

"Different from what?" I asked.

"From what everybody thinks. You know, especially about the Sudhalter crap about the family being ashamed of him. That never, ever, ever happened. Richard took all that stuff and decided he'd write the Great American Novel. And the story about the records in the closet? Never happened. It's just all b.s. Makes for a good story, though."

"It *does* make for a good story," I said. "But how do we know it's not true?"

"Well, I can tell you exactly how you can confirm it," he said.

"The story started with Bix's Davenport friend Esten Spurrier, didn't it?"

"Well, he augmented a story. You see, Esten hated Burnie, Bix's brother. When people started going Bix-crazy, Esten just—[if] anybody from Davenport said they were friends with Bix, Esten called them a liar. And he put himself up as quote, 'Bix's father-confessor.' He knew Bix, yes. Maybe played a couple jobs with him, yes. But Bix had one close friend and that was [the clarinetist] Don Murray. And that was his best friend. I mean, he was close with a lot of people—"

"So where did this story start if it didn't start with Esten?"

"Okay. The story goes back to 1933, I think. Marshall Stearns"—a jazz researcher who founded the Institute of Jazz Studies at Rutgers University before dying suddenly in 1966—"went to visit the Beiderbecke family, and he took a bunch of records that were in mint condition in one of the closets. That was Bix's own record collection. And Bix's collection consisted of mostly classical, but he had a complete set of New Orleans Rhythm Kings. He kept them in mint condition. Those were it. And out of Bix's entire collection, I thought there was only one that was historically significant. There's a copy of 'Tiger Rag' by the Original Dixieland Jazz Band that's so worn out you can hear both sides when you play it."

"Is that the one Burnie brought home from—"

"When he was a kid, that's when he started playing the cornet."

"Wow."

"And he played it over and over and over again."

"So he kept that record his whole life."

"Yeah, yeah. And it's neat. That's a great record. But there were no test pressings [that Bix was supposed to have sent home to his parents]. The family loved the guy, supported him, and were behind him. And all of that stuff about Bismark? None of it is true. He's a very nice man. Easygoing guy. Played a lot of baseball. And, like I said, Richard put all that stuff in the book because he was trying to identify himself through his own father, who told him he would never amount to anything as a musician. It's just a bunch of crap. What can you do? It's in print and people now think it's gospel."

We were inching closer and closer to Judas.

"Phil was a real pack rat," Black continued. "It's almost a sickness. I've got at least a dozen new photographs of Bix that haven't been seen before, including one from about four months before he died. He looks great. He looks absolutely great. He wasn't the run-down, sickly, desperate character that he was portrayed to be. He never lost his lip. In the spring of '31, he was playing better than ever, according to a lot of people who heard him."

"Are you saying that he wasn't killing himself with booze? That's wrong?"

"What happened was, he went on the wagon quite a bit. But when you go off the wagon, it's going to be memorable. It's like picking up where you left off. He'd be sober for months at a time and most people either don't remember or don't want to remember that time because, you know, well, he's just playing great. But when he'd screw up or be drunk, he'd be really, really drunk. And his family was never ashamed of him. He was more ashamed of himself. He was hardest on himself over that. And the big reason—he had a place at the 44th Street Hotel for years and years, and one guy in particular liked to get him drunk, keep him up playing all night."

Wait for it.

"It was Tommy Dorsey."

"Tommy Dorsey?"

"Tommy Dorsey."

"The Sentimental Gentleman?"

"That's right. Dorsey would get done doing his radio shows, nightclub things, and he'd drag a bunch of guys up to Bix's room to have him play piano. And they'd keep him up until six or seven in the morning. And so if Bix had, say, an audition to do at ten in the morning, a radio show or something, he was glassy-eyed, hungover, and not completely sober yet. And Tommy used to tell all the drunk-Bix stories to everybody, so who'd want to hire him, really?"

"What was going on with Dorsey that he did this?" I asked.

"He was a sadistical son of a bitch, that's what."

Black went on to accuse Dorsey's wife of murdering him in his sleep. He verified that, indeed, Bix "could not say no to his friends," and he sighed at the sheer number of dollars Bix lost in the Crash. "He was making enough with Whiteman in 1929, just a straight salary, that he could buy a new car every week," Black said. "But by '31, he couldn't even make his room rent at the hotel."

And Black talked at length about the various wrongs perpetrated against his friend and mentor, Phil Evans. For instance, there are the original photographs Evans loaned a documentary filmmaker that, according to Black, she didn't return. ("Why he gave her the originals, I don't know.") There's the executive producer credit on a radio documentary that Black says was stolen from Evans. And, of course, there's the book *Bix: Man & Legend*. "It's unbelievable the lengths that people have gone to steal this material from the guy," Black said. "If people were just honest, he was so open in those days to share whatever material he had; he was happy to share. But people would borrow something and say, 'Look what I found! Look what I found!' And completely exclude Phil from being in the equation, which just isn't right."

He complained that "life has passed me by" and that his many flatterers had ripped off his music in order to make a quick buck . . .

The Phil Evans whom Scott Black describes begins to sound a lot like the Bix Beiderbecke Scott Black describes—loved by his friends, tortured and misunderstood by the world, naive certainly. Most of all, though, he was a victim. Says Black:

"It's a terrible thing to know that his love of Bix, and his life's work is what killed him in the end . . ."

"There are many things in this life that I'd love to forget. And Phil Evans's last couple of months on this earth is one of them . . ."

"He became sick and heartbroken [after the publication of *Man & Legend*] because he was afraid that all of those amazing musicians and friends of Bix would feel that Phil had sold them and their friendship out for the almighty dollar and cheap fame . . ."

"Phil Evans was a man of honor. And if you don't believe me, ask anyone out there who really knew him . . ."

According to this template, friendship is akin to a knight bravely defending his maiden against all comers. It is the rare soul—at least where Bix or Phil Evans are concerned—who admits it might be more complicated than that. On Haim's forum, Brad Kay recalled visiting Evans at his California home sometime in the 1990s. "I finally got up the nerve to ask Phil what was so wrong with 'Man & Legend,'" Kay wrote. Evans responded with the usual list of factual errors and a promise to publish something more definitive, something that would put Sudhalter "in his place." "He talked like a man obsessed, *à la* Captain Ahab," Kay wrote. "This was even more saddening. . . . I sincerely hoped that Phil could direct his considerable talent and energy in a healthier direction. We would run into each other at jazz festivals and such. We always maintained friendly rapport, but I could see plainly that the bitterness and obsession were consuming him, and finally they did."

What is a good friend to do in that moment? Late in Lucy Grealy's life, Ann Patchett was willing to fly from Nashville to New York in order to be at her friend's bedside for one more in a long line of surgeries. "You're such a good friend," Grealy told her. "What did I ever do to deserve a friend like you?"

"You're a good friend to me, too," Patchett replied.

"Oh no I'm not," Grealy said. "Not like you. But at least I can make you feel like a saint. That's what you've always wanted."

And maybe it was. Patchett's book doesn't offer much of a defense. Sometimes the knight acts out of love and loyalty alone. But sometimes the knight wants glory. And sometimes the knight just wants a good story.

I asked Scott Black whether, after listening to his hundred hours of tape, after reading his thousands of pages of letters, he felt like he knew Bix.

"I know enough about him, let's put it that way," he said. "The first time I heard him on a record, I just loved it. I still do. And there was something right there, you know, geez, this is, wow. You can't describe it."

But the mythmakers want to turn all that into something it's not, Black told me. The cornetist Jimmy McPartland used to go on about his old friend Bix, Black said. "That's all he talked about, what a regular guy Bix was. Besides being a musical genius, he was just a sweet, wonderful guy you just loved spending time with. They used to double-date all the time."

Black paused.

"People would always say Bix was a misunderstood genius," Black said. "He was a genius. You bet he was. But there wasn't anything mystical about it."

Apparently neither of Bix's potential jobs panned out and I imagine that remaining at the Gavittes' place would have been rather awkward. As such, he secured the new apartment in Queens, #1-G, and it was from there on the night of August 6 that George Kraslow heard noises. The day before, Dr. Haberski had asked the rental agent if he knew Bix's next of kin. Kraslow suggested calling Paul Whiteman, who was playing in Chicago. "Whiteman came rushing over," the cornetist Andy Secrest said, "and he called for Tram. 'Come quickly, Tram,' he said. 'It's Bix!' Bix was in need of immediate medical care and refused to enter a hospital. Tram put a call to the Beiderbecke home in Davenport, and advised them of the seriousness of the situation: Bix's mother caught the first train to New York. Then we waited for word." And that's where things stood when Kraslow heard what sounded like screaming.

"His hysterical shouts brought me to his apartment on the run," he said. "He pulled me in and pointed to the bed. His whole body was trembling violently. He was screaming there were two Mexicans hiding under his bed with long daggers. To humor him, I looked under the bed, and when I rose to assure him there was no one hiding there, he staggered and fell, a dead weight, in my arms. I ran across the hall and called in a woman doctor, Dr. Haberski, to examine him. She pronounced him dead."

The official time was 9:30 P.M.

A letter, dated a week earlier, lay on the nightstand, unfinished.

Dearest Folks:—

By now you have Alice's picture—what do you think of her? We're together constantly—I dragged her in one of those Photomators on B'way & for a buck we had that made & enlarged. The little sweetheart framed it, packed it, and sent it to you when she knew—you wanted it.

The exact cause of Bix Beiderbecke's death has always been a matter of dispute. On the one hand, most historians are content to say that booze killed him—as many as three milk bottles full of gin and orange juice a day, according to Sudhalter and Evans—and lobar pneumonia, which was listed on the death certificate, only speeded things up. On the other hand, Bing Crosby claimed, remarkably, that Bix wasn't an alcoholic; he was just exhausted. Red Nichols blamed Bix's friends, and Hoagy Carmichael pointed his finger at the girl. Eddie Condon, meanwhile, thought it was those fans in Bix's room: "Bix had a hell of a cold and he would put fans on either side of his bed blowing down on him as he slept. I am convinced that was the final blow that did him in." The most poetic explanation was submitted by a friend named Frank Norris. "Bix Beiderbecke didn't die of a cold," he said. "He died of *everything*!"

But he did die, and that's what's important. We *needed* him to die— he died for his friends and for his legend; he died, without a doubt, for us—a state of affairs that always made the jazz writer Gene Lees eloquently angry. "There is an implicit condescension in this process: I can admire him because I feel sorry for him, affirming my own superiority," he writes. "Condescension to brilliance is the ultimate arrogance. America, land of ambition and success, has paradoxically, an ongoing love affair with failure and premature death." It's a love affair that has consequences, Terry Teachout told me: "Bix is a self-image. He is the ideal of the Romantic jazz musician, the first one that we have, the Romantic self-destructive musician, and you know how influential that must have been. He did a lot of damage. Bix Beiderbecke killed a lot of people."

Agatha and Bix's brother, Burnie, escorted the body home from New York, arriving in Davenport late in the evening on August 9. The service was held two days later at Hill & Fredericks' funeral home and burial followed, at Oakdale Cemetery—the same place where Burnie worked. Tucked away in a quiet east-side neighborhood and easy to miss despite its postcard beauty and skyscraper oaks, this was where the family gathered. Agatha, I imagine, barely held up; Bismark was stiff and nonplussed.

Unlike Berton, I doubt that Agatha cried crocodile tears that day. How could she after the arrest, the school expulsion, the Keeley Institute, after staying up past midnight to hear him on the radio with Whiteman? In fact, I wonder whether it's fair to suppose that mere music could ever redeem her pain. We are the callous ones, I think— all too willing to trade her Little Bickie for those shooting shafts of light in "I'm Coming Virginia."

CODA

On March 12, 2010, I boarded a plane to Racine, Wisconsin, where a Bixophile named Phil Popsychala was staging his twenty-first annual Bix Fest, scheduled each year for the week of Bix's birthday. Although I planned to skip the grueling, daylong bus tour of Chicago-area Bix sites, I looked forward to meeting in person a number of Bixophiles I otherwise knew only online or over the phone, including Brad Kay, Scott Black, Barb Wascher, and others.

A few weeks earlier, Barb had come up with the idea of staging a reenactment of Bix and Hoagy's hot night listening to *The Firebird* at the Kappa Sig house—minus the kinky stuff, of course, but complete with a red light bulb, just as Bix had used with several of his friends. It sounded vaguely ridiculous, certainly necrophilic, but also kind of perfect. A member of the Beiderbecke family had recently told me that she enjoyed a mystical connection with Bix, that he was likely even guiding her e-mail to me. (She signed off, "Bix Lives!") Well, maybe this was *my* chance at such a connection.

I told Barb to count me in, and by the time I arrived, she and her husband Paul's room at the Marriott had already been set up, with a vintage 1925 recording of *The Firebird Suite*, conducted by Leopold Stokowski, ready to go. The only question was who besides the three of us would come. "Brad's going to play it by ear," Barb said as she stood outside the hotel's front entrance, taking a smoke break. A restless, fiercely intelligent Midwesterner, she liked nothing better than to drag on a cigarette and talk about Hoagy, Bix, and their music. Her sweatshirt read, "Et in Arcadia ego."

I had forgotten that Brad Kay had been invited. That night I introduced myself to him outside a small, windowless room where mostly male Bixophiles took turns spinning their favorite 78s. A bit bleary from his long flight, he wore round glasses, a neat black suit jacket, and a porkpie hat that reminded me of Lester Young; he was as quiet now as he had been talkative over the phone. As Barb gently scolded him for being out of touch, a commotion from inside the spinning room interrupted us. Apparently a record that had been the subject of a recent debate on Albert Haim's forum was about to be played, and several men loudly disparaged Haim's view of things.

"No speeches," one of them joked, half standing up. "Just let it be said that the Little Professor was wrong again!"

The room filled with laughter.

Barb and Brad rolled their eyes. Feuds between Haim—the Little Professor—and various others occurred regularly in the Bixophile community, resulting in the occasional online tantrum and Haim banning someone from his forum. A few times disputants had cc'd me on e-mails that argued their points—messages distinguished by a mix of discographical minutiae and gleeful ad hominem—and on one occasion such an e-mail had even contained a glib but creepy joke about murdering Haim in Racine. (Haim did not attend the conference.) It all became exhausting after a while. And yet the next morning I couldn't resist approaching one of these Bixophiles over breakfast and asking him for an interview. We sat on a flat uphol-stered bench in the hotel lobby and talked for almost an hour.

In a genial baritone he told me about his introduction to record collecting as a pimply teenager, his obsession with 78s and early jazz (and, in particular, with white jazz), and finally his introduction to the magical, bell-like sound that emanated from the horn of Bix Beiderbecke. He described a hajj-like first trip to Davenport and how he toured the house on Grand Avenue on Bix's birthday. Imagining the wails of a newborn baby Bix, he found himself overcome with tears—although for ethical reasons, he said, he and his companions had avoided the actual room where Agatha gave birth.

He got emotional just thinking about it, he said. And it *was* a moving story. But it was also frustrating. After all, if you so much as raise the question of Bix's arrest to many hard-core Bixophiles, they will ridicule you for caring not about his solos but about sex and perversion. So what, I wondered, does Bix's nativity have to do with his music? For that matter, what does his house or his hometown?

The Bixophile who sat opposite me made no attempt to hide his idolization of Bix, suggesting that the musician represented all that was beautiful and right in the world. Surprisingly, though, he was more than willing to acknowledge the arrest and even conceded that yes, it did happen.

What happened? I asked.

What Bix was accused of, he said. And for all we know, he may have been guilty of something worse, but so what? All adolescent boys do that sort of thing. It happens frequently in English boarding schools, he said. But what does that prove, putting Bix up on a cross for the crime of getting caught?

The Bixophile's smooth surface had suddenly rippled. I tried to fight back, pointing out that no, we *don't* all do it, not even when we're drunk; that Bix was not in an English boarding school; that the alleged victim was not a fellow teenager but a five-year-old girl. But he had stopped listening, his face now a Bixian shade of blank.

I left the interview feeling appalled, even as I wished that I, too, could so easily cast aside this inconvenient episode in our hero's life. I wished that Bix the clever excuse-maker did not so often overwhelm my picture of him. After all, there are consequences to this state of affairs. I've begun to listen to Bix's music less and less, and to worry more and more about the opinions of people like Albert Haim and his belief in the "living principle" of Bix's innocence. In Davenport, meanwhile, the original records of the arrest seem to have gone missing from the courthouse. Even a photocopy of one of the documents, for years publicly displayed by the library, has disappeared. "I think some folks around here don't like what those documents represent," a librarian told me. "They think Bix is some kind of god."

And for a while so did I. But after years of studying Bix, of poring over books and records and arrest reports, of trying to crack his "private astronomy" and fretting over the implications of that "absence" so many people seemed to notice in him, I've begun to wear down, to feel like someone caught up in a bad relationship. According to a friend of his, Rich Johnson "was completely, totally in love with Bix," and my own experience with the man confirms this to be true. (His license plate read "BIXNME.") But even the best kinds of love can make us crazy now and again, and I have come to wonder whether my persistent, maybe even my chronic inability to find Bix is a failure of love. If I loved "Singin' the Blues" or "In a Mist" or "Sorry" just a smidgen more—if I wept at the memory of his birth, like that Bixophile, or fainted onto a davenport, like Hoagy Carmichael—would that clarify for me the mysteries surrounding Bix? Would I be able, finally, to block out the ugliness?

I doubt it, even if I were the weeping type. Still, I would open myself up to *The Firebird* and see what happened.

That night, after watching Scott Black perform, I met Barb and Paul in their room, where the music was cued up and a nice bottle of Russian vodka opened. I was depressed but also strangely energized by the things the Bixophile had said.

"This is what Bix looks like inside Bix's head most of the time," Barb joked as Paul switched on the red light bulb.

"I think we need to leave the red light bulb here when we leave," he said.

"Oh god, I'm sure they've seen worse," Barb said.

I took a gulp of the vodka.

Brad Kay had decided not to come. He was downstairs listening to 1920s jazz—music Bix played—while we listened to music Bix loved. *Which would bring me closer?* I wondered. *And what would that feel like?*

Paul, meanwhile, was explaining that the Kappa Sigma house in Bloomington wasn't built until 1926, even though Hoagy's story takes place in 1924. "Which tells me there's something amiss," he said. "I don't know if there was a Kappa Sig house—"

"—of an earlier vintage?" I said.

"Yes, and it may be that there was. I don't know. The twenties were when fraternity houses really sprouted up on American campuses. So I'm not sure if there was, or if they just made this shit up. I'm thinking there's some made-it-up in there."

"There usually is," I said, as Paul hit PLAY.

The violins sounded ominous. "It's a creepy forest," Barb said after I asked her to narrate what was happening in the ballet. "We have a generic Prince Ivan poking around the creepy forest, hunting."

The strings suddenly erupted, swirling and hysterical. "The firebird," Barb explained, as the pizzicato mixed with the cracks and the pops of the old recording and the shadows cast by the red light. I took another glug of the white mule liquor. "Think of 'In a Mist' when you hear some of these rhythms," she said.

Even as my head started turning, the music calmed down. "Twelve human princesses are behind a barrier made of horrible vines and spider webs and stuff," Barb said. "And they're playing an elaborate game of catch with golden apples from the tree. Because this is a suite, we missed Ivan capturing the firebird and the deal where he lets her go. In the end, he gets a feather, and the firebird tells him, 'If you're in trouble, you can summon me with this.'"

The three of us sank into the quiet for what was only a few moments but felt longer. "This part of the suite doesn't really match the emotional urgency of the rest of it," Barb said. "It's just kind of like, you know, emotional oatmeal. It's very bland and pretty."

Which was true, I suppose, but I liked it. My mind drifted to the Kappa Sig house. Whatever Hoagy made up—the torts, the tarts, the drunken entrechat—he didn't make up those dreadful urges. Those belonged to him, along with the terrible longing and the wonderful desires. Did he see them in Bix? And what did he know about the arrest?

I imagined that garage at the corner of Locust and Grand, and Bix taking the partially blind young girl by the hand and leading her in out of the cold, pelting rain. Bix represents all that was beautiful in the world, the Bixophile had said, and even if that were true, it's just so very bland and pretty. I thought about Hoagy and the ballet dancer Gene Berton and little Sarah Ivens, and I realized that perhaps I didn't need Bix to be wonderful. For better or for worse, I just needed him to be *interesting*.

Barb was speaking: "So the princesses are playing this stupid game with the apples, and you get the impression that they're being held there against their will, and they're kind of out of it. And the prince decides he wants to set them free—and one in particular he's really interested in. So he decides that he's going to get in somehow."

The music turned crazy again.

"And he does, but then he's captured by a bunch of demons and taken to the immortal Koshchei. That's when Prince Ivan whips out the feather, and the firebird shows up. And she makes all of the demons—and the enchanted girls—dance this freaky dance."

"Where does this story come from?" I asked.

"Russia."

"It's Russian folklore?"

"Very old. Actually almost every culture has a firebird. It's what the southwestern Navajo and other Native Americans call the thunderbird. It's basically the same idea."

The idea being that the firebird is the object of a hero's quest—a beautiful, entrancing creature that can also bring trouble.

"And he's a tricky source of inspiration," Barb was saying. "You know, the firebird can burn you."

I thought of the glowing red plumage blinding the good and the evil alike. "The firebird is just as unnatural as these demons," Barb said, "so it's kind of a tricky bargain. Ivan doesn't know how the firebird's going to help."

NOTES

EPIGRAPHS

page ix, *"When you leap"*: Donald Barthelme Literary Papers, 1956–2001, University of Houston.

page ix, *"He is the ideal"*: Interview with Terry Teachout on March 11, 2006, in Manhattan.

1

page 1, "We had been listening": I took the trolley tour, which included a tour of the Beiderbecke family home, as well as Bix's grandparents' home, in July 2005.

page 2, "the twin lines of descent": Terry Teachout, "Homage to Bix," *Commentary*, September 2005, 65.

page 2, "a common cultural ground": Amiri Baraka (LeRoi Jones), *Blues People: Negro Music in White America* (1963; New York: William Morrow, 1999), 150.

page 2, "And that's a profoundly racist argument": Interview with Teachout on March 11, 2006.

page 2, "a few hundred recordings": Approximately 250, according to Richard M. Sudhalter in his foreword to Jean Pierre Lion, *Bix: The Definitive Biography of a Jazz Legend* (New York: Continuum, 2005), vii.

page 2, "I remember the day": Richard M. Sudhalter and Philip R. Evans with William Dean-Myatt, *Bix: Man & Legend* (New Rochelle, NY: Arlington House, 1974), 7. The authors identify the speaker only as "a veteran saxophonist of the era."

page 2, "this quiet, deferential": Sudhalter and Evans, *Bix: Man & Legend*, 7.

page 3, "cardboard martyr": "Bix Beiderbecke," in Benny Green, *The Reluctant Art: Five Studies in the Growth of Jazz*, expanded edition (1962; New York: Da Capo, 1991), 20.

page 3, "jazz's Number One Saint": Green, *Reluctant Art*, 19.

page 3, "Bix was as usual gazing off": Ralph Berton, *Remembering Bix* (1974; New York: Da Capo, 2000), 254.

page 3, "Berton one-ups": Berton, *Remembering Bix*, xi.

page 3, "a young James Dickey": From his unpublished essay, "The Rebel Soul—1931" (1943), in James Dickey, *Crux: The Letters of James Dickey*, ed. Matthew J. Bruccoli and Judith S. Baughman (New York: Knopf, 1999), 3–5.

page 3, "Bix did not let anything at all": In Nat Shapiro and Nat Hentoff, eds., *Hear Me Talkin' to Ya: The Story of Jazz as Told by the Men Who Made It* (1955; New York: Dover, 1966), 158.

page 3, "focus their book": In the introduction to Sudhalter and Evans's *Bix: Man & Legend*, Sudhalter writes: "If an anecdote was based in fact, it would appear, correct, in its proper place in the narrative. If not, its omission would speak clearly enough" (11).

page 4, "40 years of underbrush": Sudhalter and Evans, *Bix: Man & Legend*, 7.

page 4, "For twenty-five years": Phone interview with Richard M. Sudhalter on March 4, 2003.

2

page 5, "downtown parking garage": This has since been painted over. Other particulars described here also have changed over the years. John O'Donnell Stadium is now Modern Woodmen Park; the baseball team is the Quad Cities River Bandits; and the Bix 7 race and the music festival no longer share a weekend.

page 5, "Bix Lives!": "The phrase 'Bix lives!' preceded the appearance of the graffito 'Bird lives,' a reference to another self-destructive jazz genius [i.e., Charlie Parker], now also part of Hollywood myth," writes Krin Gabbard in *Jammin' at the Margins: Jazz and the American Cinema* (Chicago: University of Chicago Press, 1996), 68.

page 5, "that there were two Mexicans": Philip R. Evans and Linda K. Evans, *Bix: The Leon Bix Beiderbecke Story* (Bakersfield, CA: Prelike, 1998), 546.

page 6, "that ancient and irresistible tradition": N. Scott Momaday, "A Divine Blindness: The Place of Words in a State of Grace," in *The Man Made of Words: Stories, Essays, Passages* (New York: St. Martin's, 1998), 81.

page 6, "like a girl saying yes": Eddie Condon with Thomas Sugrue, *We Called It Music: A Generation of Jazz* (1947; New York: Da Capo, 1992), 85. A similar locution—influenced by Condon?—can be found in Philip Larkin's "For Sidney Bechet," first published in 1954.

page 7, "surefooted as a mountain goat": Mezz Mezzrow and Bernard Wolfe, *Really the Blues* (1946; New York: Citadel Underground, 1990), 80.

page 7, "like a mallet": Quoted in Richard M. Sudhalter, *Stardust Melody: The Life and Music of Hoagy Carmichael* (New York: Oxford University Press, 2002), 72.

page 7, "I just sat there": Max Kaminsky and V. E. Hughes, *Jazz Band: My Life in Jazz* (1963; New York: Da Capo, 1984), 13.

page 7, "One cannot hear Bix Beiderbecke": Concert notes by James Dugan and John Hammond for "From Spirituals to Swing," performed December

23, 1938; in *Keeping Time: Readings in Jazz History*, ed. Robert Walser (New York: Oxford University Press, 1999), 103.

page 7, "sounded nothing like him": "These assertions can be taken with a grain of salt," the jazz historian James Lincoln Collier wryly asserts, because "most people who heard Bix in the wee hours . . . were drunk." Collier, *The Making of Jazz: A Comprehensive History* (Boston: Houghton Mifflin, 1978), 169.

page 8, "Well, what's wrong with gaslight?": Ciaran Carson, *Last Night's Fun: In and Out of Time with Irish Music* (New York: North Point, 1997), 2.

page 8, "Although the majority of its citizens": Charles Wareing and George Garlick, *Bugles for Beiderbecke* (London: Sidgwick and Jackson, 1958), 1.

page 8, "Like Jesus, Van Gogh": Berton, *Remembering Bix*, xi.

page 9, "The first time I heard Bix": Shapiro and Hentoff, *Hear Me Talkin' to Ya*, 158.

page 9, "from the *New York Times* obituaries": Steven Heller, "James Flora, 84, Author and Album Cover Illustrator, Dies," *New York Times*, July 18, 1998.

page 9, "extraordinary, Picassoesque album cover": This is Flora's cover art for the 1947 Columbia release *Bix and Tram*. See Irwin Chusid, *The Mischievous Art of Jim Flora* (Seattle: Fantagraphics Books, 2004), 30.

3

page 10, "rose violently from the piano": From *Jazz Banders: A Rhapsody in Mud*, by Hoagy Carmichael, an unpublished manuscript on file in the Archives of Traditional Music at Indiana University. Quoted in Sudhalter, *Stardust Melody*, 72.

4

page 11, "a long, largely positive review": "Davenport Blues" was published first in *Icon* (June 29, 2000), a now-defunct alternative weekly newspaper in Iowa City, then republished in the Davenport weekly *River City Reader* (July 11, 2000), where Beiderbecke first saw it. The *Reader* is now RCReader.com.

page 11, "more ass than a toilet seat": E-mail received from Scott Black on June 17, 2005.

page 11, "snatched out of a cradle": Mezzrow and Wolfe, *Really the Blues*, 78.

page 13, "The family ignored and deplored": Berton, *Remembering Bix*, 13.

page 14, "**Bix** and Pee Wee Russell had dinner": Evans and Evans, *Bix: The Leon Bix Beiderbecke Story*, 208.

page 14, "**Bix** came in and borrowed": Evans and Evans, *Bix: The Leon Bix Beiderbecke Story*, 208.

page 14, "So as not to confuse the reader": Evans and Evans, *Bix: The Leon Bix Beiderbecke Story*, xiv.

page 14, "anti-**Bix**": In an "Editor's Foreword" to Evans and Evans's *Bix: The Leon Bix Beiderbecke Story*, Norman Gentieu writes that "wishful thinking overroad [*sic*] historical evidence. Self-anointed gurus of the jazz vernacular promulgated arbitrary aesthetic principles, often painfully politically correct and occasionally anti-**Bix**. Worst of all, perhaps, were the imaginary conversations conjured up all too glibly out of the very thin air of reckless fantasy. What a mess that wrong stuff was (and is)!" (*Bix: The Leon Bix Beiderbecke Story*, xvii). Gentieu, an advertising executive and jazz pianist from Philadelphia, died in 2009 at the age of ninety-four.

page 15, "Trumbauer always told": Quoted in Lion, *Bix: The Definitive Biography*, 140.

page 15, "Happily, the error-ridden glut": Gentieu in Evans and Evans, *Bix: The Leon Bix Beiderbecke Story*, xvii.

5

page 16, "One of the things I like about jazz, kid": Shapiro and Hentoff, *Hear Me Talkin' to Ya*, 158. A similar quotation can be found in Evans and Evans, *Bix: The Leon Bix Beiderbecke Story*, 539. Bix's idea echoes the more cynical words of Thelonious Monk: "I don't know where jazz is going. Maybe it's going to hell. You can't make anything go anywhere. It just happens"; quoted in Scott DeVeaux, "Constructing the Jazz Tradition," in *The Jazz Cadence of American Culture*, ed. Robert G. O'Meally (New York: Columbia University Press, 1998), 483.

6

page 17, "Bix's brother Burnie claimed": Evans and Evans, *Bix: The Leon Bix Beiderbecke Story*, 17.

page 17, "from the county registrar": Evans and Evans, *Bix: The Leon Bix Beiderbecke Story*, 17. See also Sudhalter and Evans, *Bix: Man & Legend*, 26.

page 17, "Well, his name wasn't Bix": Interview with Rich Johnson on June 21, 2005, in Davenport, Iowa.

page 17, "What a wonderful, impossible name!": Anton Myrer, *A Green Desire: A Novel* (New York: Putnam, 1981), 288.

page 17, "Fantastic Names of Jazz": Hayden Carruth, "The Fantastic Names of Jazz," in *Doctor Jazz* (Port Townsend, WA: Copper Canyon, 2001), 107.

page 17, "Daddy's listening": "Family Circus" cartoon reprinted in Evans and Evans, *Bix: The Leon Bix Beiderbecke Story*, 522.

page 17, "mouth-pleasure": "Everyone was once an infant who took mouth-pleasure in gurgle and shriek, accompanied by muscle-joy as small limbs clenched and unclenched. Poetry starts from the crib," Hall writes in "The Unsayable Said," in *Breakfast Served Any Time All Day: Essays on Poetry New and Selected* (Ann Arbor: University of Michigan Press, 2003), 1.

7

page 19, "They did, according to Aggie": Evans and Evans, *Bix: The Leon Bix Beiderbecke Story*, 19.

page 19, "dangerous habit": Evans and Evans, *Bix: The Leon Bix Beiderbecke Story*, 19.

page 19, "When it was built in 1893": Evans and Evans, *Bix: The Leon Bix Beiderbecke Story*, 11. Sudhalter and Evans have Bismark and Agatha marrying in 1894 instead of 1893 and moving into "a roomy new white frame house" (*Bix: Man & Legend*, 19). Lion has them marry in June 1893 and, in a footnote, informs readers that the house at 1934 Grand Avenue was originally painted green (*Bix: The Definitive Biography*, 3).

page 19, "graduated to Liszt": In his memoir *Sometimes I Wonder*, coauthored with Stephen Longstreet (1965; New York: Da Capo, 1999), Hoagy Carmichael claims that "when only three, Bix could play the melody of the Second Hungarian Rhapsody" (111). Wareing and Garlick add, rather ungenerously, "Not quite the progress one expects from genius, however juvenile, but, nevertheless, praiseworthy in a normal child" (*Bugles for Beiderbecke*, 2).

page 19, "the *Davenport Democrat* dispatched": "7-Year-Old Boy Musical Wonder; Little Bickie Beiderbecke Plays Any Selection That He Hears," *Davenport Daily Democrat*, March 10, 1910; reprinted in Sudhalter and Evans, *Bix: Man & Legend*, 27; Evans and Evans, *Bix: The Leon Bix Beiderbecke Story*, 24–25; Lion, *Bix: The Definitive Biography*, 5.

page 20, "His feet were swollen": Condon, *We Called It Music*, 216, 217.

page 20, "follow him there": The pianist Brad Kay suggested to me the connection between these two passages. "This was the best and most accurate reporting and observation of Bix in action that anyone wrote during his lifetime," he said, referring to the piece in the *Democrat*. "All the articles that came later [were] pure bullshit." Phone interview with Kay on May 4, 2009.

8

page 21, "a few days before Christmas": Lion (*Bix: The Definitive Biography*, 12) writes that Burnie purchased the Victrola and several records on his way home from military training in Louisville, Kentucky. Evans and Evans (*Bix: The Leon Bix Beiderbecke Story*, 40) quote Burnie as saying he bought the Victrola when he got home and the records were thrown in for free.

In Sudhalter and Evans (*Bix: Man & Legend*, 35) Burnie is quoted again, this time having it both ways. He buys the records and gramophone (now a Columbia) both before *and* after he returns home: "I had a fair amount of loose cash with me. So a little while after I got home—must have been sometime in December—I bought a Columbia gramophone, the old windup type, and later a few records to go with it, and brought them home for the family."

page 21, "that *he* had invented jazz": H. O. Brunn, *Story of the Original Dixieland Jazz Band* (1960; New York: Da Capo, 1977), 251–53. Brunn describes how in the 1950s LaRocca launched a war against critics who did not properly credit him for the invention of jazz: "Newspaper columnists, authors, jazz club officials, radio networks—none who confused the provable facts of jazz history were safe. The letters, although shocking in their unrestrained vernacular, in many cases hit their mark. Whatever else may be said of the LaRocca crusade, it must be admitted that he gave no quarter." In *Lost Chords: White Musicians and Their Contribution to Jazz, 1915–1945* (New York: Oxford University Press, 1999), Richard M. Sudhalter quotes from those letters. As early as 1936, LaRocca was telling *Metronome* magazine that although "many writers have attributed this rhythm we introduced as something coming from the African jungles, and crediting the negro race with it," the truth is that "negroes learned to play this rhythm and music from the whites" (*Lost Chords*, 753). Sudhalter calls this "calumny" while still appealing to his readers not to dismiss the band's importance (*Lost Chords*, 17).

page 21, "The trombone 'chokes and gargles'": F. T. Vreeland, "Jazz, Ragtime By-Product, Revives a Lost Art of Rhythm," New York *Sun*, November 4, 1917, 50. Quoted in Charles Hersch, *Subversive Sounds: Race and the Birth of Jazz in New Orleans* (Chicago: University of Chicago Press, 2008), 181.

page 22, "meant to be used up": Scott DeVeaux, *The Birth of Bebop: A Social and Musical History* (Berkeley: University of California Press, 1997), 40. See also Scott DeVeaux and Gary Giddins, *Jazz* (New York: W. W. Norton, 2009), 150–51.

page 22, "the announcement, in 1919": H. L. Mencken, *The American Language: An Inquiry into the Development of English in the United States*, 4th edition and the two supplements, abridged, with annotations and new material by Raven I. McDavid Jr., with the assistance of David W. Maurer (1963; New York: Knopf, 1977), 743; italics in the original.

page 22, "a community steeped": Ted Gioia, *The History of Jazz* (New York: Oxford University Press, 1997), 71.

page 22, "glimpse at Davenport": Mark Twain, *Life on the Mississippi* (1883; New York: Harper and Brothers, 1901), 411. Quoted in Sharon E. Wood, *The*

Freedom of the Streets: Work, Citizenship, and Sexuality in a Gilded Age City (Chapel Hill: University of North Carolina Press, 2005), 10.

page 23, "founded Davenport": This is a fact that Bix biographies continue to get wrong. Sudhalter and Evans call Davenport "Col. Davenport's fledgling community" (*Bix: Man & Legend*, 17). Lion states that Winfield Scott drove out the Fox Indians, "permitting Colonel Davenport to found 'his' town in 1832" (*Bix: The Definitive Biography*, 2). Evans and Evans are silent on who founded the town, but they do correctly note that Colonel Davenport was the first to claim the land after it was won in the Black Hawk War (*Bix: The Leon Bix Beiderbecke Story*, 1).

page 23, "a regional entrepôt": Wood, *Freedom of the Streets*, 9.

page 23, "In 1884 the state legislature": Wood, *Freedom of the Streets*, 110.

page 23, "first German mayor . . . *die Frei Staat Scott*": Wood, *Freedom of the Streets*, 3, 115–16.

page 23, "Davenport's Storyville": "There was no Storyville in Davenport, no font of jazz creativity," writes Martin W. Laforse in *Popular Culture and American Life: Selected Topics in the Study of American Popular Culture* (with James A. Drake; Chicago: Nelson-Hall, 1981), 88, and it's true that the brothels of Bucktown were shut down in 1909, a month after Bix's sixth birthday. But it was not because of some new wave of Corn Belt conservatism sweeping over Davenport. Rather, as Wood points out, it was because of a new state law holding local mayors and police chiefs personally responsible for not enforcing state law (*Freedom of the Streets*, 161). By 1919, when Bix bought his first horn, licensed prostitutes were long gone, but at least something of the German-run city's rebellious nature likely remained.

page 23, "One such wife": *Davenport Democrat-Gazette*, April 8, 1888; quoted in Wood, *Freedom of the Streets*, 27.

page 23, "the wickedest city": *Hearst's Chicago American*, January 28, 1903; quoted in Wood, *Freedom of the Streets*, 237–38.

page 24, "with the same expression": From a lecture by the Davenport physician Jennie McCowen, "Shinbone Alley," published in the *Journal of the Iowa Auxiliary of the American Educational Aid Association* (March 1889, 9–10); quoted in Wood, *Freedom of the Streets*, 105.

page 24, "by the brook": Sudhalter and Evans, *Bix: Man & Legend*, 17.

page 24, "The pulse of that wonderful music": Interview with Alphonso "Bay" Henry, in Evans and Evans, *Bix: The Leon Bix Beiderbecke Story*, 25.

9

page 25, "sold Bix his Conn Victor": Sudhalter and Evans, *Bix: Man & Legend*, 40; Evans and Evans, *Bix: The Leon Bix Beiderbecke Story*, 45; Lion, *Bix: The Definitive Biography*, 13.

page 25, "At least one biographer": Lion, *Bix: The Definitive Biography*, 13. Lion may be following Carmichael, who writes in *Sometimes I Wonder* that Bix's unusual use of the third valve "was all wrong according to the teachers, but he got a good flow into his horn chords" (111). See also Sudhalter and Evans, *Bix: Man & Legend*, Appendix C, "And a Word about That Elusive Third Valve," 473–78.

page 25, "barely scraping through": Richard Hadlock, *Jazz Masters of the Twenties* (New York: Macmillan, 1965), 77.

page 25, "Bix is sitting at the piano": Hadlock, *Jazz Masters*, 85. His source was likely Condon, *We Called It Music*, 121.

page 25, "the cool ethos in formation": Ted Gioia, *The Birth (and Death) of the Cool* (Golden, CO: Speck, 2009), 63–64.

page 26, "Obviously, even at an early age": Collier, *The Making of Jazz*, 168–69.

page 26, "always forgot his horn": Wareing and Garlick, *Bugles for Beiderbecke*, 10–11.

page 26, "grandfather Carl . . . at First Presbyterian": Wareing and Garlick, *Bugles for Beiderbecke*, 3, 4.

page 27, "the tom-tom": Hoagy Carmichael, *The Stardust Road* (1946; New York: Da Capo, 1999), 28, 29.

page 27, "than about the fate of their one black-sheep son": Berton, *Remembering Bix*, 380.

page 28, "It's not so much that he disappointed his family": Interview with William H. Roba on March 5, 2006, in Davenport, Iowa.

page 28, "Iowa governor W. L. Harding": This history is neatly summarized in Dale Maharidge and Michael Williamson, *Denison, Iowa: Searching for the Soul of America through the Secrets of a Midwest Town* (New York: Free, 2005), 46–60.

page 29, "May 8, 1918": In "Bix Beiderbecke as a German-American," *Yearbook of German-American Studies* 45 (2010): 173, Roba cites an article in the student newspaper: *Blackhawk* 1, no. 12 (May 17, 1918).

page 29, "adult life may be viewed": Sudhalter and Evans, *Bix: Man & Legend*, 255–56.

10

page 30, "On the last day": Sudhalter and Evans, *Bix: Man & Legend*, 42; Evans and Evans, *Bix: The Leon Bix Beiderbecke Story*, 49; Lion, *Bix: The Definitive Biography*, 18.

page 30, "Fritz Putzier, meanwhile": Sudhalter and Evans, *Bix: Man & Legend*, 47–48; Evans and Evans, *Bix: The Leon Bix Beiderbecke Story*, 53; Lion, *Bix: The Definitive Biography*, 21–22.

page 30, "piles of jack": In a letter to Vera Cox dated July 10, 1920, Bix brags that he is "making piles of jack in preparation for a good time next fall with you?" (Sudhalter and Evans, *Bix: Man & Legend*, 45; Evans and Evans, *Bix: The Leon Bix Beiderbecke Story*, 52; Lion, *Bix: The Definitive Biography*, 20).

page 31, "put his arm around Bix": Interview with Fritz Putzier in the documentary film *Bix: Ain't None of Them Play Like Him Yet* (1981), written and directed by Brigitte Berman.

11

page 32, "one biographer says as much": Lion, *Bix: The Definitive Biography*, 93–94.

page 32, "It begins in *le printemps*": Grégory Elbaz, *Bix* (Bordeaux, France: Les Éditions de la Cerise, 2008). The book has no page numbers.

13

page 35, "the very best class of people": Laurence Bergreen, *Louis Armstrong: An Extravagant Life* (New York: Broadway Books, 1997), 151.

page 35, "Louis told Bix he didn't have a horn": Baby Dodds, *The Baby Dodds Story: As Told to Larry Gara*, revised edition (Alma, MI: Rebeats, 2002), 24.

page 35, "*should* meet there on the Mississippi": There has always been something mythically all-American about this particular bend in the river. It's where, for instance, a young militiaman named Abraham Lincoln battled the wizened chief Black Hawk, and a young army engineer named Robert E. Lee surveyed the rapids. On what was once Rock Island and is now Arsenal Island, the English-born trader George Davenport was murdered in his home on the Fourth of July and Dred Scott first planted his feet on free soil. Davenport, of course, is where Bix and Louis may have met, but it's also where Philip Roth's mischievous boy Portnoy travels by train one Thanksgiving in search of some "real American ass!" There, in the folds of his girlfriend's family, he finds a sun-drenched, heartfelt place that transforms him almost unwillingly into a "veritable geyser of good mornings." It was a *shiksa* paradise, the center of the world. "I pledge allegiance," he gushes, "to the twat of the United States of America—and the republic for which it stands: Davenport, Iowa!" Philip Roth, *Portnoy's Complaint* (New York: Random House, 1967), 221, 236.

page 35, "Bix was (comparatively) rich": Compared to Armstrong and his family, the Beiderbeckes were indeed rich, although reasonable people can argue whether they were middle, upper middle, or upper class.

page 36, "Sanctified Saints": For a summary of the role of religion and dancing in Armstrong's upbringing, see Thomas Brothers, *Louis Armstrong's New Orleans* (New York: W. W. Norton, 2006), 31–54.

page 36, "Bix tried to get me up there": From a 1959 interview with *Down Beat* magazine quoted by the *Chicago Tribune* in Armstrong's obituary (July 7, 1971).

page 36, "legendmongers": Berton, *Remembering Bix*, 24.

page 36, "has insisted that a white man": "A Fabrication, in My Opinion," by Albert Haim, posted on the Bixography Discussion Group, December 20, 2001. "Dreams are nice," Haim writes, "but reality is not made up of dreams."

page 37, "It was there that I met": Louis Armstrong, *Satchmo: My Life in New Orleans*, with a new introduction by Dan Morgenstern (1954; New York: Da Capo, 1986), 209.

page 37, "carefully orchestrated": William Howland Kenney, "Negotiating the Color Line: Louis Armstrong's Autobiographies," in *Jazz in Mind: Essays on the History and Meanings of Jazz*, ed. Reginald T. Buckner and Steven Weiland (Detroit, MI: Wayne State University Press, 1991), 38; quoted in Gabbard, *Jammin' at the Margins*, 214.

page 37, "uses words like he strings notes together": Quoted in Gary Giddins, *Satchmo: The Genius of Louis Armstrong* (1988; New York: Da Capo, 2001), xvi.

page 37, "justly renowned": Giddins, *Satchmo*, xvi, xvii.

page 37, "Not even the inscription": Albert Murray, "Jazz Lips," *New Republic*, November 22, 1999, 29. Murray's essay is a review of *Louis Armstrong, in His Own Words: Selected Writings* by Louis Armstrong, edited and with an introduction by Thomas Brothers (1999). In his foreword to Louis Armstrong, *Swing That Music* (New York: Da Capo, 1990), Dan Morgenstern doesn't deny that Armstrong wrote the inscription but calls it, "shall we say, politically incorrect" (ix).

page 37, "And why are scholars intent": Henry Louis Gates asks a similar question in a *New Yorker* essay examining black reactions to the not-guilty verdict in the O. J. Simpson trial. When black people stick up for Simpson's innocence, he writes, they're treated like "millenarian cultists in Texas, or Marxist deconstructionists in the academy: as things to be diagnosed, deciphered, given meaning—that is, *another* meaning." It is important that black folk not actually mean what they say "because the alternative is a population that, by [official culture's] lights, is not merely counter-normative but crazy. Black folk may mean anything at all; just not what they say they mean" ("Thirteen Ways of Looking at a Black Man," *New Yorker*, October 23, 1995).

page 38, "musicologists, while recognizing": Teachout, "Homage to Bix," 65.

page 38, "choose Louis as a subject": In my March 11, 2006, interview of Teachout, he said: "I think probably *Man & Legend* was the first jazz biography that could be compared with any accuracy to a good biography of a major writer. . . . It attempted to do what that kind of biography does. And we still have almost no jazz biographies that have been good in that way. That is my mental model in writing my Armstrong book. That's the kind of biography I want to write."

page 38, "The heart of the matter": Teachout interview on March 11, 2006.

page 39, "intruders . . . certain self-styled . . . as great performers": Albert Murray, *Stomping the Blues* (1976; New York: Da Capo, 2000), 50.

page 39, "the Bix Beiderbecke of rap": The All About Music website no longer exists, although the phrase remains as a kind of Internet detritus.

page 39, "well-meaning amateurs": In the preface to *Early Jazz: Its Roots and Musical Development* (New York: Oxford University Press, 1968), Gunther Schuller writes: "The majority of books [about jazz] have concentrated on the legendry of jazz, and over the years a body of writing has accumulated which is little more than an amalgam of well-meaning amateur criticism and fascinated opinion" (vii).

page 39, "he calls Beiderbecke an 'innovator'": Baraka, *Blues People*, 149.

page 39, "a common cultural ground": Baraka, *Blues People*, 150.

page 40, "The white middle-class boy from Iowa": Baraka, *Blues People*, 153–54.

page 41, "John F. Szwed has singled out Sudhalter": In Will Friedwald et al., *The Future of Jazz*, ed. Yuval Taylor (Chicago: A Cappella Books, 2002), various critics and scholars write and respond to each other. In "Black and White and Turning Gray: Jazz and Race," Szwed writes: "The mention of Sudhalter's *Lost Chords* gives me an opportunity to comment on the persistence of efforts to deny African and African American contributions to world culture. We are aware of the perniciousness of such projects when they surface as heavily publicized books from right-wing think tanks, but less likely to see their damage when they come from our own ranks. . . . [Sudhalter] conflates race ('color') and culture in order to portray anyone as a racist who makes a claim for black preeminence in jazz" (*Future of Jazz*, 36).

page 41, "to read Lincoln Collier": "Jazz & the White Critic: Thirty Years Later," on Baraka's website. The term *Ubermenschlichkeit* comes from Nietzsche and refers to the "whole man" who has reconciled the warring opposites within him, such as passion and reason or, in this case, black and white.

page 41, "LeRoi Jones is always signifyin' like hell": Interview with Fredrick Woodard on April 9, 2006, in Iowa City.

page 42, "Beiderbecke ceases": Stanley Crouch, "The Negro Aesthetic of Jazz," in *Considering Genius: Writings on Jazz* (New York: Basic *Civitas* Books, 2006), 212. Crouch was reacting to this, from the same essay: "Martin Williams, the late, great jazz critic and himself a white Southerner, told me [i.e., Crouch] once that there used to be a group of white jazz musicians who would say, when there were only white guys around, 'Louis Armstrong and those people had a nice little primitive thing going, but we really didn't have what we now call jazz until Jack Teagarden, Bix, Trumbauer, and their gang gave it some sophistication'" (*Considering Genius*, 212).

page 43, "Faite Maribores bunch": In *Jazz on the River* (Chicago: University of Chicago Press, 2005) William Howland Kenney writes: "His precision about the location indicates that he had encountered Marible's orchestra not in Davenport but rather in a chance meeting of riverboats in July 1921, when he was playing in Doc Wrixon's Ten *Capitol* Harmony Syncopators" (123). The letter, which is dated September 17, 1921, and addressed to his siblings Burnie and Mary Louise, is reprinted in Evans and Evans, *Bix: The Leon Bix Beiderbecke Story*, 68–70. See also Lion, *Bix: The Definitive Biography*, 33.

page 43, "Other historians have pointed out": Sue Fischer, "Bix Beiderbecke and the New Orleans Rhythm Kings," a lecture delivered at the Bix Beiderbecke Memorial Jazz Festival in Davenport, July 2008.

page 43, "Still, Teachout wasn't convinced": To be clear, I did not present Teachout specifically with Bix's letter or Fischer's research.

page 43, "This is not a joke": In his novel *Sophie's Choice*, William Styron memorably describes Guy Lombardo's music as "glutinously innocuous," while the early jazz critic Otis Ferguson calls it "a scrupulously edited version of nothing at all." William Styron, *Sophie's Choice* (1979; New York: Vintage International, 1992), 215; Otis Ferguson, "Jazz at Random," in *The Otis Ferguson Reader*, ed. Dorothy Chamberlain and Robert Wilson (Highland Park, IL: December, 1982), 108.

page 43, "all of a sudden": Shapiro and Hentoff, *Hear Me Talkin' to Ya*, 158–59. Ellipses are in the original.

page 44, "not necessarily a compliment": Kenney, *Jazz on the River*, 123.

14

page 45, "I'm sitting here": Tom Hallett, "Whoops! A Little Lesson in Jazz History," *Pulse of the Twin Cities*, February 19, 2003.

15

page 46, "funny-looking man": In *Movers and Shakers: Volume Three of Intimate Memories* (New York: Harcourt Brace, 1936), Luhan describes the "funny-looking man [sitting] opposite me. . . . His name was Carl Van Vechten and he came of Dutch parentage; this, perhaps, explained the porcine texture of his skin and the suggestion of the wild boar in him, for many Hollanders have that quality" (15). She goes on to describe how "when he laughed, little shrieks flew out between the slits in his big teeth" (15). Van Vechten's biographer, Bruce Kellner, was also impressed by Van Vechten's teeth, calling them "incredible" and writing, "He looked like a genial walrus." Bruce Kellner, *Carl Van Vechten and the Irreverent Decades* (Norman: University of Oklahoma Press, 1968), xi.

page 46, "propinquity": On May 8, 2006, Teachout wrote about Van Vechten on his blog, About Last Night, confessing to his envy "of what you might call his achievements in the field of propinquity. Among many, many other things, he attended both the Armory Show in New York *and* the Paris premiere of *The Rite of Spring*, at which he shared a box with Gertrude Stein and Alice B. Toklas, who subsequently became his lifelong friends."

page 46, "Van Vechten admitted to feeling": Ann Douglas, *Terrible Honesty: Mongrel Manhattan in the 1920s* (New York: Noonday, 1996), 288.

page 46, "he went so far": John Gennari, *Blowin' Hot and Cool: Jazz and Its Critics* (Chicago: University of Chicago Press, 2006), 32.

page 46, "prompted *Vanity Fair* to accuse him": Kellner, *Carl Van Vechten*, 198.

page 46, "The Mexican painter Miguel Covarrubias": Kellner, *Carl Van Vechten*, 198. Covarrubias was a protégé of Van Vechten and introduced him to photography.

page 47, "Van Vechten even appended a footnote": Carl Van Vechten, *Nigger Heaven* (1926; Urbana: University of Illinois Press, 2000), 26. Countee Cullen, whose poetry provides the novel's epigraph, "turned white with rage" at Van Vechten's choice of words and gave Carlo the silent treatment for fourteen years (*Nigger Heaven*, xiv).

page 47, "express our dark-skinned selves": Langston Hughes, "The Negro Artist and the Racial Mountain," *Nation*, June 23, 1926; quoted in Gennari, *Blowin' Hot and Cool*, 30.

page 47, "honorary Negro": Quoted by Emily Bernard in her introduction to Langston Hughes, *Remember Me to Harlem: The Letters of Langston Hughes and Carl Van Vechten* (New York: Vintage, 2002), xix.

page 47, "he took literally": Douglas, *Terrible Honesty*, 288. Gennari contrasts Van Vechten's attempts at passing with those of the seminal jazz critics John Hammond and Leonard Feather. The former's fantasy was to be "the kind of Jew who helped blacks," while the latter, who was British, "understood that the key to his insider status was his foreignness. His cachet in the black community came from whiteness—a whiteness that was different from the American whiteness that blacks couldn't help but distrust" (Gennari, *Blowin' Hot and Cool*, 32).

page 47, "A major way many white youth": Michael Eric Dyson, *Open Mike: Reflections on Philosophy, Race, Sex, Culture and Religion* (New York: Basic Civitas Books, 2002), 193.

page 48, "I get around": Condon, *We Called It Music*, 121.

page 48, "Ellison calls to mind": Letter dated June 2, 1957; in Ralph Ellison, *Living with Music: Ralph Ellison's Jazz Writings*, ed. Robert G. O'Meally (New York: Modern Library, 2001), 240–44.

page 48, "Jazz is musical humor": "Bix Beiderbecke," *Davenport Democrat and Leader*, February 10, 1929; reprinted in Evans and Evans, *Bix: The Leon Bix Beiderbecke Story*, 430–32. See also Sudhalter and Evans, *Bix: Man & Legend*, 267–69; Lion, *Bix: The Definitive Biography*, 209–10.

page 48, "the innocent who": Scott Yanow, *Trumpet Kings: The Players Who Shaped the Sound of Jazz Trumpet* (San Francisco: Backbeat Books, 2001), 49.

page 48, "naive," "a trusting sort": Sudhalter and Evans, *Bix: Man & Legend*, 325. Challis was suggesting that admirers such as Eddie Condon hung around Bix too much and kept him drunk. Bix trusted everybody, Challis said, and "was well-liked by most people. But the thing is, they made fun of his drinking. They made fun of his remarks. Good old Bix—everything was funny to them."

page 48, "this big overgrown kid": Mezzrow and Wolfe, *Really the Blues*, 78.

page 48, "he of the funny little mouth": Carmichael, *The Stardust Road*, 65.

page 49, "a lost child": Collier, *The Making of Jazz*, 169.

page 49, "like flowing water": Woodard interview on April 9, 2006.

page 49, "As Bix might have said": Berton quotes his brother Eugene: "*You know his favorite phrase: 'What the hell.' That was about where he stood, on nearly everything but his music: What the hell*" (*Remembering Bix*, 392).

page 49, "lithe African beauty": Quoted in Gennari, *Blowin' Hot and Cool*, 32, from Van Vechten's 1930 novel, *Parties: Scenes from Contemporary New York Life*. Carlo's language is similar in *Nigger Heaven* (the word "lithe" appears in the second sentence); elsewhere he refers to one woman's "queenly African manner" (21).

page 49, "it's an obsession with 'the primitive'": Kathleen Pfeiffer, in her introduction to Van Vechten's *Nigger Heaven*, notes Kellner's point that "Van Vechten himself never used the term 'primitive,' the one adjective which, ironically, is most often hurled at him by hostile critics" (xxxiv). I am not at all hostile to Van Vechten; still, my reaction to that is so what? One hardly needs to use the word "primitive" to invoke it as an idea.

page 49, "the negroes are rhythmic as rain": Corby's poem is titled "Trumpeter"; Wareing and Garlick, *Bugles for Beiderbecke*, v. It first appeared in Herbert Corby, *Time in a Blue Prison* (London: Fortune, 1947), 41.

page 49, "People used to ask Bix": Shapiro and Hentoff, *Hear Me Talkin' to Ya*, 157–58. See also Evans and Evans, *Bix: The Leon Bix Beiderbecke Story*, 539.

page 49, "Jazz and freedom go hand in hand": Quoted in Dan Morgenstern,

"Integrating Jazz," in *Reading Jazz*, ed. Sheldon Meyer (New York: Pantheon, 2004), 667.

page 50, "I use the term 'jazz' here": Cornel West, *Race Matters* (New York: Vintage, 1994), 150.

page 50, "Jack Kerouac, for instance": Quoted in David Sterritt, "Revision, Prevision, and the Aura of Improvisatory Art," *The Journal of Aesthetics and Art Criticism* 58, no. 2 (Spring 2000): 163.

page 50, "Malcolm Lowry . . . claimed": Letter to the Irish writer and translator James Stern dated May 7, 1940; in Malcolm Lowry, *Selected Letters* (Philadelphia: Lippincott, 1965), 28. Lowry is arguing that a good short-story writer "is capable of writing the best kind of novel, something that is bald and winnowed, like Sibelius, and that makes an odd but splendid din, like Bix Beiderbecke."

page 50, "Sometimes I think that his idea": From Malcolm Cowley's introduction to Ferguson, *Otis Ferguson Reader*, xi. Cowley was one of Ferguson's editors at the *New Republic*; here he is quoting Ferguson from "Young Man with a Horn," which appeared in the *New Republic* on July 29, 1936, 354–55, and is reprinted in Ferguson, *Otis Ferguson Reader*, 19–21.

page 50, "Leon Wieseltier once tried": Leon Wieseltier, "All and Nothing at All: The Unreal World of Cornel West," *New Republic*, March 6, 1995, 31–36. The jazz scholar Robert G. O'Meally argues that jazz—especially in the academy—has come to stand for everything, not just freedom and democracy. "What is bowling? What is biology? What's a poem?" he asks. "They are not structures in a numbered series of disappearing 'texts'; that was last year. Now they are jazz." Ironically, this was written by way of introduction to *The Jazz Cadence of American Culture* (1998; ix), an anthology that commits exactly these sorts of so-called sins. I imagine that this is O'Meally's Van Vechtean way of saying that he knows what he's doing, even if it isn't right. Although perhaps "right" isn't the right word. It's not about right or wrong. Jazz is a metaphor, and an apt one for many circumstances. But jazz is also *not* a metaphor. It's a complicated and beautiful and real thing. As Wieseltier said, it's art, and therefore has no more to do with freedom than the structure of a sonnet has to do with fascism.

page 50, "Music is a brilliant agent of ideology": Ruth Padel, *I'm a Man: Sex, Gods and Rock 'n' Roll* (London: Faber and Faber, 2000), 6.

page 50, "You hear a song . . . second-hand myths": Padel, *I'm a Man*, 9.

16

page 51, "belted it out": Ethel Waters with Charles Samuels, *His Eye Is on the Sparrow: An Autobiography* (New York: Da Capo, 1992), 189.

page 51, "he eschews the gutbucket growls": A version of this description of "I'm Coming Virginia" was originally published in Brendan Wolfe, "The Dozens: Essential Bix Beiderbecke," Jazz.com, March 9, 2008.

page 51, "'correlated' phrases": Sudhalter, *Stardust Melody*, 110.

page 51, "Caravaggio-like shafts of light": Sudhalter, *Lost Chords*, 419.

page 51, "The world of Greek mythology": Edith Hamilton, *Mythology: Timeless Tales of Gods and Heroes* (Boston: Little, Brown, 1942), 10.

page 52, "I lifted the platter": Gary Giddins, *Weather Bird: Jazz at the Dawn of the Second Century* (New York: Oxford University Press, 2004), xvii.

17

page 53, "There is always a poignancy": Randy Sandke, *Bix Beiderbecke: Observing a Genius at Work* (self-published, 1996), 16; quoted in Lion, *Bix: The Definitive Biography*, 135. Sandke is widely considered to be the best cornetist in the Bixian style working today. His comment reminds me of Steven Spielberg, who once described Michael Jackson as being "like a fawn in a burning forest" (quoted in Michael Kinsley, "The Prisoner of Commerce," *New Republic*, April 16, 1984, 4).

18

page 54, "likening himself to Billy the Kid . . . got me high": Baraka, *Blues People*, vii.

page 54, "Well, first of all": Phone interview with Amiri Baraka on December 18, 2009. I have edited portions of the interview transcript for clarity.

page 54, "go inside an idea": Woodard interview on April 9, 2006.

page 55, "his long poem about 9/11": The poem is reprinted on Baraka's website.

page 55, "a 'detonation'": Baraka writes: "The poem's own detonation caused the author's photo and words to be splashed across the pages of New York's *Amsterdam News* and the *New York Times* and to be featured on CNN."

page 55, "The Newark public schools": Andrew Jacobs, "Criticized Poet Is Named Laureate of Newark Schools," *New York Times*, December 19, 2002.

page 56, "My thing about Sudhalter": I have edited Baraka's remarks here for clarity. The original transcript reads: "My thing about Sudhalter is him claiming that the music rose up spontaneously within the Afro-American community post-slavery and a white origination, which would either make slavery a common cultural background or at least diminish the influence that slavery, and the Afro-American culture that developed out of that, had on the rest of the United States."

page 57, "The article to which Baraka referred": Richard M. Sudhalter, "A Racial Divide That Needn't Be," *New York Times*, January 3, 1999.

page 58, "became Young's chief inspiration": The critic Martin Williams suggests that Bix, too, influenced Young's famously cool style. "I doubt if a man who carried *Singin' the Blues* around in his tenor case was unaffected by Bix's part in it," Williams writes in *The Jazz Tradition* (New York: Oxford, 1993, 1970), 69.

page 58, "research into the origins": Sudhalter, *Lost Chords*, xvii.

page 58, "This earned him a rebuke": Jason Berry, "White Men Can Jam," *New York Times*, July 11, 1999.

page 58, "a tradition now known to be shared": Quoted in Berry, "White Men Can Jam."

page 59, "Marsalis talks constantly": Eric Nisenson, *Blue: The Murder of Jazz* (New York: Da Capo, 1997), 31.

page 60, "must have been much like tasting real eggs": Baraka, *Blues People*, 147.

19

page 62, "the apparent delusion of parents": Lion, *Bix: The Definitive Biography*, 30.

page 62, "unexcused absences": For a summary of Bix's short time at Lake Forest, see Sudhalter and Evans, *Bix: Man & Legend*, 61–75; Lion, *Bix: The Definitive Biography*, 29–44. See also Evans and Evans, *Bix: The Leon Bix Beiderbecke Story*, 63–109, but I'd hardly call the latter a summary. The authors are typically exhaustive, informing readers, for instance, that Bix's Lake Forest baseball team was shut out by Marquette Academy 5–0 in May 1922 (precise date unclear) (*Bix: The Leon Bix Beiderbecke Story*, 109).

page 62, "He was finally expelled": See Sudhalter and Evans, *Bix: Man & Legend*, 77–98; Evans and Evans, *Bix: The Leon Bix Beiderbecke Story*, 110–40; Lion, *Bix: The Definitive Biography*, 44–61.

page 63, "The more I read about Bix": E-mail received from Barbara Wascher on November 25, 2009.

page 63, "a note to Agatha": Evans and Evans, *Bix: The Leon Bix Beiderbecke Story*, 105–6.

page 63, "By a faculty vote": Evans and Evans, *Bix: The Leon Bix Beiderbecke Story*, 109.

page 64, "Mr. Richards noted": Lion, *Bix: The Definitive Biography*, 42–44.

20

page 65, "It was the spring of 1924": My ideas in this section have been heavily influenced by an unpublished essay by Barbara Wascher and the e-mail conversation between us that inspired it.

page 65, "The moon was always out . . . I like it different": Carmichael, *The Stardust Road*, 65–66.

page 66, "So he wrote this": Carmichael, *Sometimes I Wonder*, 127.

page 66, "clumsy, half-loaded . . . moaning softly . . . the music filled us both": Carmichael, *Sometimes I Wonder*, 127.

page 66, "One morning Bix and I came out": Evans and Evans, *Bix: The Leon Bix Beiderbecke Story*, 190.

page 66, "When we all got high": Sudhalter and Evans, *Bix: Man & Legend*, 145. See also Evans and Evans, *Bix: The Leon Bix Beiderbecke Story*, 194.

page 67, "Paul Mertz recalled": Interview with Mertz in Berman, *Ain't None of Them Play Like Him Yet*.

page 67, "hurts you across . . . another long pause": Carmichael, *The Stardust Road*, 68.

page 67, "Bix fixation borders": Peter B. Lowry, untitled review of *Stardust Melody: The Life and Music of Hoagy Carmichael* by Richard M. Sudhalter, *IAJRC Journal* 39, no. 3 (August 2006): 88.

21

page 68, "We had more than you think . . . by a 'fling'?": Berton, *Remembering Bix*, 391–92.

22

page 69, "whom he had first met in Davenport": Sudhalter and Evans, *Bix: Man & Legend*, 86; Evans and Evans, *Bix: The Leon Bix Beiderbecke Story*, 125–26; Lion, *Bix: The Definitive Biography*, 49.

page 69, "Ted Jansen band . . . Bix takes Ruth bowling": Sudhalter and Evans, *Bix: Man & Legend*, 354. Phil Evans took this chronology and expanded it for the book he wrote with his wife. For instance, we now know that on the next day, November 6, Bix didn't just attend the St. Louis Symphony; he heard Beethoven's *Egmont Overture* and Dvořák's *New World Symphony* (Evans and Evans, *Bix: The Leon Bix Beiderbecke Story*, 198–99).

page 69, "In Dayton": Sudhalter and Evans, *Bix: Man & Legend*, 360.

page 69, "Band in Scranton": Sudhalter and Evans, *Bix: Man & Legend*, 361.

page 69, "Whiteman records for Victor": Sudhalter and Evans, *Bix: Man & Legend*, 365.

page 69, "Whiteman records for Victor on February 7 . . . September": Sudhalter and Evans, *Bix: Man & Legend*, 366–69.

page 70, "One night, when Bix didn't show up": Interview with Karl Spaeth, in Evans and Evans, *Bix: The Leon Bix Beiderbecke Story*, 198.

page 70, "looked like a farmboy": Berton, *Remembering Bix*, 49.

page 70, "under the rusty tux": Otis Ferguson, "Young Man with a Horn Again," *New Republic*, November 18, 1940, 693; in Ferguson, *Otis Ferguson Reader*, 28. Does Ferguson mean "dusty" here?

page 70, "unkempt, even smelly": In an article about the origins of the word "funky," the folk-etymologist Peter Tamony points out that "the celebrated Bix Beiderbecke was said to have been funky because of his careless personal habits." An earlier article from the same publication also mentions Bix, referring to his "inability to take care of himself," and positing that his "smoke-filled, whisky-saturated surroundings" were at least partly to blame: "The jazz man feels deeply the frustration of his environment and responds to it with self-abandon and, often, self-violation." Peter Tamony, "Funky," *American Speech* 55, no. 3 (Autumn 1980): 212; Robert S. Gold, "The Vernacular of the Jazz World," *American Speech* 32, no. 4 (December 1957): 279.

page 70, "Who is this guy": Carmichael, *Sometimes I Wonder*, 128.

page 70, "According to the one-armed trumpeter": Wingy Manone with Paul Vandervoort, *Trumpet on the Wing* (New York: Doubleday, 1948), 59.

page 71, "the usual dilemma . . . Bix said": Condon, *We Called It Music*, 122.

page 72, "a false, or pivot, tooth": Sudhalter and Evans, *Bix: Man & Legend*, 185; Evans and Evans, *Bix: The Leon Bix Beiderbecke Story*, 230–31; Lion, *Bix: The Definitive Biography*, 125–26. See also Bill Crow, *Jazz Anecdotes: Second Time Around* (New York: Oxford University Press, 2005).

23

page 73, "walking barefoot . . . *untalented bastards*": Berton, *Remembering Bix*, 183.

page 73, "almost totally ineffectual": Collier, *The Making of Jazz*, 168.

page 73, "an impossible little shit": E-mail received from Barbara Wascher on April 3, 2009.

page 73, "I never said more than two words": Gene Lees, "Emily Remler," in *Waiting for Dizzy: Fourteen Jazz Portraits* (New York: Cooper Square, 2000), 136.

page 74, "At bottom the man": Burnett James, *Bix Beiderbecke* (London: Cassell, 1959), 25. James argues that Bix's personality contributed to his style but also to his death. "Which is not, of course, to argue that a man's biography is reproduced in his work," he writes. "That is a stupid and flabby notion against which criticism has to be constantly on its guard."

page 74, "Talent and character": Interview with Geoff Muldaur on May 18, 2009, in Charlottesville, Virginia.

page 74, "Bix's personality problems": Collier, *The Making of Jazz*, 169.

page 76, "an idealized image . . . resemblance to its model": Lion, *Bix: The Definitive Biography*, 60.

24

page 78, "*une Bixographie spirituelle*": This is the title of Thierry Smolderen's preface to Elbaz, *Bix*.

page 78, "The drawings are horrendous": "A Weird Book about Bix," by Albert Haim, posted on the Bixography Discussion Group, July 7, 2008.

page 79, "Gregor awoke to find himself an *Ungeziefer*": See Franz Kafka, *The Metamorphosis*, introduction and explanatory notes by Stanley Corngold (1915; New York: Random House, 1986), 63.

page 79, "Think of the painting": See Susan Power Bratton, *Environmental Values in Christian Art* (Albany: State University of New York Press, 2008), 191.

page 80, "perfectly normal": Ferguson, "Young Man with a Horn Again," in *Otis Ferguson Reader*, 29.

page 80, "simple goodness and loyalty": Ferguson, "Young Man with a Horn Again," in *Otis Ferguson Reader*, 28.

page 80, "swinging free . . . herd of mustangs": Ferguson, "Young Man with a Horn," in *Otis Ferguson Reader*, 20, 21.

page 80, "so generally hardy": Ferguson, "Young Man with a Horn Again," in *Otis Ferguson Reader*, 28.

page 80, "Jazz was the country": Ferguson, "Young Man with a Horn Again," in *Otis Ferguson Reader*, 31.

page 80, "gross": "gross grosz," by Callum Kenmuir, posted on the Bixography Discussion Group, November 19, 2008.

page 80, "really revolting . . . Just ugly drawings": "I Agree," by Laura Demilio, posted on the Bixography Discussion Group, November 1, 2008.

page 80, "Poor Bix!": "A Weird Book about Bix," by Albert Haim, posted on the Bixography Discussion Group, July 7, 2008.

page 81, "It's obvious that [Bix]": "I Agree," by Laura Demilio, posted on the Bixography Discussion Group, November 1, 2008.

page 81, "Looks more like Henry Busse": "Re: Poor Bix!!" by Hal Smith, posted on the Bixography Discussion Group, October 31, 2008.

page 81, "Still another": "gross grosz," by Callum Kenmuir, posted on the Bixography Discussion Group, November 19, 2008.

page 81, "The expression on the face": A version of this description of "Way Down Yonder in New Orleans" was originally published in Wolfe, "The Dozens: Essential Bix Beiderbecke," Jazz.com, March 9, 2008.

26

page 83, "October 12, 1926": As if to mock my attempt to make dramatic hay of this date, the books can't agree on October 12. Lion gives that date

(*Bix: The Definitive Biography*, 126) while Evans and Evans seem to prefer October 6 (*Bix: The Leon Bix Beiderbecke Story*, 227), as do Sudhalter and Evans (*Bix: Man & Legend*, 183). It seems to be the case that Goldkette opened at the Roseland on the sixth, and Henderson not until the twelfth, when both bands shared the stage for the first time. Sudhalter and Evans, however, seem to conflate the two dates, making the battle happen a week earlier than it did.

page 83, "Two of the finest": *New York Times*, October 12, 1926, 31. Quoted in Evans and Evans, *Bix: The Leon Bix Beiderbecke Story*, 232.

page 83, "the *New York Daily News* promised": *New York Daily News*, October 12, 1926. Quoted in Lion, *Bix: The Definitive Biography*, 125.

page 83, "it was very quiet": Interview with Willcox in Berman, *Ain't None of Them Play Like Him Yet.*

page 84, "Bix left Detroit for Iowa City": Sudhalter and Evans, *Bix: Man & Legend*, 132–33; Lion, *Bix: The Definitive Biography*, 94–95. William P. Fleckenstein played for the Chicago Bears from 1925 until 1930. Sudhalter and Evans spell his name Flechenstein.

page 84, "That a place of instruction should refuse": Green, *Reluctant Art*, 29.

page 85, "I mean, put it this way": Sudhalter and Evans, *Bix: Man & Legend*, 185; italics in the original. Rex Stewart tells the same story in Rex Stewart, *Jazz Masters of the Thirties* (New York: Macmillan, 1972), 11-12.

page 86, "As humiliating as it may have been": The Fletcher Henderson Orchestra recorded "Singing the Blues (Till My Daddy Comes Home)," featuring Rex Stewart on cornet, on October 15, 1931.

page 86, "I bumped into two of those": Evans and Evans, *Bix: The Leon Bix Beiderbecke Story*, 233.

27

page 87, "he twined the herky-jerky": A version of this description of "In a Mist" was originally published in Wolfe, "The Dozens: Essential Bix Beiderbecke," Jazz.com, March 9, 2008.

page 87, "feels a bit clunky": In a journal entry dated August 24, 1939, the Trappist monk Thomas Merton disagreed, suggesting that "In a Mist" has a "very complicated perfect ending," one that calls forth a "movement of light . . . and for a tenth of a second it was like being lifted through the sky: and things almost all stopped and lost their diversity and knit themselves together as they ought to be, and then I caught my breath and fell out of it laughing and crying." See Thomas Merton, *Run to the Mountain: The Story of a Vocation; The Journal of Thomas Merton, Volume 1: 1939-1941* (New York: HarperCollins, 2009).

page 87, "I'm in a fog": Sudhalter and Evans, *Bix: Man & Legend*, 217. Sudhalter and Evans peppered their book with speculative dialogue based on descriptions of scenes and conversations.

page 88, "number-one recording artist": An inference drawn from Elijah Wald, *How the Beatles Destroyed Rock 'n' Roll: An Alternative History of American Popular Music* (New York: Oxford University Press, 2009), 76–77. Wald writes, "When *Talking Machine Journal* announced in 1923 that Whiteman had become the best-selling artist on Victor—the most popular record label in the world—he was taking over that honor from Enrico Caruso."

page 88, "the self-proclaimed Calathumpic": Don Rayno, *Paul Whiteman: Pioneer in American Music, Volume I: 1890–1930* (Lanham, MD: Scarecrow, 2003), 94.

page 88, "a bladderish man": Niven Busch Jr., "The Paid Piper," *New Yorker*, November 27, 1926, 25.

page 88, "jazz classique": Rayno, *Paul Whiteman*, 34.

page 88, "formed in December 1918": Rayno, *Paul Whiteman*, 25–26.

page 88, "Paul got the music out of the cellars": Rayno, *Paul Whiteman*, xxiii.

page 88, "seventeen-story skyscraper": "Aeolian Hall Sold," *Time Magazine*, August 11, 1924.

page 88, "There, on February 12, 1924": Rayno, *Paul Whiteman*, 84–86.

page 88, "was a huge success": So long as success isn't judged by the balance sheets. Whiteman actually lost $7,000 on the concert (Rayno, *Paul Whiteman*, 86).

page 88, "an amusing mountebank . . . incessant Chesterfields": Busch, "The Paid Piper," 25, 26.

page 89, "Bix Beiderbecke lived very briefly . . . humble and right": Ferguson, *Otis Ferguson Reader*, 19.

page 89, "A people can no more indulge": Interview with Alfred Hertz, "Thinks Jazz Music Allied to Alcohol," *Santa Barbara Daily News*, June 5, 1919; quoted in Rayno, *Paul Whiteman*, 29.

page 89, "The cultural critic Curtis White": See Curtis White, *The Middle Mind: Why Americans Don't Think for Themselves* (San Francisco: HarperSanFrancisco, 2003).

page 89, "a gorgeous piece of impudence": Olin Downes, "A Concert of Jazz," *New York Times*, February 13, 1924; quoted in Rayno, *Paul Whiteman*, 84.

page 89, "the inspiration for the writing of this book": Dorothy Baker, *Young Man with a Horn* (1938; New York: Press of the Readers Club, 1943), xi.

page 90, "a bed of his own": Baker, *Young Man with a Horn*, 9.

page 90, "The story ends with death": Baker, *Young Man with a Horn*, 4.

page 90, "the slick fellow": Baker, *Young Man with a Horn*, 149. For more on Baker's novel and Bix, see John Paul Perhonis, *The Bix Beiderbecke Story: The Jazz Musician in Legend, Fiction, and Fact; A Study of the Images of Jazz in the National Culture: 1930–Present* (unpublished dissertation, University of Minnesota, March 1978), 97–143.

page 90, "It had been a cash deal": Baker, *Young Man with a Horn*, 155.

page 90, "looked at Smoke Jordan's black face": Baker, *Young Man with a Horn*, 161.

page 90, "was at home now": Baker, *Young Man with a Horn*, 163.

page 91, "It was an organization . . . people out on the floor": Baker, *Young Man with a Horn*, 170–71.

page 91, "Boy, you must have got good": Baker, *Young Man with a Horn*, 163.

page 91, "I don't know what the hell that boy": Baker, *Young Man with a Horn*, 230.

page 91, "In the first place maybe he shouldn't": Baker, *Young Man with a Horn*, 9.

page 91, "knew Bix's worth": James, *Bix Beiderbecke*, 15.

page 92, "playing a lot of music": James, *Bix Beiderbecke*, 18–19.

page 92, "If his destiny had led him": James, *Bix Beiderbecke*, 77.

page 92, "title of a Sex Pistols song": "The Great Rock 'n' Roll Swindle," off the 1979 album of the same name.

page 92, "for himself he gets a chateau": Robert Pattison, *The Triumph of Vulgarity: Rock Music in the Mirror of Romanticism* (New York: Oxford University Press, 1987), 149.

page 93, "So far from being a moral coward": Green, *Reluctant Art*, 38.

page 93, "a mediocre vaudeville act . . . the pitiful gulf": Green, *Reluctant Art*, 38, 39.

28

page 94, "The records Bix made with Paul Whiteman": Berton, *Remembering Bix*, 367.

page 94, "colleagues . . . feeling bound or stifled": Sudhalter, *Lost Chords*, 423.

page 95, "admirable . . . no question it was admired": Schuller, *Early Jazz*, 192. Publishing in 1968, Schuller bravely defends Whiteman, but only in a footnote.

page 95, "even Duke Ellington loved Whiteman": Wald, *How the Beatles Destroyed Rock 'n' Roll*, 74. Wald quotes Ellington as calling Whiteman "one of the truly great musicians of the jazz era," and then suggests that Ellington modeled his approach to jazz on Whiteman's.

page 95, "as Grover Sales has done": Grover Sales, *Jazz: America's Classical*

Music (New York: Da Capo, 1992), 5. Sales compares Ellington's music, and that of Charlie Parker and John Coltrane, to "the Beethoven Quartets and Bach's *Goldberg Variations.*"

page 95, "It is an irony of fate": Norman Gentieu, "Some Comments," in Rayno, *Paul Whiteman*, ix.

page 95, "tended toward ballyhoo": Rayno, *Paul Whiteman*, 94.

page 95, "that fictitious superlative": Rayno, *Paul Whiteman*, 94.

page 96, "Calathumpian music": Louis C. Elson, *Elson's Music Dictionary; Containing the Definition and Pronunciation of Such Terms as Are Used in Modern Music* (Boston: Oliver Ditson, 1905), 44. Elson was a professor of music theory at the New England Conservatory.

page 96, "an assortment of Calathumpians": Thomas Pynchon, *Mason & Dixon* (New York: Henry Holt, 1997), 582.

page 96, "The man with the clarinet": Olin Downes, "A Concert of Jazz," *New York Times*, February 13, 1924; quoted in Rayno, *Paul Whiteman*, 84.

page 97, "When [the audience] laughed": Paul Whiteman and Mary Margaret McBride, *Jazz* (1926; New York: Arno, 1974), 104; quoted in Rayno, *Paul Whiteman*, 84.

page 97, "Ann Douglas points out": Douglas, *Terrible Honesty*, 75–76. Elsewhere in *Terrible Honesty* she notes: "In later, still more successful presentations of the Aeolian Hall material, Whiteman made less and less effort to instruct his listeners as to what was serious, what burlesque, what good, what bad. Who, after all, could say?" (350–51).

29

page 99, "Whiteman just agonizingly": Muldaur interview on May 18, 2009.

page 99, "waxed just days before": Lion, *Bix: The Definitive Biography*, 160. The recording date was October 25, 1927.

page 99, "the way its opening, grenade-burst staccato": A version of this description of "Sorry" was originally published in Wolfe, "The Dozens: Essential Bix Beiderbecke," Jazz.com, March 9, 2008.

page 99, "Lion twice uses the word 'astonishing'": Lion, *Bix: The Definitive Biography*, 161.

page 99, "I have never felt better": Evans and Evans, *Bix: The Leon Bix Beiderbecke Story*, 297. The quotation, which originally comes from Esten Spurrier, appears in slightly different form in Lion (*Bix: The Definitive Biography*, 161).

page 99, "recorded a month later": Lion, *Bix: The Definitive Biography*, 316. The recording date was November 25, 1927.

page 100, "Gioia writes that the jazz . . . called it 'hot music'": Gioia, *The Birth (and Death) of the Cool*, 58.

page 100, "There was a surface level . . . to the whole proceedings": Gioia, *The Birth (and Death) of the Cool*, 58–59.

page 100, "we encounter all the inner contradictions . . . cool personified": Gioia, *The Birth (and Death) of the Cool*, 60.

page 100, "the most fascinating": Gioia, *The Birth (and Death) of the Cool*, 61.

page 100, "the forerunners of the personality type": Gioia, *The Birth (and Death) of the Cool*, 60.

page 100, "the Kurt Cobain of the 1920s": Chris Lehmann, "In a Mist," a review of the novel *1929*, by Frederick Turner, *Washington Post*, June 22, 2003.

page 100, "the malleability of his life": Gioia, *The Birth (and Death) of the Cool*, 62.

page 101, "reinvented his life": Gioia, *The Birth (and Death) of the Cool*, 63.

page 101, "approximates a feeling": Robert S. Greene, "Bix," *The Record Changer* 8, no. 5 (May 1949): 8; quoted in Perhonis, *Bix Beiderbecke Story*, 153. Greene writes: "Legend has a trick of aging the memory, and with Bix the legend and the man, his music and his life, have gradually all come together into what approximates a feeling rather than an historical fact."

page 101, "Bix was never actually a person": Condon, *We Called It Music*, 102.

page 101, "the best thing about it": Vance Bourjaily, "In and Out of Storyville: Jazz and Fiction," *New York Times*, December 13, 1987.

page 102, "there is absolutely no connection": "A Grotesque Distortion of Bix's Legacy," by Albert Haim, posted on the Bixography Discussion Group, April 15, 2005.

page 102, "Bix could have kicked": "Bix could have kicked Elvis' ass in a race anyday . . ." by Bridget [Calzaretta], posted on the Bixography Discussion Group, April 15, 2005.

page 102, "the symbol, or the byword": Gilbert Seldes, *The Seven Lively Arts* (1924; New York: Sagamore, 1957), 83.

page 102, "jazz has come to stay": Kathy J. Ogren, *The Jazz Revolution: Twenties America and the Meaning of Jazz* (New York: Oxford University Press, 1989), 7; quoted in Mitchell Breitwieser, "Jazz Fractures: F. Scott Fitzgerald and Epochal Representation," *American Literary History* 12, no. 3 (Autumn 2000): 368.

page 102, "the perfect music for Bix": As much as Bix can be seen as proto-cool, his music was the *opposite* of cool by the time the Glenn Ford movie *Blackboard Jungle* was released in 1955. Famous for its use of Bill Haley's "Rock Around the Clock," the film also features a nerdy teacher who attempts to impress his inner-city students with Bix's "Jazz Me Blues."

They respond by destroying his records and rioting—well, dancing to swing music.

page 102, "F. Scott Fitzgerald, like Bix": In an endnote, Breitwieser wonders why more hasn't been made of the similar narrative arcs followed by Bix and Fitzgerald: "The resonances are many: in addition to death from drinking, they share an upper Midwestern origin, rapid and somewhat scandalous celebrity, the pressure of coming to terms with the constraints imposed by success, and a fine strain of alluring and disturbing melancholia" ("Jazz Fractures," 379).

page 102, "writer who'd given the word 'jazz'": Bourjaily, "In and Out of Storyville: Jazz and Fiction," *New York Times*, December 13, 1987.

page 103, "A society jazz orchestra": Breitwieser, "Jazz Fractures," 362. The orchestra's performance and Nick Carraway's reaction to it can be found in F. Scott Fitzgerald, *The Great Gatsby: The Authorized Text* (New York: Scribner's, 1991), 54.

page 103, "Breitwieser argues that this is likely a veiled reference": Breitwieser, "Jazz Fractures," 370.

page 103, "an aesthetics of jazz": Ted Gioia, *The Imperfect Art: Reflections on Jazz and Modern Culture* (New York: Oxford University Press, 1988), 55; quoted in Breitwieser, "Jazz Fractures," 367.

page 103, "Emerson's 'Representative Man,'": Breitwieser, "Jazz Fractures," 376.

page 103, "power was embodied": Claude Lefort, *Democracy and Political Theory*, trans. David Macey (Minneapolis: University of Minnesota Press, 1988), 17; quoted in Breitwieser, "Jazz Fractures," 378.

31

page 105, "taken a lesson": Sudhalter and Evans, *Bix: Man & Legend*, 151; Lion, *Bix: The Definitive Biography*, 106. Joseph Gustat, first trumpet with the St. Louis Symphony, told Bix that his style of playing would not fit in a symphony hall, and anyway, "Trying to change someone like you would be putting a wild animal in a cage—and to what end?" In 1939, however, Gustat began giving lessons to a thirteen-year-old trumpeter named Miles Davis. Gerald Early, ed., *Miles Davis and American Culture* (St. Louis, MO: Missouri Historical Society, 2001), 210.

page 105, "writing a jazz symphony": Shapiro and Hentoff, *Hear Me Talkin' to Ya*, 157–58; Lion, *Bix: The Definitive Biography*, 211.

page 105, "extremely interested": Evans and Evans, *Bix: The Leon Bix Beiderbecke Story*, 340; Lion, *Bix: The Definitive Biography*, 182.

page 105, "He's got to sit up there": Lion, *Bix: The Definitive Biography*, 187.

page 105, "he missed his train": Evans and Evans, *Bix: The Leon Bix Beiderbecke Story*, 416; Lion, *Bix: The Definitive Biography*, 202.

page 106, "waxed three extant takes": A version of this description of "From Monday On" was originally published in Wolfe, "The Dozens: Essential Bix Beiderbecke," Jazz.com, March 9, 2008.

page 106, "the Davenport paper ran a feature": "Jazz Trumpeter and Soloist of Whiteman's Orchestra Is Former Davenport Lad," *Davenport Democrat and Leader*, April 25, 1928, 19. See also Lion, *Bix: The Definitive Biography*, 185.

page 106, "a peak in Bix's professional career": Lion, *Bix: The Definitive Biography*, 200.

32

page 107, "suffered a severe nervous breakdown": Sudhalter and Evans write that "Bix's Cleveland 'breakdown' was in all probability an acute attack of delirium tremens" (*Bix: Man & Legend*, 264). Lion calls the breakdown "a severe nervous crisis" and notes Frank Trumbauer's diary entry from December 2: "Bix still gone. Stayed in Cleveland with DTs. I spent four years with him to no avail" (*Bix: The Definitive Biography*, 203). See also Evans and Evans, *Bix: The Leon Bix Beiderbecke Story*, 418–19. In *Jazz and Death: Medical Profiles of Jazz Greats* (Jackson: University Press of Mississippi, 2002), Frederick J. Spencer is highly skeptical of claims that Bix on this or other occasions suffered from delirium tremens and questions the qualifications of a British physician quoted by Sudhalter and Evans, as well as the claim by Sudhalter and Evans that Bix "may have continued to harbor pneumonia sub-clinically" (*Bix: Man & Legend*, 102–3).

page 107, "Bix and another friend were badly beaten up": Evans and Evans, *Bix: The Leon Bix Beiderbecke Story*, 427.

page 107, "couple of sailors": Evans and Evans, *Bix: The Leon Bix Beiderbecke Story*, 427.

page 107, "approached him for an interview": This is my speculation.

page 107, "the feature appeared prominently": "Bix Beiderbecke," *Davenport Democrat and Leader*, February 10, 1929; reprinted in Evans and Evans, *Bix: The Leon Bix Beiderbecke Story*, 430–32. See also Sudhalter and Evans, *Bix: Man & Legend*, 267–69; Lion, *Bix: The Definitive Biography*, 209–10.

page 109, "wordless": Berton, *Remembering Bix*, 381. He writes: "To the end of his life [Bix] tried to make friends again with that tribe of smug philistines, tried to persuade them in his own wordless way that becoming one of the two most famous trumpet players in the world was no crime."

page 110, "'ear-tickling,' 'nerve-harrowing'": Henry O. Osgood, *So This Is Jazz* (Boston: Little, Brown, 1926), 6, 7.

page 110, "'nerve-tickling, toe-inciting'": Osgood, *So This Is Jazz*, 131.

page 110, "he argues that Whiteman's famous concert": Osgood, *So This Is Jazz*, 138.

page 110, "there is better popular music today": Abbe Niles, "Ballads, Songs and Snatches," *Bookman* 67, no. 2 (April 1928): 170.

page 111, "Osgood also happens to use that word . . . *blooey*": Osgood, *So This Is Jazz*, 7, 63.

page 111, "That's why Geoffrey C. Ward": Geoffrey C. Ward, *Jazz: A History of America's Music* (New York: Knopf, 2000), 155.

page 111, "and why Stephan Talty": Stephan Talty, *Mulatto America: At the Crossroads of Black and White Culture: A Social History* (New York: HarperCollins, 2003), 119.

page 112, "Still, Ward scoffs": Ward, *Jazz*, 155.

page 112, "little more than the convoluted view": Sudhalter and Evans, *Bix: Man & Legend*, 267. As we'll see, Sudhalter and Evans may have been keeping a big secret about Bix when they penned their biography. Their language here makes me wonder whether they also knew more about this interview than they were telling.

page 112, "placing the word in scare quotes": Sudhalter and Evans, *Bix: Man & Legend*, 269.

page 112, "Bix is quoted as saying . . . supposedly emphasized": Lion, *Bix: The Definitive Biography*, 209.

page 112, "This long interview gives": Lion, *Bix: The Definitive Biography*, 210.

page 112, "Bix Sounds Off on Jazz": John Willard, "Bix Sounds Off on Jazz, the Word," *Quad-City Times*, July 12, 2005.

page 113, "quotes *Merchant of Venice*": Osgood, *So This Is Jazz*, 6.

page 113, "'serious jazz' that is also 'funny'": Osgood, *So This Is Jazz*, 139–40.

page 113, "As the musician Brad Kay pointed out": Phone interview with Kay on May 4, 2009. Kay also posted about the subject on the Bixography Discussion Group: "Check This Out:" August 24, 2009.

page 114, "the head of this journeyman news reporter": Phone interview with Kay on May 4, 2009.

page 114, "in the fashion of a Bixophile": "Bix Speaks . . ." by Peter Curry, posted on the Bixography Discussion Group, February 25, 2002.

page 115, "movie-shy": On the Bixography Discussion Group ("Movie-Shy," posted February 6, 2010), Robert Spoo, a law professor at the University of Tulsa, points out that a song of that title was copyrighted by John Tally, of Chicago, in 1926.

page 115, "It was a newspaper article": Louise Garwood, "The Official How and Why of Jazz—From a Lawyer," *Evening Independent* (St. Petersburg, Florida), September 1, 1928. The same article appeared elsewhere, including, for instance, the *Reading Times* (Reading, Pennsylvania), on August 18, 1928.

page 115, "an associate at the Wall Street firm": Elliott S. Hurwitt, "Abbe Niles, Blues Advocate," in *Ramblin' on My Mind: New Perspectives on the Blues*, ed. David Evans (Urbana: University of Illinois Press, 2008), 106.

page 115, "the author of *Encyclopaedia Britannica*'s entry on jazz": Garwood, "The Official How and Why of Jazz—From a Lawyer." See also Hurwitt, "Abbe Niles," 105.

page 116, "even called him 'Bill'": Hurwitt, "Abbe Niles," 107.

33

page 117, "hail it as 'important'": This and subsequent comments were left by Hans Eekhoff on the post "Bix Beiderbecke (The Fake Interview)" at the author's blog, The Beiderbecke Affair, on February 7–8, 2010. The post is dated February 6, 2010. The blog has since been deactivated but can be accessed through the Internet Archive Wayback Machine. Eekhoff is not alone in making these arguments; a former employee of the *Quad-City Times* defended the article. See "Bix and Plagiarism," by Albert Haim, posted on the Bixography Discussion Group, March 1, 2010.

page 118, "I'm almost done writing": Comment posted on February 8, 2010.

34

page 119, "snatch of newsreel": Lion, *Bix: The Definitive Biography*, 186.

35

page 121, "Bix was drinking pretty heavily again": Sudhalter and Evans, *Bix: Man & Legend*, 283; Lion, *Bix: The Definitive Biography*, 224.

page 121, "By September 1929": Sudhalter and Evans, *Bix: Man & Legend*, 289–96; Evans and Evans, *Bix: The Leon Bix Beiderbecke Story*, 491–501; Lion, *Bix: The Definitive Biography*, 230–32. The Keeley Institute was the nation's premier alcohol rehabilitation facility, and a week into Bix's stay, a doctor wrote to inform Agatha Beiderbecke about her son's condition upon arrival. He described "loss of appetite, gas on the stomach, diarrhea at times, palpitation of the heart, shortness of breath, nervousness, neuritis in the feet, lapses of memory, dizziness, insomnia, etc." Bix's breathing was "very harsh," "heart sounds . . . short and soft," liver and pupils enlarged, and throat congested. In addition, Bix had trouble with his balance and exhibited a tremor in his fingers. See Keeley Institute Records at the Abraham Lincoln Presidential Library and Museum; Box 138, Bix Beiderbecke Folder.

page 121, "the golden door": Green, *Reluctant Art*, 42.

page 121, "Come the end of 1930": Sudhalter and Evans, *Bix: Man & Legend*, 311–13; Evans and Evans, *Bix: The Leon Bix Beiderbecke Story*, 525–26; Lion, *Bix: The Definitive Biography*, 257–62.

page 121, "alcoholic polyneuritis": Lion, *Bix: The Definitive Biography*, 220. See also Spencer, *Jazz and Death*, 99–106.

page 121, "We can only try to conceive": Berton, *Remembering Bix*, 381.

page 122, "jazz cornet player exiled": Rod Jellema, "Bix Beiderbecke Composing Light, 1927–1931," in *A Slender Grace: Poems* (Grand Rapids, MI: William B. Eerdmans, 2004), 50.

page 122, "His mother was very pleased": Evans and Evans, *Bix: The Leon Bix Beiderbecke Story*, 302; Lion, *Bix: The Definitive Biography*, 167.

page 122, "Bix's brother, Burnie": Sudhalter and Evans, *Bix: Man & Legend*, 249; Evans and Evans, *Bix: The Leon Bix Beiderbecke Story*, 387; Lion, *Bix: The Definitive Biography*, 193.

page 122, "Bix's parents saw him play": Evans and Evans, *Bix: The Leon Bix Beiderbecke Story*, 417–18; Lion, *Bix: The Definitive Biography*, 202–3. In Sudhalter and Evans, Mr. and Mrs. Beiderbecke skipped the show: "Only brother Burnie was on hand to represent the Beiderbecke family" (*Bix: Man & Legend*, 259).

page 123, "I respected him and loved him": Carmichael, *Sometimes I Wonder*, 229.

page 123, "that the real Bix": Berton, *Remembering Bix*, xii.

page 123, "rebellious gestures": Theodor W. Adorno, *Prisms: Essays on Veblen, Huxley, Benjamin, Bach, Proust, Schoenberg, Spengler, Jazz, Kafka*, translated from the German by Samuel and Shierry Weber (1967; Cambridge, MA: MIT Press, 1981), 122.

page 123, "Even given a certain amount . . . his reported response": Sudhalter, *Lost Chords*, 802.

36

page 125, "begin with the police blotter": Lion transcribes the police blotter and Ivens's affidavit in a footnote (*Bix: The Definitive Biography*, 26). In *Bix: The Davenport Album*, cowritten with Jim Arpy and Gerri Bowers (Barnegat, NJ: Razor Edge, 2009), Rich Johnson transcribes the police report (442–43). He mistakenly lists Ivens's address as 1700 Iowa Street; a partial image of the document on page 453 shows it to have been 1703 Iowa Street.

page 126, "Bix had been picked up for speeding": Johnson, *Bix: The Davenport Album*, 442.

page 126, "I live at 3030 Grand Ave.": Johnson, *Bix: The Davenport Album*, 443; Lion, *Bix: The Definitive Biography*, 26. In "Sep 26, 1921: State of Iowa vs. Leon B. Beiderbecke," posted on the Bixography Discussion Group on May 17, 2014, Albert Haim provides a link to digital images of Ivens's affidavit.

page 126, "B. J. Palmer directed the Palmer School . . . Cornelius H. Murphy": Johnson, *Bix: The Davenport Album*, 443–44. Johnson mistakenly refers to Murphy's given name as Conrad.

page 127, "As Rich Johnson points out": Johnson, *Bix: The Davenport Album*, 443.

page 128, "the possibility that Bix had been gay": Berton never actually claims Bix was gay. He reports his brother as telling him that "Bix was about as 'homosexual' as you are, brother. I mean let's face it—it meant absolutely nothing to him one way or the other. I don't even know how much girls meant to him, if it comes to that—or let's say sex" (*Remembering Bix*, 392).

page 128, "it is useful to consider . . . Beiderbecke's short life": Sudhalter, *Lost Chords*, 802–3.

page 129, "it sure all fits": Interview with Teachout on March 11, 2006.

page 129, "I interviewed Sudhalter": Phone interview with Sudhalter on March 4, 2003.

page 129, "Phil Evans knew of this story": E-mail received from Jean Pierre Lion on April 9, 2009; ellipses in the original. Lion goes on to say that "Sudhalter didn't know about this incident; he only had rumours that something naughty was hidden in Davenport."

page 129, "At nineteen, he was arrested": Ward, *Jazz*, 83.

page 130, "Bix had probably drunk a bit too much": E-mail received from Jean Pierre Lion on March 30, 2009; ellipses in the original.

page 130, "I believe Bix was a bit 'hot'": E-mail received from Jean Pierre Lion on April 9, 2009; ellipses in the original.

page 130, "a four-page primer": Johnson, *Bix: The Davenport Album*, 438–41.

page 130, "The Espionage Act expired": Johnson, *Bix: The Davenport Album*, 441.

page 130, "According to Bill Roba": Johnson, *Bix: The Davenport Album*, 441.

page 131, "Ivens apparently became incensed": Roba, "Bix Beiderbecke as a German-American," 158.

page 131, "a stronghold of anti-chiropractic belief": Roba, "Bix Beiderbecke as a German-American," 158.

page 131, "check a few things": E-mail received from William H. Roba on March 31, 2010. Roba graciously credited my comments in the endnotes of the published version of his article ("Bix Beiderbecke as a German-American," 173).

page 132, "the idea of trying to exert influence": E-mail received from Christopher Bix Beiderbecke on February 7, 2010.

37

page 133, "Apparently Berton, who died in 1993": Lion, *Bix: The Definitive Biography*, 79. Lion cites Chip Deffaa, *Voices of the Jazz Age: Profiles of Eight Vintage Jazzmen* (Urbana: University of Illinois Press, 1990), 221. Deffaa writes that in a phone interview Berton "spoke of Beiderbecke's open personality and general willingness to try anything, and confirmed having attended a drag party with his brother Gene and Beiderbecke and having learned from Gene in a kitchen conversation shortly after Beiderbecke's death, that Gene had a brief homosexual involvement with Beiderbecke."

page 133, "incongruous features": Laura Mazzuca Toops, *Hudson Lake* (Kingsport, TN: Twilight Times Books, 2005), 13.

page 133, "The great American icons": Lee Siegel, "Hound Dog Hybrid," *New Republic Online*, May 9, 2005.

38

page 135, "cute as a bug's ear . . . just out of this world": Sudhalter and Evans, *Bix: Man & Legend*, 145.

page 135, "I found him a kindly . . . Whatever the case . . .": Sudhalter and Evans, *Bix: Man & Legend*, 146.

page 135, "A baby's a wonderful thing": Sudhalter and Evans, *Bix: Man & Legend*, 158.

page 135, "He was smiling at her": Sudhalter and Evans, *Bix: Man & Legend*, 158.

page 135, "If only I could relive my life": Sudhalter and Evans, *Bix: Man & Legend*, 159.

page 136, "Impossible is a ridiculous word": Sudhalter and Evans, *Bix: Man & Legend*, 158.

page 136, "In December [of 1926] she had noticed": Lion, *Bix: The Definitive Biography*, 108; ellipsis in the original.

39

page 138, "the sacredness of privacy": "Addendum: Bix Speaks," by Albert Haim, posted on the Bixography Discussion Group, April 15, 2001.

page 138, "the presumption of innocence": "Calling a lawyer, calling a lawyer" by Albert Haim, posted on the Bixography Discussion Group, December 24, 2009.

page 138, "Bix is not guilty": "You write . . ." by Emrah Erken, posted on the Bixography Discussion Group, December 25, 2009.

page 139, "said something to a little girl in braids": Carmichael, *The Stardust Road*, 16. Barbara Wascher called my attention to this possible reading of Carmichael's memoirs.

page 139, "a blue-eyed blonde with a baby stare": Carmichael, *Sometimes I Wonder*, 28.

page 139, "acted like a movie version": Carmichael, *Sometimes I Wonder*, 28–29.

page 139, "the vices of . . . Oscar Wilde": Carmichael, *Sometimes I Wonder*, 28.

page 139, "Did this really happen?": E-mail received from Barbara Wascher on January 4, 2010. Wascher notes that the incident goes unmentioned in Sudhalter's biography of Carmichael, an omission that might suggest Sudhalter's view that it never happened.

40

page 140, "In 1947 Columbia Records": My thinking about Bix and Tram owes much to my conversations with Barbara Wascher.

page 140, "finally, race is no longer": Alfred Appel Jr., in *Jazz Modernism: From Ellington and Armstrong to Matisse and Joyce* (New York: Knopf, 2002), mentions race in the context of Flora's Louis Armstrong cover: "The flat sepia hues of Armstrong's skin, the banjo, clarinet bell, piano trimming, and HOT-titled pennant would reduce or remove the issue of race. Color becomes a matter of pure play" (192).

page 141, "spun out . . . from a silver spool": Kaminsky and Hughes, *Jazz Band*, 16; quoted in Berton, *Remembering Bix*, 362.

page 141, "to swipe a word": Hadlock, *Jazz Masters*, 90; quoted in Berton, *Remembering Bix*, 363.

page 141, "In the notice, the *Times* explains": Heller, "James Flora, 84, Author and Album Cover Illustrator, Dies."

page 141, "I had heard Bix . . . I was determined": Philip R. Evans and Larry F. Kiner with William Trumbauer, *TRAM: The Frank Trumbauer Story* (Newark, NJ: Institute of Jazz Studies, Rutgers—The State University of New Jersey; Metuchen, NJ: Scarecrow, 1994), 51–52.

page 141, "When Bix got so loaded": Interview with Vernon Brown, in Evans and Evans, *Bix: The Leon Bix Beiderbecke Story*, 205.

page 142, "Or when Bix just didn't show up": Interview with Karl Spaeth, in Evans and Evans, *Bix: The Leon Bix Beiderbecke Story*, 198.

page 142, "Bix forgot to bring his cornet": Interview with Vernon Brown, in Evans and Evans, *Bix: The Leon Bix Beiderbecke Story*, 206.

page 142, "it was the 'catalyst'": Evans and Evans, *Bix: The Leon Bix Beiderbecke Story*, 218–19.

page 142, "his fellow musicians 'merely travelled'": Evans and Evans, *Bix: The Leon Bix Beiderbecke Story*, 200.

page 142, "Bix had a screwy way": Evans and Kiner, *TRAM*, 54.

page 142, "Bix, meanwhile, was up all night": Interview with Matty Matlock, in Evans and Evans, *Bix: The Leon Bix Beiderbecke Story*, 214.

page 142, "didn't even want her to meet with us": Evans and Evans, *Bix: The Leon Bix Beiderbecke Story*, 211.

page 142, "We just kick it around": Interview with Marlin Skiles, in Evans and Evans, *Bix: The Leon Bix Beiderbecke Story*, 211.

page 142, "I admit that Bix is a great cornet player": From Frank Trumbauer's unpublished writings, in Evans and Kiner, *TRAM*, 56.

page 143, "Bix has changed": Evans and Kiner, *TRAM*, 56.

page 143, "Fortunately we had a Greek restaurant": Interview with Fred Bergin via Bob Harrington, in Evans and Evans, *Bix: The Leon Bix Beiderbecke Story*, 217.

page 143, "like the actor who portrays him": Mark Sovel plays Frank Trumbauer in *Bix: An Interpretation of a Legend*.

page 143, "It's that stare": Recall that description from Eddie Condon: "When I looked at his face and saw the absence there . . . things got cold and tight around me and I stiffened my drink."

page 144, "Tram had an adult": E-mail received from Barbara Wascher on December 4, 2009.

page 144, "Bix and Tram launch into": "Bill Challis did the arrangement on BORNEO, but the idea of the Bix-Tram chase chorus, was Trumbauer's idea," Evans and Evans write. "It was based on an idea Bix and Tram had developed during their St. Louis days. Many of the Whiteman musicians felt the chase chorus was an innovation that Bix and Tram introduced into American jazz music" (*Bix: The Leon Bix Beiderbecke Story*, 345–46).

page 144, "covered 'Borneo' in 1963": The first track on *Geoff Muldaur Rare and Unissued: Collectors' Items 1963–2008* is "Borneo," performed live by Kweskin's calathumpian band, including Muldaur, on the Oscar Brand Radio Show in New York, on September 25, 1963.

page 144, "There's something conversational": Muldaur interview on May 18, 2009; I have edited the transcript very slightly to remove some redundancy.

page 144, "Tram told of his trepidation": Evans and Evans, *Bix: The Leon Bix Beiderbecke Story*, 346.

page 145, "their instruments converge": A version of this description of "Borneo" was originally published in Wolfe, "The Dozens: Essential Bix Beiderbecke," Jazz.com, March 9, 2008.

page 145, "Bix was now getting out of hand": Evans and Kiner, *TRAM*, 102.

page 145, "I guess I am a minus quality": Letter reprinted in Evans and Evans, *Bix: The Leon Bix Beiderbecke Story*, 433. I don't know whether the error—i.e., "that" should be "than"—is by the Evanses or Bix.

page 145, "Frank Trumbauer's foibles": Spurrier quoted in Lion, *Bix: The Definitive Biography*, 235.

page 145, "He says Mitzi would've said no": E-mail received from Barbara Wascher on December 4, 2009.

page 146, "Tram gets word": Lion, *Bix: The Definitive Biography*, 278.

page 146, "portrayed, unexpectedly": Romano Orzari plays Carmichael, although Orzari is actually Quebecois by birth.

page 146, "his professional future": For example, *Sexual Response* (1992), *Virtual Seduction* (1995). Levisetti is now a television director and producer.

41

page 147, "our conversation": Phone interview with Kay on May 4, 2009.

42

page 154, "dust everywhere": Berton, *Remembering Bix*, 7.

page 154, "The temperature had reached": Sudhalter and Evans, *Bix: Man & Legend*, 329.

page 154, "Bix had fixed up an electric fan . . . call the ambulance": Berton, *Remembering Bix*, 7.

page 154, "He seldom went out": Sudhalter and Evans, *Bix: Man & Legend*, 327. In Evans and Evans, Kraslow's words are slightly different: "During the next few weeks Bix did no outside work of any kind and did not leave the building save to buy gin" (*Bix: The Leon Bix Beiderbecke Story*, 544). Lion uses the Sudhalter and Evans wording (*Bix: The Definitive Biography*, 277).

page 154, "Bix's landlady is actually a landlord": See, for example, Crow, *Jazz Anecdotes*, 253. George Hoefer, author of *Music on My Mind: The Memoirs of an American Pianist* (1964), is quoted in various places suggesting that Kraslow was actually a bass player and Bix's roommate. However, he may have been thinking of Rex Gavitte, whom we'll meet soon.

page 154, "halfheartedly": Sudhalter and Evans, *Bix: Man & Legend*, 327; Evans and Evans, *Bix: The Leon Bix Beiderbecke Story*, 544; Lion, *Bix: The Definitive Biography*, 277.

page 154, "the most private recital possible": Frederick Turner, *1929: A Novel of the Jazz Age* (New York: Counterpoint, 2003), 353.

page 155, "The tenants explained": Sudhalter and Evans, *Bix: Man & Legend*, 327. Evans and Evans do not include the last two sentences (*Bix: The Leon

Bix Beiderbecke Story, 544). See also Lion, *Bix: The Definitive Biography*, 277.

page 155, "served as her husband's nurse": Lion, *Bix: The Definitive Biography*, 278.

page 155, "forced to remove doors from their hinges": Bergreen, *Louis Armstrong*, 321.

page 155, "Musicians explained to Phil Evans": Evans and Evans, *Bix: The Leon Bix Beiderbecke Story*, 506. In *Babe: The Legend Comes to Life* (New York: Simon & Schuster, 1992, 1974), Robert W. Creamer mentions, parenthetically, that the ballplayer "used to drink occasionally with Bix Beiderbecke, the near legendary cornetist" (238). *Near* legendary! I guess not everyone can be the Babe.

page 155, "He had a very bad cold": Shapiro and Hentoff, *Hear Me Talkin' to Ya*, 162.

page 155, "Princeton University was putting on a dance": Sudhalter and Evans, *Bix: Man & Legend*, 316–18; Evans and Evans, *Bix: The Leon Bix Beiderbecke Story*, 523–38; Lion, *Bix: The Definitive Biography*, 268–71.

page 155, "When he learnt that his absence": James, *Bix Beiderbecke*, 22.

page 155, "sounded a lot like Bix": Berton, *Remembering Bix*, 385.

page 156, "Bix's characteristic courtesy": James, *Bix Beiderbecke*, 22–23.

43

page 157, "In his memoir": The material in this section was published, in slightly different form, as "Bixology (An Excerpt)" on Jazz.com, March 9, 2008.

page 157, "Bix nearly got run over": Mezzrow and Wolfe, *Really the Blues*, 126–27.

page 158, "He drank so much for so long": Whitney Balliett, "Even His Feet Looked Sad," *New Yorker*, August 11, 1962; reprinted in *Reading Jazz: A Gathering of Autobiography, Reportage, and Criticism from 1919 to Now*, ed. Robert Gottlieb (New York: Vintage, 1996), 377.

page 158, "Gin and weed? Hell!!": Carl Cons, "'Musicians Killed Bix Beiderbecke': 'Bix Died of a Broken Heart,' Says Famous Leader of Five Pennies," *Down Beat* 4, no. 8 (August 1937). See *DownBeat—The Great Jazz Interviews: A 75th Anniversary Anthology*, ed. Frank Alkyer and Ed Enright (New York: Hal Leonard, 2009), 6.

page 159, "three of his bandmates": Sudhalter and Evans, *Bix: Man & Legend*, 310.

page 159, "He told me that every time": Sudhalter and Evans, *Bix: Man & Legend*, 310. Ciricillo actually said "off the wagon," but the context strongly suggests that he meant the opposite.

page 159, "People came around, sure": Sudhalter and Evans, *Bix: Man & Legend*, 324.

page 159, "[Bix] had a lot of admirers": Sudhalter and Evans, *Bix: Man & Legend*, 326.

page 159, "he was still a kid": Sudhalter and Evans, *Bix: Man & Legend*, 325.

page 159, "couldn't say no to anybody": Lion, *Bix: The Definitive Biography*, 252.

page 160, "In defense of their fumbling": Berton, *Remembering Bix*, 46.

page 160, "He had completely ruined me": Quoted in Sudhalter, *Stardust Melody*, 72.

page 160, "bitter and lasting": Sudhalter, *Stardust Melody*, 144.

page 160, "anecdotage . . . Carmichael had either": Green, *Reluctant Art*, 31.

page 161, "I remember trying to explain Bix": Carmichael, *The Stardust Road*, 51.

page 161, "We didn't have a drink": Carmichael, *The Stardust Road*, 136.

page 161, "maddening": "From a literary point of view, Carmichael made two bad mistakes in the construction of his short story," Green writes. "A best friend doesn't ask a languishing hero to play the trumpet at a time like that. The introduction of a symbolically mysterious woman who, like the population of Davenport, had no idea who Bix was, is an excellent box-office ending ruined by Carmichael's maddening last sentence" (*Reluctant Art*, 44–45).

page 161, "He learned that you can't say everything": Quoted in Sudhalter, *Stardust Melody*, 278. Sudhalter credits Krin Gabbard for noticing the similarity between this passage and one from Carmichael's *The Stardust Road*: "Bix, the incomparable genius, but a human being with it all, subject to the ills of the flesh, the tortures of the spirit. And no way to say it except with the horn and the horn wouldn't say it all" (Carmichael, *The Stardust Road*, 135).

page 162, "Reading Lucy's work": Sven Birkerts, "Brave Face: When the Writer Lucy Grealy Died, Some of Our Most Consoling Notions Went with Her," *Boston Globe*, February 2, 2003.

page 162, "His reply was quick and fierce": E-mail received February 6, 2003. Name of author withheld by request.

page 163, "What she was suffering from": Ann Patchett, "The Face of Pain," *New York*, March 3, 2003, 30–37.

44

page 164, "Dearest Mom & Dad": Reprinted in Evans and Evans, *Bix: The Leon Bix Beiderbecke Story*, 540–41. See also Lion, who calls the letter "unbelievable" (*Bix: The Definitive Biography*, 274).

page 164, "sounds like Aunt Blanch": According to Albert Haim on the
Bixography Discussion Group (April 19, 2009), Aunt Blanch was Blanch
Kidd, a New York–born cousin of Agatha Beiderbecke.

page 165, "I'm certain that I never met her": Evans and Evans, *Bix: The Leon
Bix Beiderbecke Story*, 542.

page 165, "About Helen Weiss": Evans and Evans, *Bix: The Leon Bix
Beiderbecke Story*, 544.

page 165, "Also that he thought": Sudhalter and Evans, *Bix: Man & Legend*, 327.

page 166, "was stunned at how good": Sudhalter and Evans, *Bix: Man &
Legend*, 327.

page 166, "I told the girl to please call me": Evans and Evans, *Bix: The Leon Bix
Beiderbecke Story*, 545.

page 166, "Or at least she had until 2012": This discovery was published in
Albert Haim and Chris Barry, "Alice and Bix," *Journal of Jazz Studies* 9, no. 1
(summer 2013): 1–52.

45

page 168, "go down to the Bellevue morgue": Sudhalter and Evans, *Bix: Man
& Legend*, 315; Evans and Evans, *Bix: The Leon Bix Beiderbecke Story*, 531;
Lion, *Bix: The Definitive Biography*, 264.

page 168, "He later asked Burnie": Sudhalter and Evans, *Bix: Man & Legend*,
315.

46

page 169, "He would have his slips at times": "Bix and Drinking . . ." by Scott
Black, posted on the Bixography Discussion Group, May 7, 2005.

page 169, "I called Black": Phone interview with Scott Black in March 2007.

47

page 175, "I finally got up the nerve": "I Remember Phil," by Brad Kay, posted
on the Bixography Discussion Group, August 15, 2005.

page 175, "You're such a good friend . . . what you've always wanted": Ann
Patchett, *Truth & Beauty: A Friendship* (New York: Harper Perennial, 2005),
225.

48

page 177, "Dr. Haberski had asked": Lion, *Bix: The Definitive Biography*, 278.
See also Evans and Kiner, *TRAM*, 142–43.

page 177, "His hysterical shouts": Sudhalter and Evans, *Bix: Man & Legend*,
329; Evans and Evans, *Bix: The Leon Bix Beiderbecke Story*, 546; Lion, *Bix:
The Definitive Biography*, 278.

page 177, "She pronounced him dead": The matter of Dr. and Mrs. Haberski is a tangled mess. In Berton's *Remembering Bix*, Bix somehow makes it to Queens General Hospital on Long Island, where the "ward nurse on duty rolled a screen around the bed, pulled the sheet up over the pale sweated face and went to notify Dr. Haberski" (6). Everyone else agrees that Dr. Haberski in fact lived across the hall from Bix. Sudhalter and Evans (*Bix: Man & Legend*, 329) identify him as Dr. John James Haberski, while Lion (*Bix: The Definitive Biography*, 278) gives him a middle initial of H. Kraslow, of course, claimed he was a woman—this despite the fact that Bix's death certificate was signed by a man—leading some, including the novelist Frederick Turner, to offer the view that there were *two* Dr. Haberskis, a husband and a wife. "As far as the Doctor Haberski picture is concerned," Kraslow told Phil Evans in a follow-up interview, "I can only tell you that I remembered a woman doctor lived across the hall and I called her in to examine Bix. If she had a father or husband, I can't recall." Bix's friend Stephen Ickes suggested another theory to Evans: "I also understand that Dr. Haberski's wife was the one who was present when Bix died. She was her husband's nurse" (Evans and Evans, *The Leon Bix Beiderbecke Story*, 546–47).

page 177, "The official time was 9:30 P.M.": Sudhalter and Evans, *Bix: Man & Legend*, 329, 334; Evans and Evans, *Bix: The Leon Bix Beiderbecke Story*, 546.

page 177, "Dearest Folks": Letter dated "July 30/31" and reprinted in Evans and Evans, *Bix: The Leon Bix Beiderbecke Story*, 545. "Bixie's letter, never finished" is written on the bottom of the page in Agatha Beiderbecke's handwriting. For a photograph of the document, see Lion, *Bix: The Definitive Biography*, 277. He notes that the date is also in Mrs. Beiderbecke's hand.

page 178, "as many as three milk bottles": Sudhalter and Evans, *Bix: Man & Legend*, 334.

page 178, "Bing Crosby claimed": In his foreword to the 2000 edition of Berton's *Remembering Bix*, Nat Hentoff writes, "I once asked Bing Crosby—who knew Bix when both were with Paul Whiteman and even better, after hours—about that explanation [i.e., alcoholism] for his early death. 'It wasn't booze that killed Bix,' Crosby told me. 'He wasn't an alcoholic. He was an absentminded fellow, sometimes quite jolly. But he was so totally immersed that he never ate or slept properly. His health broke from exhaustion. Of course, it seemed that none of us went to bed in those days. It's amazing that some of us survived'" (*Remembering Bix*, xvi–xvii).

page 178, "Bix had a hell of a cold": Evans and Evans, *Bix: The Leon Bix Beiderbecke Story*, 545.

page 178, "Bix Beiderbecke didn't die of a cold": Quoted in Studs Terkel, *Giants of Jazz: Revised Edition*, with Milly Hawk Daniel (1957; New York: Thomas Y. Crowell, 1975), 60. Turner ends his novel *1929* with a "stooped old man in his John Deere cap," "his voice like an aged raven," responding to a woman who asked him what Bix died of: " 'Everything!' he calls after her. 'He died of everything!' " (390).

page 178, "There is an implicit condescension": Gene Lees, *You Can't Steal a Gift: Dizzy, Clark, Milt, and Nat* (New Haven, CT: Yale University Press, 2001), 40.

page 178, "a self-image. He is the ideal": Teachout interview on March 11, 2006.

page 178, "The service was held": Lion, *Bix: The Definitive Biography*, 279–80.

226 CODA

page 180, "Et in Arcadia ego": Wascher was being cheeky and a little dark: Her sweatshirt recalled the Arcadia Ballroom in St. Louis, where Bix and Tram first played together, while more directly referencing the classical land of Arcadia, a supposed utopia in ancient Greece. The Latin inscription, *Et in Arcadia ego*, which may have first accompanied a seventeenth-century painting, is widely interpreted to mean that even in Arcadia goes death.

page 181, "contained a glib but creepy joke": E-mail received February 11, 2010.

page 181, "one of these Bixophiles": Interview on March 13, 2010, at the Marriott Hotel in Racine, Wisconsin.

page 182, "I think some folks around here": Visit to the Davenport Public Library, in downtown Davenport, Iowa, on February 12, 2014.

INDEX

Illustrations are indicated in *italics*